SCC Library

3 3065 00348 9907

Santiago Canyon College
Library

D0575303

Santiago Canyon College
Library

THE
WORLD
OF
THE
VIKINGS

DL
65
.H33
2007

THE
WORLD
OF
THE
VIKINGS

RICHARD HALL

with 330 illustrations, 141 in color

Thames & Hudson

OCM 85481777

Santiago Canyon College
Library

CONTENTS

For Ailsa,
and for Alasdair and Guy, 'barely perceptible'

(Half-title) Silver pendant representing a stylized Viking man's
head, made in c. 800, found in a female cremation burial at Aska
in Östergötland, Sweden. Height 3.4 cm (1¹/₃ in).
(Title Page) The Imme Gram, a reconstruction of the early
tenth-century Ladby ship built in 1963 by Scouts in southern
Jutland, Denmark.
(This page) Viking Age sword hilts from Sweden.

© 2007 Richard Hall

All Rights Reserved. No part of this publication may be
reproduced or transmitted in any form or by any means,
electronic or mechanical, including photocopy, recording or
any other information storage and retrieval system, without
prior permission in writing from the publisher.

First published in 2007 in hardcover in the United States
of America by Thames & Hudson Inc., 500 Fifth Avenue,
New York, New York 10110

thamesandhudsonusa.com

Library of Congress Catalog Card Number 2005911189

ISBN-13: 978-0-500-05144-3
ISBN-10: 0-500-05144-5

Printed and bound in China by Everbest Printing Co Ltd

I · WHO WERE THE VIKINGS?

The world of the Vikings was defined by raiding, trading and settlement.
Their sphere of activity extended far beyond their homelands in Scandinavia
and the adjacent coastal lands around the Baltic Sea, they reached not only
the northern tip of Europe but also its western, southern and eastern limits.
The Vikings' initial impact upon the Christian communities of western Europe
in the late eighth and ninth centuries caused the greatest damage and most
vocal outrage, but their power, influence and contacts were probably at a
peak in the generations either side of the year 1000. They crossed vast tracts
of uncharted waters to explore and colonize new lands in the west; they made
long, arduous and dangerous journeys along the river systems of central
Europe to Russia and Byzantium. For short periods they were active not only
in Europe but also in North America and Asia.

The experiences and circumstances that shaped the mindset and lifestyle
of someone living in Viking Age Scandinavia varied considerably, depending
upon his or her status in society and where she or he lived. Moreover, across
the centuries there were changes in these experiences and circumstances –
the Viking Age wasn't a frozen, timeless world, but a dynamic one that both
shaped events and had to change in response to external and internal
pressures. Between the beginning and end of the Viking Age the political,
religious and social scene in Scandinavia had been transformed. And for
communities far beyond their own shores with whom contact was made,
the Age of the Vikings was a formative period.

*A Viking warrior's iron helmet from Gjermundbu, Norway, a functional object without
any horns. This is the only reasonably complete helmet to survive from the Viking Age,
although late Viking Age representations (see p. 68) show that pointed helmets, rather
than rounded ones, were popular then. This scarcity of archaeological remains of
helmets suggests that they were unusual, the preserve of the wealthy and very
successful; perhaps the average Viking wore a skull protector of hardened leather
that would not survive for the archaeologist to find.*

WHO AND WHAT WAS A VIKING?

Vikings were warriors. More precisely, Vikings is the name by which Scandinavian seaborne raiders of the early medieval period are now commonly known. Although not invincible, they were hugely successful in plundering silver and other wealth. Of course, not all Scandinavians were Vikings. In the late ninth century the English King Alfred, scourge of Vikings, welcomed a Norwegian merchant adventurer to his court and ordered that his traveller's tales be recorded; and Alfred's royal grandson Athelstan patronized a Scandinavian court poet. For the vast majority of early medieval Europeans, however, any meeting with a Scandinavian most probably came in the form of an encounter with a fearsome heathen warrior.

Yet Vikings were not professional privateers or full-time soldiers – or, at least, not at first. Originally, they were farmers and fishermen who spent much of the year at home working the land or otherwise providing food for themselves and their dependants. Only in the summer calm did they rally to the ship of some charismatic local leader and venture across the seas in order to raid, to trade, or to seek out new lands to settle. The Vikings' 'multi-tasking' does, however, explain the need to look beyond questions of tactics and weapons; any review of the world of the Vikings requires an overview of their homes, families, and every aspect of their everyday life.

Finding the Vikings

For many people today, a first introduction to the world of the Vikings comes from reading translations of the sagas, written in Iceland in the thirteenth century and later. These stories paint a vivid picture of the world of the Vikings, not only in Iceland but across a vast territorial sweep from Vinland to Byzantium. Classic accounts of the deeds of heroes, or epic tales of love, passion, greed and honour, they are a vital part of the Icelandic legacy. They provide dramatic glimpses of all sorts of human situations; they take us into the minds of legendary figures. But we now realize that their detailed descriptions of such things as clothing,

The stylized head of a Viking man carved in wood, from the side of the cart found in the burial dated c. 834 at Oseberg, Norway.

THE MEANING OF 'VIKING'

Even before the earliest Viking raids on Anglo-Saxon monasteries, the Anglo-Saxons used an Old English word *wicing*. However, *wicing* wasn't a word that the Anglo-Saxons used often or exclusively for the Scandinavian raiders who gave them so much grief in the ninth and tenth centuries. Instead they used it of all comers, in the sense of 'a pirate' or 'piracy'. It was only in the late tenth to early eleventh century that, in Anglo-Saxon poems such as *The Battle of Maldon*, the word *wicing* came to mean 'a Scandinavian sea-raider'.

The Old Norse language spoken in Scandinavia had a word *víkingr*, but apart from appearing on a few rune stones it was not recorded in written records until the twelfth century, and its origins are therefore uncertain. The explanation currently favoured is that it originally designated a seaman who came from the Vík district of Oslo Fjord, and then came to mean 'seaborne warrior', firstly one from that area and latterly from anywhere in Scandinavia.

RUNES

First-millennium AD Scandinavia was not a zone of total illiteracy. By the second century a distinctive alphabet made up of letters known as runes had been invented, perhaps in Denmark, and it remained in use throughout the Viking Age. At first there were 24 letters; the first six represented the sounds f, u, th, a, r, k, and so the whole alphabet became known as the *futhark*. Its linear and angular shapes reveal that it was designed to cut short messages easily into wood, bone and (later) stone, although it could also be scratched on to metalwork. It could be written from left to right, from right to left, or in opposite directions on alternate lines. By about AD 700 a 'younger *futhark*' of only 16 letters was introduced, with the major variants being Danish 'common' runes and Swedo-Norwegian 'short-twig' runes. With over 3,000, Sweden has the most surviving inscriptions; Norway has over 1,000 and Denmark more than 700.

When some of the peoples later known as Anglo-Saxons emigrated from the northwest of continental Europe to England in the fifth and sixth centuries, the ability to write in runes was transplanted with them. Runic inscriptions there, usually very short and sometimes unintelligible, occur on pagan cremation urns and a miscellany of other objects; later they are found on coins and Christian memorial stones, and, for example, on the wooden coffin of St Cuthbert, made in the late seventh century; there is nothing specifically pagan about their use. By the mid-ninth century, however, they were becoming a rarity, as the Latin script became the norm.

The Vikings gave a new lease of life to the use of runes in Britain and Ireland, but only to a limited extent, and not at all in Wales. Neither Scotland, England nor Ireland has very many Viking Age inscriptions, and although new discoveries are being made, the overall total stands at a relatively modest 90. Dublin, for example, has yielded about 15 runic items, to add to just a handful from the rest of Ireland. Numbers in mainland Scotland, in Orkney, and in England are, in each case, less than 20; there are no certain runic inscriptions from York. The Isle of Man therefore stands out for the 30 or so inscribed memorial slabs that attest specific fashions for the script there.

f u þ a/æ r k g w h n i j ï p z s t b e m l n o d
   (th)   (R)   (ng)

f u þ a r k h n i a s t b m l R
   (th)

(Above) The 24-character futhark.

(Left) The 16-character 'younger futhark' Danish runes.

(Left) Rune stone from Tullstorp, Skåne, Sweden, c. 1000, reading 'Kleppe and Åse raised this monument in memory of Ulv'; the ship, the great beast and the rune ribbon's gaping jaws refer to Ragnarök, the apocalyptic battle at the end of the world.

weaponry, ships and customs are more relevant to the time of their composition than the circumstances several hundred years earlier, and that their version of legend and history was carefully crafted to satisfy the writers' patrons.

For contemporary accounts of the Viking world we rely almost exclusively upon the verdict of their victims. Monks in the British Isles and continental Europe wrote yearly accounts of important events in their region; Arabs and Byzantines who encountered Vikings also recorded their impressions. It is not surprising that these documents, although both welcome and important, are generally brief, biased and limited in their content.

Yet in England, for example, the information they contained was sometimes copied into later medieval histories, and thus the Vikings remained a part of the national historical consciousness, if only as nasty, brutish barbarians who had finally been overcome.

The Vikings left little obvious imprint on the landscapes they inhabited. Their only monumental legacy that could be fairly easily identified in later centuries was a series of memorial stones inscribed with runic inscriptions. Thus it was only with the gradual increase in antiquarian interest and then, from the late nineteenth century, archaeological skills, that buried traces of the Viking Age

DATING THE VIKINGS

Until quite recently, attributing a date to any Viking Age object involved firstly an assessment of where it fitted into an evolutionary framework that had been built up by generations of scholars. Underpinning this framework were the twin piers of typology (the study of the evolution of objects' shape or form) and art-historical analysis of its decorative style.

Given the vagaries of artistry – the counterpoint of innovation and tradition, the idiosyncrasies of individual craftsmen, the preferences of patrons and the differences of taste from one region to another – there is room for experts to vary in their views. So, for all these reasons, deciding where pieces should be placed within this evolutionary framework is not an exact science, but an art.

Nonetheless, having determined an object's likely position in the evolutionary sequence, its calendar (absolute) date could then be estimated by reference to items of related

style found in association with datable coins. Chains or clusters of these somewhat hypothetical relationships could thus be developed, with concomitant leeway in the possible date range of any particular object's manufacture. Further complexity and ambiguity comes with the tricky question of how long a given item had been in use before it was lost, discarded or deliberately buried.

Beset by all these uncertainties, experts' estimates of an object's date could sometimes vary by as much as half a century and nothing more precise than a span of several decades could normally be suggested.

The advent of new scientific dating techniques in the second half of the twentieth century, and particularly the development of dendrochronology (tree-ring dating), has added a welcome number of precise chronological indicators to the framework. However, the dating of inert materials such as stonework or

metalwork remains stubbornly dependent on the traditional, somewhat subjective, methods of the art historian.

No pieces of Viking Age art incorporate a date expressed in terms of calendar years, but a few classes of object, principally from the end of the Viking Age, do provide broad clues about their date. Some rune stones, particularly from the Uppland area of Sweden, include in their design a cross motif that would only have been acceptable after the adoption of Christianity by that kingdom in the early eleventh century. Other rune stones have inscriptions that refer to events and leaders, and these can sometimes be associated with historically attested episodes or individuals. Most famously, the large decorated stone at Jelling, in Jutland, Denmark (see p. 182), is inscribed with a proclamation about the king who erected it; this allows the monument, and the decorative style, to be dated fairly precisely to the 960s.

Coins

From about the year 1000 onwards, coins minted in Scandinavia bear the name of the ruler under whose authority they were struck. The same is true for the ninth- and tenth-century coins which both Viking warriors and traders brought from England, Europe and the Islamic world. The periods when these named individuals ruled are known, thanks to the records made by contemporary or near-contemporary European and Islamic chroniclers. The important outcome of this is not so much the provision of an absolute date in calendar years for the coins themselves, but for what we can infer about the dating of any objects found buried together with such coins, or even in a looser stratigraphic association with them.

Two Viking Age coins: minted by King Alfred of Wessex (left) who was king of Wessex from 877–99, and Olof Skötkonung (right) the first Swedish king to issue coinage.

came to be uncovered and identified. By charting where different sorts of artifacts have been found, by identifying variations in the pattern of human settlement, and by working out when different types of archaeological remains appear and disappear over the centuries, archaeologists have begun to sketch in an increasingly detailed picture of conditions in Scandinavia in the first millennium AD.

Increasingly careful recovery of evidence, coupled with the deployment of a steadily growing array of analytical techniques, has brought virtually all aspects of Viking life within the archaeologists' view. Of key importance has been the ability to determine the date of many kinds of objects.

Radiocarbon dating can often indicate the age of organic remains such as bone, wood, textile and leather to within a century or less. Dendrochronology, which recognizes patterns of tree-ring growth in excavated timbers and places them against lengthy master patterns that extend back for thousands of years into the past, can pinpoint the precise year in which that tree was cut down. Studies that identify species of plants, beetles and animals illuminate topics such as climate, diet, health and the ancient environment. Armed with these and a battery of other scientific methods, archaeologists are now able to unlock the world of the Vikings to an extent hitherto thought impossible.

A manuscript of Vápnafirðinga Saga, The Saga of the People of Vápnafjord ('Weapon's Fjord'), which tells the story of a power struggle between two young chieftains and their descendants in northeast Iceland. Saga stories dealt with kings, with chieftains, with real and invented heroes and heroines, in several different genres.

CRADLE OF THE VIKINGS

The very different landscapes throughout Scandinavia played a crucial role in determining the course of history. The Jutland peninsula, and the islands of Fyn, Sjaelland and other smaller islands to the east were low lying, with Jutland itself rising to only 175 m (575 ft) above sea level. Nowhere was more than about 75 km (50 miles) from the coast. Sailing to the north of Jutland across the Skagerrak, with the habitable coastal strips of southeast Norway to port and southwest Sweden to starboard, the waters gradually narrowed into the funnel of the Oslo Fjord. Rising up behind the Norwegian coast was the imposing, ridge-like range of mountains known as 'the keel' which ran for almost all of the

(Right) Scandinavia, the Baltic Sea and surrounding countries, seen from a NASA satellite; snow covers much of the area.

(Opposite) Fjord landscape at Sognefjord, Norway. Both images emphasise the importance of seaborne communication to the Vikings; and also hint at the conditions that led some to seek permanent settlements in less harsh climes.

very considerable 1,750-km (1,100-mile) length of the country, up towards North Cape, some 650 km (400 miles) inside the Arctic Circle. Only Norway's southern coast posed a danger to sailors. A safe sailing route up the Atlantic western coast of Norway from Stavanger to North Cape was formed by a protective barrier of skerries and islands. It was known as leið (ð is pronounced th), literally 'the way'; it was a 'north way' that assisted the country's eventual unification and gave it its name. It passed a landscape where low coastal areas suitable for settlement were punctuated by long narrow fjords penetrating into the mountainous interior.

Inland from the west Swedish coastal strip were large areas of virtually impenetrable forest, bog and lakes. To the north were the much more accessible areas around waterways of the Lake Mälaren area, in the vicinity of modern Stockholm, and beyond that the lands bordering the Gulf of Bothnia, with Lapland to the north and Finland to the east.

These landscapes spawned the traders, raiders and colonists whose travels pushed back the frontiers of the Viking world. The motives and circumstances that prompted their journeys can be traced far back into the early first millennium AD. That is a time when there were no contemporary writings to chart social customs and political events; in this prehistoric period it is archaeological remains that paint a picture of everyday life and death. Study and interpretation of these remains reveals the Vikings' antecedents, and creates a 'family tree' for the Vikings both more mundane and more believable than their own later attempts to trace their ancestry.

Thanks mainly to discoveries made over the last few decades, we can now see how the influence of distant contacts with the advanced European civilization of Rome affected Scandinavia in the early and middle centuries of the first millennium, and contributed to internal developments there that culminated in the emergence of Vikings.

WHAT'S IN A NAME?

The names which archaeologists in Denmark, Norway and Sweden have given to their subdivisions of the first millennium AD usefully reflect key aspects of this period:

1–400: Early (Roman) Iron Age (Denmark, Norway, Sweden). A time when the proximity of the Roman Empire had a major impact upon Scandinavia, particularly in the south.

400–550: Early (Germanic) Iron Age (Denmark); Migration Period (Norway, Sweden). The era after the decline of the western Roman Empire, traditionally associated with wholesale folk migrations across large tracts of Europe.

550–800: Later (Germanic) Iron Age (Denmark); Merovingian Period (Norway); Vendel Period (Sweden). Political and economic contacts with the consolidating states of western Europe such as the Merovingian kingdom in France and Germany gain importance; richly appointed Svear burials at Vendel demonstrate the growing wealth and power of aristocrats and rulers.

800–1050: Later Iron Age or Viking Age (Denmark, Norway, Sweden).

BEFORE THE VIKINGS: SCANDINAVIA AND THE ROMAN EMPIRE

Warrior gear sacrificed to the gods through deposition in a bog at Illerup Ådal, Jutland, in c. AD 200.

Personal jewelry of high quality, including gold armrings and bracteates, and everyday items, including knives and a fish-hook, from Lundeborg, the manufacturing and exchange site associated with Gudme, on Fyn, Denmark.

The Romans never invaded Scandinavia, let alone conquered any of it. Their frontier along the Rivers Rhine and Danube defended the empire against Germanic tribes, while permitting diplomatic and commercial interchange. Germanic warriors could come south to serve as Roman auxiliary troops, and Roman luxury goods such as glassware could be traded to the north. The frontier protected the empire from a turmoil beyond it that is unknown in the documentary sources but clearly visible in the archaeological record. Large quantities of weapons (and occasionally ships) that had been captured from defeated invaders and then

'sacrificed' to the gods in bogs or pools during the first five centuries AD have been found at some 50 places. A few are on Sjaelland, Bornholm, in south Sweden and on Gotland and Öland, but most are in central and south Jutland and on the neighbouring island of Fyn, which appear to have been the main targets for successive waves of invaders.

At Illerup Ådal, in north-central Jutland, for example, equipment for about 350 warriors – swords, shields, lances, archers' gear, together with warhorses – was offered to the gods in c. AD 200. Differences in the sacrificed weaponry reflect the origins of successive waves of attackers. The earliest came from Germany; then, from c. 200 onwards, from Norway; and finally, from c. 300 onwards, from central and northern Sweden. Most of the offerings were made from c. 200–300, mute testimony to a dangerously unsettled era.

Chiefdoms

Strong leadership and military prowess were needed in the face of these threats, and so the more egalitarian, clan-based tribal society of the early centuries AD was replaced with more hierarchical chiefdoms. Archaeologically these changes are reflected in several ways. Instead of farms and houses being uniform in size, the norm was now for one farm in a settlement to stand out as larger.

The ultimate architectural expressions of rank and status were 'halls', large timber buildings that formed the setting for impressive displays of power, wealth, influence and prestige at aristocratic residences. These so-called 'magnate centres' or 'central places' were the theatres where the scenes of lordly magnificence and feasting portrayed in early medieval epic poems could be played out, together with cultic religious practices.

The earliest site with an enormous hall is at Gudme, a name that means 'home of the gods', on southeast Fyn. There, in c. 250, a huge building measuring over 47 m (155 ft) long by 10 m (33 ft) wide was erected, its roof supported by eight sets of posts, each more than 80 cm (32 in) in diameter. Immediately to the south and in part contemporary, a series of smaller but still impressive buildings was built and rebuilt on the same spot

Excavating the mid-third-century 'hall' at Gudme, Fyn, Denmark. Dark soil had backfilled the holes (outlined in white) in which wall timbers and internal roof supports had stood. The human figure shows how big these holes were.

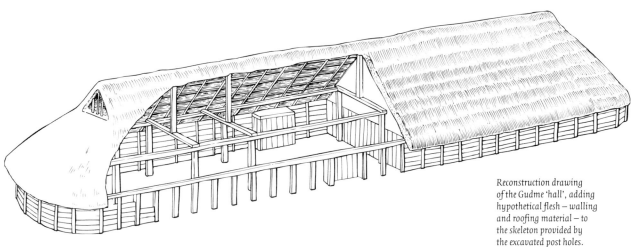

Reconstruction drawing of the Gudme 'hall', adding hypothetical flesh – walling and roofing material – to the skeleton provided by the excavated post holes.

between 200 and 500. Over 100 Roman silver coins, gold ornaments from Russia and Ukraine, decorated silverwork and a hoard of gold were all found there.

On the nearby coast, at Lundeborg, exchange and manufacture took place; as well as gold and silver there are craft products including glass, copper alloy, ironwork, amber and antler, and imported items such as opal, amethyst, garnet and carnelian. This collection, as well as 102 gold foils (see p. 17), all emphasize the enormous wealth and power concentrated at the Gudme/Lundeborg complex. Whoever lived there might be described as a king – but was he the first king of the Danes, or merely one of a series of local rulers in southern Scandinavia?

Newly erected defensive works also demonstrate the fear that pervaded Jutland and south Scandinavia, as well as the authority of those leaders who had to counter it. A 12-km (7.5-mile) long earthen rampart at Olgerdiget, in south Jutland, erected in 219, shows how large-scale human effort could be harnessed to defend regional communities. Smaller-scale but still impressive works include those at Eketorp, on the Swedish island of Öland. There, a 57-m (187-ft) diameter ringfort with a stone rampart was erected in c. 300 to protect 20 houses; in c. 400 it was rebuilt with an 80-m (260-ft) diameter rampart, now with houses, cattle byres and storehouses inside.

This is just one of 19 such forts on Öland that are believed to be approximately contemporary; they could be interpreted as the works of local families competing to flaunt their status, but are just as likely to have been inspired by external threats.

Air view of the reconstructed fortified village at Eketorp, on Öland, Sweden, as it is believed to have looked in its second phase of occupation, c. 400–650.

NEW SIGNS OF POWER

The Romans' Rhine frontier was overwhelmed by invading German tribes in AD 406, and during the fifth century the western half of the Roman Empire shrank and disintegrated. In a new era that combined threat with opportunity, the peoples of Scandinavia had to adapt. The tribal offerings of war booty peter out after about 500, either because there was greater stability in southern Scandinavia, or because the new elite decided on new cult practices.

Novel forms of conspicuous display now appeared. Some grave deposits became much more ostentatious, as the living elite honoured the elite dead. Bracteates – small gold discs modelled ultimately on Roman imperial medallions – became fashionable across southern Scandinavia. Their designs, it is suggested, reflect the god Odin's journey to the otherworld where, it was believed, he could contact the ancestors. Rich burials and Odin/ancestor worship may both have appealed to the new elite as means to legitimize their role and bolster their standing in society. Another symbol of wealth and power was the ring sword, named after the ring on their elaborate hilts. Embellished with gleaming gold and glistening garnets, ring swords were a sign of status across the Germanic world, not least in Anglo-Saxon England.

In Jutland part of the wealth available to the elite accrued simply because of the region's strategic position as the point of intersection between the Baltic and western Europe. At Dankirke, near the base of Jutland's west coast, an unusual assemblage of late Roman silver coins, over 1,300 shards of Frankish glass beakers and many metal objects all testify to links with the south in the fifth to seventh centuries. Presumably Dankirke was where a local aristocrat controlled and profited from the exchange of luxury items, and gained prestige by overseeing the conduit which brought them to the area.

From c. 500, so-called gold foil figures – small sheets of thin gold, typically 10–30 mm (less than 1 inch) tall, stamped with impressions of either one or two figures – appear to be another insignia of power. Approximately 3,000 gold foils are known, of which an amazing 2,345 come from one site at Sorte Muld on the island of Bornholm. Like the bracteates before them, and the ring swords (which

are represented on two of the Sorte Muld foils), these are virtually a pan-Scandinavian phenomenon. The stamped impressions on them are thought to signify either gods or rulers. Indeed, the double figures may combine a political and cultic significance, depicting the marriage of the god Freyr (representing secular power) to a giantess, Gerd (symbolizing the land). Some foils have been found deliberately placed in the foundations of aristocratic 'halls', such as that at Slöinge, in Halland, Sweden, where the associated timber post is dated c. 710–20. Possibly this is some sort of ritual or dedicatory deposit, indicating that the buildings (and their powerful owners and occupiers) exercised a religious function in society.

Another notable example of a probable temple has been found at Uppåkra, 4 km (2.5 miles) south

Gold bracteate, perhaps fifth-century, found at Gerete, Fardhem, Gotland, Sweden. The central figure amidst the die-stamped decoration may represent Odin.

(Left) Bronze and silver beaker, embellished with six bands of decorated gold foil, from Uppåkra, Sweden. It is 17 cm (6¾ in) tall, and dates to the sixth century.

(Below) Four of the 2,345 tiny gold foils known from Sorte Muld, Bornholm, Denmark, embellished with representations of gods or rulers.

of Lund in Skåne, southwest Sweden. There was a large and important settlement there throughout the first millennium, changing emphasis with the times but always manifesting itself archaeologically as the focal point within its region. In the period AD 1–400 the site was large and unusually rich; in the Migration Period (400–550) it is distinguished by the quantity of imported glass and jewelry from Europe, and by its array of metalworking which includes bracteates, gold foils and elaborate brooches. Inside a bow-side timber building measuring 12.6 by 5.6 m (41 by 18 ft) internally, its roof supported by four substantial posts, were found about 110 gold foils; in its centre a two-coloured glass bowl and a metal beaker with decorated gold foil bands had been carefully placed in what must have been a ceremonial act of ritual dedication. Equally remarkably, the structure seems to have remained in use for several centuries, into the early Viking Age.

A sixth-century ring sword found in Grave V at Snartemo, Vest Agder, Norway. Gold plate on the grip and silver-gilt mounts beside the lower guard's ring have so-called Style I animal-based decoration.

POLITICAL MERGERS:
THE RISE OF THE REGIONS

It may be that local differences within the Danish archaeological record during the period c. 250–550 represent the characteristics that distinguished individual tribes; a lessening of these distinctions in the fifth and sixth centuries may point to the formation of larger tribal confederacies, although precisely where their boundaries lay isn't certain. South Jutland, Fyn and west Sjaelland may have been one political unit; central Jutland a second; north Jutland and the Oslo Fjord region a third; and east Sjaelland and southwest Sweden a fourth. By the later sixth and seventh century archaeologically detectable distinctions had largely disappeared in south Scandinavia; so had ring swords and helmets, the ostentatious markers of an emerging aristocracy desperate to impress its relatively new and somewhat fragile superiority upon the population. This suggests that Denmark was a relatively unified area; in contrast, in south Norway, Uppland and Gotland the continuing currency of these objects indicates that contests for power were still the order of the day.

Norway: A Network of Chiefdoms

In southern Norway an expansion of the settled area during the fourth to sixth centuries suggests a growing population. The locations of rich aristocratic graves and the distribution of the hillforts settled and used at this time indicate that southern Norway was subdivided into 10 chiefdoms. All but one were sited in coastal areas, about 100 km (60 miles) apart from each other, either on the coast itself or some way up the fjords. The exception was inland in Vest Agder, where there seems to have been a power base that flourished through controlling the supply of pelts and furs from the mountain-dwelling hunters to the chiefs who lived along the coast.

Some of these Norwegian chiefs were buried within impressive burial mounds grouped as dynastic graveyards. At Borre in Vestfold, for example, the earliest mounds are dated to c. 600, and mark the start of a lordship that continued to bury its dead there until c. 900, well into the Viking Age. These chiefs may have reorganized where people lived – many farms in south and west Norway were abandoned in the sixth and seventh centuries, perhaps because the chiefs moved them to new sites which were more directly under their own control. With these semi-independent chiefdoms spread over long distances, the difficulties of uniting the whole coastline into one dominion are obvious, although there are hints that the ten chiefdoms were coalescing into a few larger political units in the seventh and eighth centuries. This geography of scattered lordship accounts for the time lag between the

PEOPLE AND PLACES – ACROSS THE CENTURIES

Writing in c. 550 the Gothic chronicler Jordanes named 30 Scandinavian tribes whose territory lay within modern Norway and Sweden. A comparison of some of these names and those of counties in Norway suggests long-term continuity of peoples and traditions:

Jordanes	Tribe	County Name
Grannii	Grener	Grenland
Augandzi	Egder	Agder
Rugi	Ryger	Rogaland
Arochi	Horder	Hordaland

The equally marked similarities between the tribal names recorded by classical writers such as Ptolemy and Tacitus and those surviving as names of districts in Jutland suggest a similar continuity there:

Classical Name of Tribe	District Name
Cimbri	Himmersyssel
Teutoni	Thysyssel
Vandalii	Vendsyssel
Harudi	Hardsyssel

creation of a Danish state and the creation of a politically unified Norway; it also emphasizes why the Norwegians, as well as the island-hopping Danes, developed such mastery of boats and sailing.

Vendel: The Rise of the Svear

In Sweden the years from 550 to 800 are called the Vendel Period. The name was coined after the discovery of a series of richly furnished boat graves uncovered in the 1880s and 1890s below mounds near the church of Vendel in Uppland, the heartland of the Svear kingdom. The mounds which had covered the burials had completely disappeared. Timbers from the 8.3-m (27-ft) long by 1.7-m (5-ft-6-in) wide boats had rotted, the graves contained no personal jewelry, and the skeletons of the dead men – for all the graves were men's – were not well preserved. What had survived to catch people's attention were remains of elaborate war gear, among which were ring swords and a remarkable series of iron helmets, as well as ornaments of outstanding quality.

From 1928 to 1952 a comparable cemetery was excavated at Valsgärde, a site which, like Vendel, lies beside a waterway that flows into Lake Mälaren. Improved excavation techniques revealed that earlier chamber graves, dated 400–600, had been reopened and emptied (looted?), probably soon after the burials, but the Vendel Period boat graves had been left undesecrated – an indication, presumably, of more settled conditions from the seventh into the eleventh century, while the graveyard remained in use. These extremely rich graves, and a few others in the region, are all found at the inland limits of the contemporary distribution of settlements; the wealth they represent may well have been generated by the control of outlying natural resources and products including iron, hides, furs and elk antler. Perhaps these goods were transported on to the coast, whence they could be redistributed more easily either within the Svear region or, indeed, beyond it, around the Baltic Sea. The dead must represent a local aristocracy, but exactly how far up the regional pecking order (aristocrats, kings?) has been much debated. The helmets buried with them indicate something of their pretensions, for they are based on types associated with Roman emperors and the imperial entourage. Presumably it had been warriors who took service as Roman auxiliary troops who had originally brought back home a knowledge of what was worn by the most powerful rulers in the world.

A Svear site at Helgö, 'the holy island' in Lake Mälaren, seems to have been a regional centre in both the Migration and Vendel Periods. In the fifth and sixth centuries jewelry and dress fittings were made there in large quantities: 90,000 fragments of clay moulds and 300 kg (660 lb) of crucible fragments have been recovered, as well as 70 late Roman gold coins, more than from any mainland Swedish site, and exceeded only on the islands of Öland and Gotland. Some of these coins came to light inside one of the buildings associated with metalworking; perhaps they were imported to be melted down and refashioned. Later, in the seventh and eighth centuries, the focus of activity had shifted slightly, and the site is remarkable for a range of objects that originated in distant lands. Exotic objects include an

(Opposite) Helmet from Grave I at Vendel, Uppland, Sweden; an iron framework supports decorated bronze plates and other embellishments. Seventh century.

THE WARRIOR'S WAY

In 1980 a warrior's grave dated to c. 600 was excavated at Rickeby in Vallentuna, Uppland, Sweden. A stone cairn about 1.6 m (5 ft) high and 13 m (43 ft) in diameter had been raised directly over the funeral pyre, encompassing the remains of the 40–50-year-old man. With him was his war gear – a sword, shield and helmet. Other objects such as glass drinking vessels, combs and gaming pieces including an antler die incised with runic letters, also indicate his high social status. So, too, do a horse and four dogs; whereas remains of sheep, cattle, pigs, hens, grouse, geese and a crane probably represent food eaten at the funeral feast. Most remarkable of all were traces of a sparrowhawk, a goshawk and two peregrine falcons – birds used in hawking, an aristocratic pursuit. An eagle owl, also found on the pyre, may have been used as a decoy to attract the hawks' prey.

The Rickeby aristocrat, depicted with the items that went with him to the otherworld.

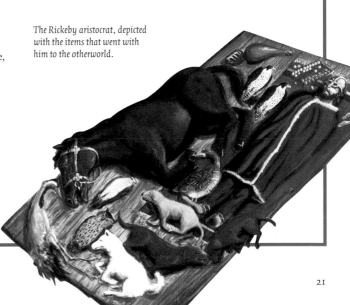

Irish ecclesiastical crozier; a Byzantine silver dish; a Coptic bronze ladle; much Rhenish glass; and a small bronze figure of the Buddha from north India. Helgö seems to have functioned, then, as a centre for commercial or politically motivated transactions.

In the Viking Age the Svears' most important cult site was at Old Uppsala where, it was said, there had been a great pagan temple. Certainly, there was a Viking Age cemetery. However, this place was already of considerable significance at a much earlier date. In c. 525–50 a boy aged between 10 and 14 and an older woman were cremated there; a pottery cremation urn was interred within a stone cairn that was capped by a 10-m (33-ft) high mound, one of three approximately contemporary 'Kings' Mounds' here. Among the diagnostic traces not totally consumed in the flames of the pyre were a decorated helmet of Vendel style, a seax (large knife) and a carved bone dove that was, perhaps, the tip of a sceptre. Such princely regalia suggest that this was a royal burial ground. A bronze mirror and a stone palette with traces of 'make-up', both unusual and prestigious objects, might have belonged to the woman. The nature of the relationship between these two individuals is not clear, however, and nor is the reason why their remains were buried together.

Danish Power in the Seventh Century

In the century or so starting about 700 there are several signs of increasingly sophisticated and co-ordinated power being wielded in south Scandinavia. Already, in the late seventh century, a defensive rampart with a ditch in front of it on its south side (part of the system known collectively as Danevirke) had been erected to defend Jutland from attack; in 737 parts of it were significantly strengthened with a strong timber-revetted facade. It ran across the base of the peninsula just south of the later town of Schleswig, between natural obstacles to invasion provided by waterways and bogs. Altogether at this stage in its development the complex ran for about 15 km (9½ miles).

Other massive earthmoving projects included the Kanhave canal, a 1-km (3,300-ft) cutting dug across the island of Samsø. It was 1.25 m (4 ft) deep and 11 m (36 ft) wide; where it passed through sand it was lined with horizontal oak planks which were pegged back into the battered sides and retained by raking posts driven into the subsoil. The posts have been dated to 726. Whether to facilitate trade or defence, the canal was a remarkable accomplishment.

There is no doubt, however, that it was trade and the economy that prompted the foundation of a

Buddha figurine of bronze, made in north India in c. 600, and found at Helgö, Sweden. Height 8.4 cm (3¼ in).

The grave mounds, looking south, at Old Uppsala, Sweden. The traditional site of the pagan temple is at or near the church at the centre left of the picture.

new sort of trading and manufacturing centre at Ribe, on Jutland's southwest coast, and this site has provided the clearest picture yet available of how such a trading centre could develop. In about 705 craftsmen, including glass bead makers, began to use Ribe; in about 710 a street running for about 200 m (650 ft) was laid out parallel to the river, and on both sides of the street ditches were dug, running back from it at 90 degrees. These ditches defined the boundaries between about 50 to 60 individual plots of land, each of which measured about 6–8 m (20–26 ft) wide by about 30 m (100 ft) long. No permanent structures, houses or workshops were erected at this stage, and it seems that the plots were occupied on a temporary or seasonal basis by itinerant craftsmen and merchants.

Vast quantities of debris from a variety of craft activities have been recovered; specialists were working antler, making textiles and leather goods, and producing iron objects, bronze and silver jewelry, glass beads and amber beads. Coins indicate contacts with western Europe, and in many ways Ribe seems to have taken over the functions of the fifth- to seventh-century settlement that stood only 4 km (2.5 miles) away at Dankirke (see p. 17). At Ribe, however, silver coins of an internationally accepted standard, called sceattas, seem to have been produced for the first time in Denmark; their designs have caused them to be called the Woden/Monster type.

All of these characteristics suggest that Ribe's planned development was the act of some overwhelmingly important regional ruler, perhaps the 'King of the Danes' called Angantyr who is named in slightly later documents. The plots may have been rented out to their occupiers by the king, who may also have taxed the commerce transacted there. Ribe was not strictly a town in its early decades, for occupation was not on a year-round basis. Nonetheless, the shape, size and plan of the early eighth-century settlement make it look more like an urban settlement than earlier places such as Gudme or Dankirke where craftsmen worked in and around an aristocratic manor. Moreover, by about 750, Ribe had permanent residents, and was truly urban.

(Above) Silver coins, known as sceattas, were minted at many places around the North Sea; these examples are of the Woden/Monster type, believed to have been struck at Ribe in the early eighth century.

(Top) Danevirke defended the south boundary of the Danish kingdom in Jutland; its grassed embankment conceals a long and complex history of reinforcement and rebuilding.

THE VIKING AGE: AN OUTLINE HISTORY

The start of the Viking Age may be defined in any one of several ways. Traditionally, it is the first precisely documented Viking raid overseas, in 793, that signals the beginning of this new era. This is indeed a convenient and valuable marker, not only because it is precisely dated but also because it is the external, seaborne depredations and adventures of the Vikings that particularly mark them out in what was generally a bloody and brutal period. Although the appearance of some characteristic artifact types of the Viking Age, such as oval brooches, may be taken back a decade or two towards the mid-eighth century, this is not sufficient reason to depart from a date of shortly before 800 as the start of the Viking Age.

The Vikings' world was simultaneously one of fission and of nucleation. During the two centuries and more that their energetic forays overseas attracted the attention of foreign writers, the medieval kingdoms of Denmark, Norway and Sweden were coalescing into recognizable entities. When Viking raids started at the end of the eighth century, most victims were terminologically inexact about the precise geographical origins of the aggressors. Nevertheless, a few Europeans, missionaries, did travel quite widely in southern Scandinavia in the first half of the ninth century. In Denmark, in particular, they could already see signs of considerable political power mobilized for substantial projects such as the earthwork rampart that defended Jutland, or in the canal that traversed the island of Samsø. Power was also manifested in extravagant funerals, such as the series of ship burials of the ninth century that have been investigated in the Oslo

Helge Ask, a replica of the Skuldelev 5 ship, a small (17.3 m) Danish warship built in about 1030.

Fjord area of Norway. And in each of the Scandinavian lands there was already a network of major international trading centres and lesser regional and local market places.

Traders, Raiders and Settlers

These international emporia attracted precious luxury goods from distant parts of Europe and the Near East. Trade and transport were the spurs for intrepid Scandinavian entrepreneurs to explore these distant lands in search of profit, and merchants were probably in the forefront of ventures that culminated in trips to the east and the west. Already, in the eighth century, Scandinavians had penetrated into what is now northwestern Russia, and this marked the start of a geographically and chronologically long association with not only Russia but also Byzantium, and beyond the Black Sea and the Caspian Sea to Arab lands, a source of great profit.

Westwards, the intermittent late eighth- and early ninth-century Viking raids lead to more frequent and concerted attacks throughout large areas of Britain and Ireland. The establishment of raiding bases in Ireland from the 840s is well documented, whereas the stages by which parts of northern and western Scotland were over-run are not at all clear. Three formerly independent Anglo-Saxon kingdoms were annexed by a great Viking army in the 870s, and Scandinavian kings ruled parts of England until 954. In a variety of ways the influence of these Scandinavian settlers in the British Isles can still be traced today. Elsewhere in continental western Europe, only Normandy experienced an influx of Scandinavian settlers, although raids are attested, historically and archaeologically, in modern Holland, Germany, Belgium, France, Portugal, Spain and Italy as Vikings ventured around the Atlantic coast and into the Mediterranean, where North Africa was also molested on occasion. The Baltic Sea was another arena for Viking activity, both raiding and, in some areas, settlement. Baltic islands, notably Gotland, became remarkably wealthy at this time.

While some Scandinavians were intent on seizing foreign wealth in long-established, prosperous and well-populated kingdoms, others set their sights on unpopulated pastures. The islands of the North Atlantic successively enticed settlers, some of whom had already experienced the ups and downs of Viking life in Britain or Ireland. Vikings had reached the Faeroes by the early ninth century; in the second half of that century Iceland's habitable areas were filling with migrant farmers; and a century later, in

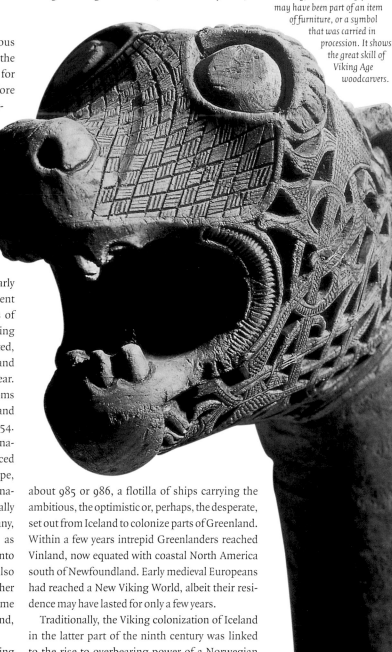

An animal-headed wooden post, one of five, all different in their decoration, found in the ship burial at Oseberg, Vestfold, Norway, dated to c. 834. It may have been part of an item of furniture, or a symbol that was carried in procession. It shows the great skill of Viking Age woodcarvers.

about 985 or 986, a flotilla of ships carrying the ambitious, the optimistic or, perhaps, the desperate, set out from Iceland to colonize parts of Greenland. Within a few years intrepid Greenlanders reached Vinland, now equated with coastal North America south of Newfoundland. Early medieval Europeans had reached a New Viking World, albeit their residence may have lasted for only a few years.

Traditionally, the Viking colonization of Iceland in the latter part of the ninth century was linked to the rise to overbearing power of a Norwegian king called Harald Finehair. Historians now believe that his successes in putting down opposition were several decades too late to have instigated a migration of defeated or dispossessed Norwegians, but he appears to represent the tendency for the

AD 1   800   900   950

SCANDINAVIA

Weapon Finds in Bogs
• Harald Finehair, King of Norway (c. 870)
• Harald Finehair wins Battle of Hafrsfjord (885/90)
Birka founded •
Håkon the Good, King of Norway (c. 934) •   • Sigtuna founded
Kaupang founded (c. 800) •   • Oseberg ship built (834)   Ravning causeway built (979/80) •
• Runes Invented   • Danevirke begun   Gorm the Old, King of Denmark (c. 950) •
• Danevirke strengthened (737)   Harald Bluetooth Christianizes Denmark (960s/70s) •
• Nydam boat (310)   • Ansgar's missions to Denmark and Sweden (826–54)
• Ribe founded (c. 705)   Death of Gorm; Harald Bluetooth's accession (958/9) •
Samsø canal (726) •   • Slav merchants move to Hedeby (808)   Danish circular camps built (980/1) •

WESTERN EUROPE

Charlemagne orders defences against the pagans (c. 800) •
• Death of Godfrid in Frisia; Siege of Paris (885)
• Raids in Spain, North Africa, Mediterranean France and NW Italy (859/60)
Rouen burned (841) •   • Deventer (Zutphen) raided (882)
Pirates on the Lower Seine (820) •   • Winter camps established on Loire and Seine (850)
Vikings bribed to leave Paris (845) •   • Hrolfr founds independent Normandy (911)
Dorestad raids (834–65) •   • Loire fleet raids Spain and Africa (844)   • Rouen replanned, mint revived (925–

EASTERN EUROPE, RUSSIA, BYZANTIUM, NEAR EAST

First Viking ventures in Russia •   Rus attack Constantinople (907) •   Slavicization of Russian state
Rus envoys go to Constantinople and on to Francia (839) •   • Traditional date for Slav invitation to Rus; Ryurikovo Gorodisce founded (862)   • Rus-Byzantine treaty (945
Rus attack across Caspian Sea (910) •   • Baghdad envoy meets Rus on River Volga (9
Rus fleet attacks Constantinople (860) •   • Oleg captures Kiev and makes it Rus capital (882)
Arab dirhams exported west to Scandinavia and Europe (780–960)

ENGLAND

Sporadic raids (800–50)   • More Viking invaders in England (892–96)
King Edmund of East Anglia killed (869) •   • Viking settlers in northwest England (c. 900)
Lindisfarne raid (793) •   • First overwintering in England; Codex Aureus ransomed (851)
'Great Heathen Army' campaigns in England (865–79) •   • Alfred becomes king of Wessex (871)
York captured (866) •   • Vikings share out and settle Northumbria (876)
'Great Heathen Army' overwinters at Repton (873/4) •   • Alfred and Guthrum divide England (880)
Vikings share out and settle and East Midlands (877) •   • More raids (885)   • Athelstan controls York (927–39)
Vikings share out and settle East Anglia (879) •   • St Edmund memorial pennies minted (895)
Cuerdale hoard deposited (905) •   Viking raids recommence (980) •
English reconquest of Midlands and East Anglia (909–18) •   • Ragnall takes control of York (c. 914)
Athelstan defeats Irish Vikings and Scots at Brunanburh (937) •

THE IRISH SEA ZONE (Western Scotland, Wales, Isle of Man, Ireland)

First Viking raids recorded (794) •   • Viking burials in Western Isles (850–75)
Vikings overwinter in southwest Wales (878) •   Wales attacked (950 onwards) •
First recorded raid on Wales (852) •   Pagan burials on Man (940s–950s) •
First Irish raid; Iona raided (795) •   Manx monuments by Gautr (930–50) •
Vikings expelled from Dublin settle in Cumbria (902) •   Olaf of Dublin buried on Iona; Dublin Vikings lose Battle of Tara (980) •
Irish defeat and kill Turgeís (845) •   Dublin 'refounded' (917) •
Dublin founded (841) •   Hiberno-Viking armrings produced (850–950)   • Dublin sacked by Irish (94
Vikings rampant in Ireland (837–45) •   Last great raid by Dublin Vikings (951) •

THE NORTH ATLANTIC (Northern Isles of Scotland, Faeroes, Iceland, Greenland, North America)

• 794 First raids on Scotland may include Northern Isles
• 892 Death of Sigurd, first earl of Orkney
825 Vikings on Faeroes •
• Iceland's main settlement according to Islendingabok (870–930)
982 Erik the Red, banished from Iceland, explores Greenland

AD 1   800   900   950

1000	1050	1100	1200	1500

● Olaf Skötkonung, King of Sweden; promotes Christianity (995)
● Olaf Tryggvason seizes Norway; promotes Christianity (995)
ath of Harald Bluetooth; Svein Forkbeard's accession (985/7)
    ● Svein Forkbeard invades England (1013)
    ● Death of Svein Forkbeard; accession of Cnut (1014)
    ● Cnut, King of Norway (1019)   ● Harald Hardraada invades England and is killed (1066)
Death of Cnut (1035) ●   ● Harald Hardraada, King of Norway (1045/7)
● Olaf Tryggvason killed at Battle of Svold (1000) ● Danish invasions of England (1069–75)
   ● Olaf Haraldsson killed at Battle of Stiklestad (1030)

● Aethelred of England flees to Normandy (1013)

● Cnut a guest in Rome (1027)

...adimir of Kiev marries Byzantine princess and
...onverts to Christianity; Varangian Guard founded (988)
   ● Ingvar's expedition to Serkland (1041)
   ● Harald Hardraada in Varangian Guard (1030s–1040s)
Kievan and Byzantine goods reach Sweden   ● Earl Rognvald of Orkney makes
   pilgrimage to Holy Land (1151–53)

● 1009–12 Thorkell's army campaigns and bought off;
   Thorkell recruited by English; heregeld levied
● 1011 Archbishop Alfheah of Canterbury abducted and killed
991 Vikings win Battle of Maldon; first Danegeld payment
● 994 Olaf Tryggvason baptized in England ● 1066 Harald Hardraada defeated at Stamford Bridge
 ● 1002 St Brice's Day massacre ● 1068 English royal family flee to Denmark
  ● 1013 Svein Forkbeard invades ● 1069/70/75 Danish raids on York
  ● 1014 Svein dies; Cnut expelled
  ● 1015 Cnut returns
...ut king (1016–35) ● ● 1035–42 Cnut's sons rule in turn
   ● 1042 English dynasty returns

...otto-Viking armrings produced (950–1050) Norwegian expedition to Western Isles (1230) ●
...Guthroth, first King of the Western Isles, dies (989) Norwegian expedition to Western Isles and Man (1263) ●
  Norway becomes overlord of Western Isles (1098) ● Scots gain control of Western Isles (1266) ●
   Anglo-Normans capture Waterford and Dublin (1265) ● ● Scots gain control of Man (1265)
  ● Manx coinage starts (1020s) ● Somerled rules Man and Isles (1120s/30s–1164)
● Dublin mints coinage (997) ● 1079–1265 Dublin dynasty rules Man ● Anglo-Normans invade Ireland (1169)
 ● Dublin sacked by Irish (999) Norwegian king killed in Ulster (1103) ●
  ● Dublin and its allies defeated at Battle of Clontarf (1014) ● 1102 Dublin slave trade with England stops

   Murder of (St) Magnus of Orkney (1117) ● ● End of Orkney earl's family dynasty (1231)
  Building Kirkwall Cathedral as shrine to Magnus (1136) ● Orkney and Shetland handed back to Scots (1468–69) ●
   Death of last bishop on Greenland (1377) ●
  Earl Rognvald of Orkney on pilgrimage to Holy Land (1151–53) ●
   Snorre Sturluson, Icelandic politician and writer (1178/9–1241) ● ● Western Settlement of
● Iceland accepts Christianity Iceland Age of Sturlungs – political feuding (1220s–1260s) ● Greenland abandoned (1350)
● c. 1000 Vinland explored Norway–Greenland regular contact severed (1367/9) ● ● Skraelings attack
...5/6 Erik the Red colonizes Greenland Norwegian overlordship of Greenland (1261) ● Greenlanders (1379)
  Norwegian overlordship of Iceland begins (1262–64) ● Greenland abandoned (c. 1450)

1000	1050	1100	1200	1500

amalgamation of petty lordships into larger kingdoms. When Harald Finehair's son, Erik Bloodaxe, the last Scandinavian king to rule in tenth-century England, was expelled in 954, a powerful royal dynasty was asserting itself in Denmark.

Over four generations the family of Gorm the Old cemented their power at home. In the second generation, Harald Bluetooth introduced Christianity as the religion of choice (or expediency); third-generation Svein Forkbeard was the most important figure in a new wave of attacks against England in the late tenth and early eleventh centuries; and in 1016 fourth-generation Cnut made himself master of England. His rule eventually extended not only to Denmark but, for some time, to parts of Norway and Sweden as well. In this he was following the precedents set intermittently over the previous two centuries, but Danish control there was never unchallenged for long. The Danes represented a foe against whom other, quasi-national dynasties could define themselves, and eventually, as the Viking Age ended, recognizable independent kingdoms of Norway and Sweden, as well as Denmark, were emerging.

The End of the Viking Age

By about 1000 much of Scandinavia was nominally Christian; indeed, King Olaf Haraldsson of Norway, a key figure in the rise of the Norwegian state, rapidly became recognized as a popular martyr saint after his death in battle in 1030, fighting against the Danes. It was his half-brother, King Harald Hardraada of Norway, whose attempted invasion of England in 1066 was defeated at the Battle of Stamford Bridge in Yorkshire; and the death of this archetypal Viking adventurer there may be said to mark the end of the Viking Age.

It did not, of course, bring down the curtain on all the Scandinavian settlements and colonies abroad. Yet they too were gradually adapting to changing circumstances. Already, by 1066 the Norsemen of Normandy had evolved into Normans, adopting the French ways of their neighbours, and the Viking

states of Russia had taken on a Slavic mantle. Iceland maintained its independence far longer, but succumbed to Norwegian control in the mid-thirteenth century. So did Greenland, where conditions slowly depleted the settlements to the point where

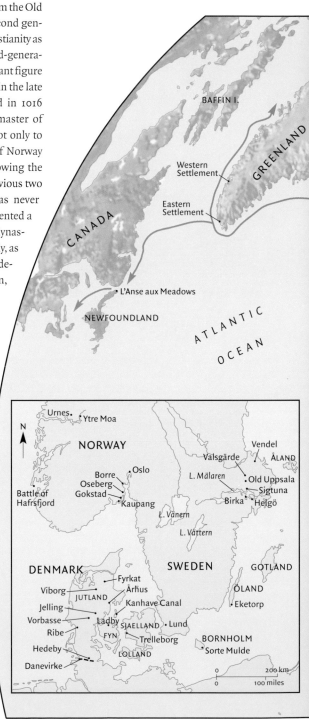

they were wholly abandoned in the early to mid-fifteenth century. Just when Norway formally took over Iceland and Greenland it lost control of its possessions in the Hebrides, off the west coast of Scotland; and by the time the Greenland settlement had disappeared, the archipelagos of Orkney and Shetland had been surrendered to the Scottish king. With this handover in 1468–69 the political legacy of the Viking Age was largely exhausted; the world that the Vikings had created was no more.

Map of the Viking world, showing the major sites mentioned in the text.

II · VIKING LIFE AND CULTURE

Throughout Viking Age Scandinavia almost everyone's main preoccupation was the production of food. Farming, together with fishing, trapping and collecting, were the main activities in the annual cycle. Communities had to be largely self-sufficient, taking advantage of fertile soils, good pasture, well-stocked fishing grounds or whatever else nature had provided. They also had to be expert in fashioning a range of raw materials into the tools and equipment that they needed; their self-sufficiency would be the envy of most modern western communities.

Geographical differences inevitably decreed that the basis of the subsistence economy would vary enormously across Scandinavia. Nevertheless, the archaeological record of house forms, jewelry, tools and other everyday equipment from across Scandinavia is sufficiently uniform to warrant labelling the period by a single name – the Age of the Vikings.

Only a very few of the inhabitants of the world of the Vikings are known to us by name. Kings and war-leaders feature in the sparse contemporary chronicles written in some neighbouring Christian states; Swedish rune stones at the end of the Viking Age commemorate the deeds of named Viking adventurers; immigrants to Iceland were recorded much later in *Landnámabók*, 'the Book of the Settlements'; the Icelandic sagas tell the stories of some believably historical characters such as Leif Eriksson. Occasionally, surviving artifacts were inscribed with their owner's (or even maker's) name – 'Ranvaig owns this casket', 'Thorfastr makes a good comb' – inviting us to speculate about these people. The nicknaming habit beloved of the Vikings conjures up cartoon images of a few individuals: 'Domnall seal's-head owns this sword' makes us wonder whether he had the flat-crowned, somewhat 'horse-faced' appearance of the grey seal; whereas Sigtryggr 'the one-eyed' or Olaf 'the little hunchback' are more readily pictured. But what of Ivar 'the boneless'?

Comments by bemused or contemptuous foreigners indicate something of the Vikings' appearance, as do the few representations of them that have come down to us. An English writer refers to the Danish fashion of 'blinded eyes' and 'bared neck', which may suggest hair styled to be long at the front and short at the back. But only in death, through the discovery and analysis of human skeletons, do we come face to face with Vikings and their contemporaries.

Reconstruction of the interior of a house from Hedeby, Schleswig.
The central hearth is enclosed with wood; there is a soapstone bowl to left foreground, and a
vessel suspended over the flames. On the raised side bench is a tub and a warp-weighted loom.
Only the pottery, such as the ring-shaped loom weights, survives in the archaeological record.

THE PEOPLES OF SCANDINAVIA

The people who lived in the Viking homelands did not think of themselves collectively as a group in the way that we today might say 'She's a Scandinavian'. Neither, at the start of the Viking Age, did they think of themselves territorially as Danes, Norwegians or Swedes; instead, these terms were used to describe three of the groups of people who were identified as living within what we know call Scandinavia. The modern country boundaries did not exist, however, and the concept of nationality was, at best, embryonic. Instead, allegiances were to individuals, kings or chiefs who ruled (or who wanted to rule) peoples who defined themselves as being different from their neighbours. For the most part these differences in Scandinavia were somewhat artificial constructs, but in some cases a feeling of independence and distinctiveness was heightened by a more overt recognition of ethnic variety.

Most obviously different was the way of life practised by the people now called Saami, previously known as Lapps. The Saami were a mobile people, whose life revolved around hunting, trapping, gathering and fishing; elk and reindeer provided many of the essentials of food, clothing, tools, and so on. Animal furs were an important commodity that attracted the attention of Viking merchants. The Saami roamed over much of the north of Norway and Sweden, as well as Finland and into Russia. It is now recognized that they ventured considerably further south than was previously thought, down towards latitude 60 degrees North, close to Oslo and Uppsala. The exploration of their contribution to Viking Age life is at a relatively early stage, but there is no doubt that Saami and Viking achieved a modus vivendi that was, at least, mutual toleration. In some places the Saami payed tribute to Viking chieftains; how much closer their relations may have become is under active discussion.

Within what is now Sweden, the Svear, whose name eventually came to embrace the whole country but whose heartland was in the hinterland of Lake Mälaren, in and beyond the Stockholm area, had rivals to their south. Known as the Goths, their former presence is echoed in the regional names Vestergötland and Östergötland. Like the Svear (but even more so) they are a people without a documented history; archaeology is the key to their existence. Areas still further south, along the coast, were under Danish control or more open to Danish influence.

Ranking the Vikings

Viewed simplistically through the prism of some documentary sources, the population of Viking Age Scandinavia can be ranked into a few, well-defined classes. At the top of the social tree were kings; they were surrounded, supported or supplanted by jarls or earls. These members of the nobility, in turn, oversaw the lives of freemen who, usually, farmed their own land or were merchants or craftsmen. The lowest of the low were slaves.

In reality, there seem to have been a great many more steps on the social ladder, as a careful reading of all the written sources demonstrates. The

Map showing the distribution and territories of the main peoples of Scandinavia. Much of the central and northern regions of Scandinavia were not inhabited during the Viking Age.

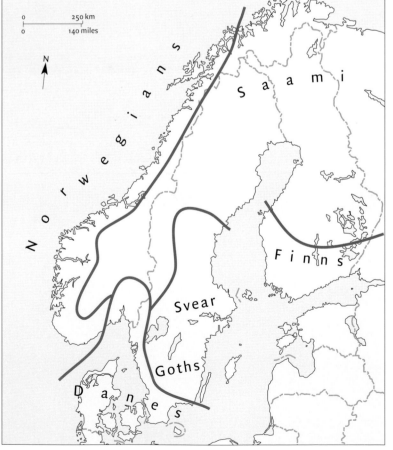

evidence of rune stones, for example, introduces a series of terms that suggest a complex and finely graded society, although the pecking order of their interrelationships is not always clear. Throughout much of northern Scandinavia during most of the Viking Age there was little difference between individuals who may have styled themselves as king and those who might have been termed an earl. Both, by later medieval and modern standards, were petty kings who were in control of relatively small areas. Their tenure was also fragile; the rather fuller written sources from Anglo-Saxon England, for example, demonstrate something of the intrigues and rivalries that could exist both within and between dynasties. Power and prestige were within the grasp of ambitious, shrewd and charismatic princelings able to command an army.

The retinues of kings and noblemen contained a variety of followers who hoped to prosper by their association with royalty and to consolidate their positions in society through rewards from their master. Closest to the kings were their húskarls (or housekarls), literally 'house men'. Best known as the innermost fighting retinue, virtual bodyguards, housekarls were entrusted with other key tasks such as diplomatic missions and collecting money owed to the king. Another key post in the court was that of 'staller', literally the royal 'stableman' but apparently more aptly described as a marshal. Both housekarls and stallers were transplanted to the Anglo-Scandinavian courts of King Cnut in the eleventh century. The rune stones also mention several other titles or positions at court, all of which presumably came with various privileges as well as responsibilities, but their fine details remain mysterious.

The ordinary freeman landowner was known as a bóndi, the equivalent of the Anglo-Saxon ceorl or churl. All freemen were not equal, however – family circumstances, the fortunes of war, innate ability, ambition, skill and sheer good luck meant that some could become more equal than others. Venturing abroad on Viking raids or trading ventures was one means of prospering, of acquiring the wherewithal to purchase lands and win the respect of your contemporaries. An Anglo-Saxon document of the early eleventh century, conceivably compiled when Cnut was on the throne, lays out the terms upon which a ceorl could raise himself to

the minor aristocracy, and it is likely that there were similarly well-recognized routes opening advancement to freemen in the Scandinavian homelands. Not all freemen automatically prospered, however, and not all of them owned the land that they worked – some were tenant farmers, paying rent to landlords. Here was another incentive to seize the chance that 'viking' offered, the chance to win a sufficient share of plunder to buy land.

Slaves

Sometimes the drudgery of working the land and undertaking menial tasks could be passed down to slaves, who were an integral part of society all over northern and western Europe at this time. A slave or thraell could be condemned to servitude by being captured on a raid or after a battle; less dramatically, he or she could reach that state as a result of economic or social pressures. Slaves were not necessarily badly treated – they had to be fit to do the work that enriched (or at least fed) their owner. And slaves could sometimes be set free – a runic inscription at Hørning in Jutland records that Toki the smith raised the stone in memory of Thorgisl, son of Gudmund, who gave him gold and his freedom.

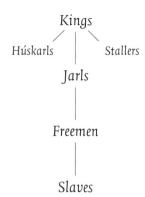

(Above) The hierarchy of the Viking world.

Rune stone from Hørning, north Jutland, Denmark, recording the freeing of a slave. The cross symbol shows it was raised after the official adoption of Christianity in Denmark. Height 1.6 m (5 ft 3 in).

VIKING WOMEN

A re-enactor tablet-weaving to produce a decorative braid like those that adorn the hem of her dress.

One of the three sleighs interred in c. 834 with the female burial in a ship at Oseberg, Norway. This and the other decorated woodwork illustrate the craftsmanship and resources at the command of high-status women in the early ninth century.

Women are outnumbered by men in both the archaeological and the documentary record of the Viking Age, yet there is evidence from both sources that women shared in many of the era's defining experiences. Some – probably only a few – accompanied their menfolk on Viking raids; the *Anglo-Saxon Chronicle* records that when the English successfully stormed a Viking camp at Benfleet, Essex, in 893 they captured women and children, including the wife and two sons of the Vikings' leader. This woman may not have been a Scandinavian (she might have been Frankish, for example, or from some other part of Europe), but hers is not (quite) the only instance of a reference to women travelling with the Viking armies.

Women of royal or aristocratic status such as this were certainly those most likely to figure in the documentary sources, and among the most striking of them all is Aud the Deep-Minded. Daughter of a Norwegian Viking who ruled in the Hebrides in the mid-ninth century, she was married to a Viking king of Dublin and had a son by him. Years later, after this son's death, she took his other son and daughters and her own household to Iceland, where she settled. This intrepid venture is not unique in the sagas – when Vinland was explored a

century later, Freydis, sister of Leif Eriksson, is reported to have gone on the last of the voyages. But whereas there are several independent sources that tell about Aud, for Freydis we have to rely exclusively on just two sagas, and there is thus the possibility that stories about her have been manufactured in the interests of the saga narrative and of its deeper meanings.

Archaeology confirms that women of high status were treated lavishly, at least in death. The famous ship burial that took place at Oseberg (see p. 225) in Vestfold, Norway, in 834, an exercise in the ostentatious disposal of wealth and an affirmation of its organizer's power and prestige, was the final resting place of two women. One was in her twenties, in her prime; the other, aged about 50, had suffered badly from arthritis. Such a magnificent funeral, it is supposed, can only represent royalty – but which one was the queen? Unfortunately the grave had been robbed in antiquity and any jewelry that might have distinguished the relative importance of the two women had been removed. Elderly queen and young female attendant; young queen and faithful old retainer; two members of the royal family who had died simultaneously? The mystery remains.

Although no comparably rich female Viking grave has ever been found outside Scandinavia, a scatter of recognizably female burials confirms the potential reality of the story of Aud. They demonstrate that the Scandinavians who settled abroad were not an all-male contingent, but included women who went to the grave bedecked in traditional Scandinavian jewelry, and who were buried with such traditional Scandinavian rites as interment in a boat.

In Scandinavia it is not only graves but, even more particularly, later Viking Age rune stones, which demonstrate the status of some women. Indeed, the very act of commissioning a rune stone was an index of wealth. On these stones such women proclaimed their status as individual land holders, their piety and generosity in paying for the building of bridges, and they often implied their legal rights to what they and their heirs inherited. Yet, at the other end of the spectrum, it seems to have been female babies who were more vulnerable to the infanticide that was apparently sometimes practised at the behest of fathers.

Reconstruction of the woman's boat burial from Røttingsnes, Tingvoll, Møre og Romsdal, Norway. Although it is the large ships from a handful of burials that have caught most attention, the majority of boat graves utilized much smaller vessels such as this.

(Above) Box-shaped brooches, like this one from Mårtens, Grötlingbo, Gotland, Sweden, were characteristic of women's costume on Gotland during the Viking Age. This one is made of gilt bronze and highlighted with panels of gold and silver.

COSTUME AND APPEARANCE

(Right) Reconstruction of the clothing worn by the aristocrat buried in c. 971 at Mammen, Jutland, Denmark. The colours, yarns and weaving techniques are correct, but the precise form of the garments is speculative. More usually, Vikings probably wore linen shirts like this reconstruction (far right) of the eleventh-century one from Viborg, Jutland, Denmark.

Reconstructing the fashions and clothing worn by Viking Age people relies on several sources of information, most of them tantalizingly incomplete. There are some small-scale representations of costume, on carvings and embroideries for example, but these are necessarily impressionistic and give only the most general of guidance rather than any detailed evidence.

Usually the fabrics from which clothing was made do not survive when buried in the ground. Archaeologists have therefore had to eke out information by looking at the corrosion products left when decaying metal brooches or buckles impregnate the textiles to which they were attached, thereby preserving the form of tiny fragments of

weave. Only in exceptional soil conditions do woollen, linen or silk garments survive, and even then it is normally only smallish fragments that remain – worn-out clothing was not usually discarded intact, but was used for anything from rags to toilet paper. Nevertheless, enough is known to allow some broad generalizations, although in the knowledge that there was regional variation across Scandinavia, and that Scandinavian settlers abroad could be influenced by the sartorial customs of their new neighbours, which they might adopt or adapt.

Garments were often essentially similar in their basic form across the social spectrum; it was quality of cloth, intricacy of decorative elements, richness of colour and opulence of accessories that distinguished the very rich from the poor.

Men's Costume

Men customarily had a long-sleeved undershirt of linen or wool, pulled on over the head and reaching down to just above their knees. Over this might be worn a tunic or kirtle of broadly similar form, with a belt or cord at the waist; or, alternatively, a pullover-type upper garment and knee-length trousers, the lower legs covered by long socks or hose, tied at the top but sometimes footless. Ankle socks are also known. Shoes took a variety of

Silver amulets/pendants from Sweden representing female figures, perhaps Valkyries, show the long trailing dresses typical of women's clothing. Their hairstyles may also indicate contemporary fashions.

forms from ankle boots to slip-ons, fastened by toggles or ties. A cloak, pinned at the right shoulder, completed the outfit. The cloak pins took many forms. In the west, the Irish ringed pin was widely adopted, and was taken by the Vikings as far as North America (see p. 161); more costly, large penannular brooches of silver were also a fashion in the British Isles, while smaller penannular brooches were a trait in the Baltic. Some men, such as the Repton warrior (see box on p. 38) wore a few beads, and, in this case, an amulet in the form of a Thor's hammer, on a thong around their neck. Other male jewelry could include a finger ring; silver and other armrings of a variety of types, worn to display wealth; and neckrings were also worn by some. Depending upon the resources available, all these might be of iron, copper-alloy, silver or gold; they range in design from the relatively simple to complex variations of elaborately inter-twisted strands.

Women's Costume

Women wore a long-sleeved ankle-length underdress that was made slightly longer at the back and thus trailed behind them in the manner that is portrayed on contemporary representations of Valkyries and other females. Over this could be worn what is often described as a pinafore dress, a calf-length garment wrapped around the body below the armpits and held over each shoulder by a strap that was fastened above each breast by a pin, most characteristically in the form of an oval ('tortoise') brooch. A third brooch, of different shape, most often of trefoil, disc or equal-armed form, was sometimes worn between and below this pair. Suspended from these brooches might be fine-linked chains, pendants and beads. The beads might be made of glass or of semi-precious stones; amber was common; carnelian from the Black Sea area, rock crystal, jet (probably from Yorkshire) and amethyst from the Middle East also appear sometimes. Over all this a cloak or cape could be worn, fastened at the throat by a disc or other brooch. Shoes were broadly similar to those worn by men.

Luxuries

The hoard found in 1834 at the Hoen farm in Eiker, Buskerud, Norway, gives some idea of the very high quality of gold jewelry available to wealthy sections of society (illustrated overleaf). Sixteen gold coins and four gilt silver coins, which between them originated in Arab, Carolingian, English, and Byzantine mints, and also included heirlooms in the form of Late Roman and Merovingian issues, all had suspension loops applied to make them pendants on a necklace. The coins had been very carefully selected so that, wherever possible, it was the side of the coin with a royal portrait that faced outwards. Of the other 52 gold and 13 silver ornaments, the majority had been made in Scandinavia, although there were also pieces of Carolingian, Anglo-Saxon and Byzantine origin.

Replicas of types of shoe found at Hedeby, Schleswig.

*Tenth-century silk headdress
from Coppergate, York.*

*(Opposite) Much of the
jewelry in the hoard from Hoen,
Buskerud, Norway, deposited
in c. 875, including neck-rings,
armrings and pendants, was
made in Scandinavia;
Carolingian pieces include the
trefoil mount that has been
refashioned as a brooch.*

The clothing of the well-to-do could be enhanced by sewing on decorative edge strips made in the technique called tablet-weaving (see p. 49). Particularly in the tenth century, gold or silver thread might be woven into the garments of the prosperous; silver wire was also used to fashion buttons of types found in cemeteries from Birka in Sweden to Peel on the Isle of Man.

The most expensive of all textiles were silks. Fragments have been found in royal graves such as that at Jelling in Denmark and Oseberg in Norway, as well as in graves at Birka in Sweden, where the silk has been attributed to a Chinese workshop. It is generally thought that most of the silk found in the Viking world came from Byzantium (see p. 99), although Baghdad is another possibility for some of it. Birka, York, Dublin and Lincoln have all produced evidence that some women wore a form of cap or bonnet on their head; others wore a tasselled, scarf-like garment.

Face to Face with the Vikings

Contemporary writings give few clues to the appearance of the people who inhabited the Viking world. Whenever human skeletons of this period are encountered, however, there is an opportunity to write biographies of these individuals and then to generalize about living conditions in that time. Ever more subtle scientific techniques available to the palaeopathologist can distinguish not only age at death and sex, but identify traces of disease, of diet, of wounds and trauma, and even indicate whereabouts childhood was spent.

Famously, in *King Harald's Saga*, King Harold of England offered the invader King Harald Hardraada of Norway 'seven feet of English ground, or as much more as he is taller than other men.' As the Anglo-Saxon king rode off, Hardraada commented 'What a little man that was; but he stood proudly in his stirrups.' The heights and appearance of the two kings are not known, but average height for adult males at this time was about 1.73 m (5 ft 8 in), and for women about 1.57 m (5 ft 2 in). These figures are not dramatically different from current average stature, and Viking Age individuals dressed in modern clothes would not stand out from their present-day descendants on account of their height. However, a crowd of people representative of Viking Age society would strike a modern observer as including rather few elderly people.

Life expectancy in the Viking Age, even for warriors not cut down in their prime, was relatively short and unpredictable – the ages reached by Anglo-Saxon kings in the tenth century, who mostly died in their twenties, thirties, forties or fifties, make the point. Infant mortality must have been high; women faced added risks of childbirth which killed an appreciable number of them (see p. 30); acute illnesses had no surgical remedy and chronic conditions such as arthritis took their toll. Life on the farm, as a fisherman or hunter, was rigorous; daily chores involved hard physical grind.

THE BITER BIT

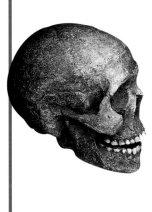

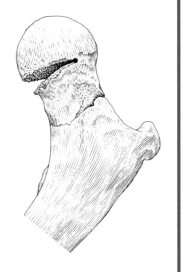

The risks that raiders ran have been graphically revealed by the skeleton of a warrior buried within the camp at Repton, in Derbyshire, where Vikings spent the winter of 873–74. Aged between 35 and 45, and 1.81 m (5 ft 11 in) tall, he was a robust individual who had ended his life fighting. Hit over the head, he had fallen to the ground and been consigned to Valhalla by a slashing blow that almost severed the joint between his hip and left leg, cutting his femoral artery and rapidly draining the lifeblood from him.
This dramatic scene, reconstructed on the basis of osteological evidence, is a typical, if particularly vivid, example of how the wounds and traumas experienced by people of the Viking Age can be identified; and it illustrates only too graphically the outcome of Viking failure.

(Left) Skull from the Repton warrior.

(Right) The fatal wound on the ball joint at the top of the Repton warrior's femur (thigh bone).

AT HOME WITH THE VIKINGS

Improved excavation techniques coupled with more opportunities to investigate individual buildings, farmsteads, hamlets and villages in advance of redevelopment projects in the last half century have greatly increased knowledge of home life in Viking Age Scandinavia. Perhaps the most remarkable advances have been the extensive programmes of large-scale investigations, particularly in Jutland at sites such as Omgård, Saedding, and Trabjerg. At Vorbasse 260,000 sq. m (2.8 million sq. ft) were excavated in 1974–87, providing an opportunity to trace that settlement's development through the entire first millennium. Especially important has been the recognition of ditched boundaries that surround and subdivide several of these settlements into their individual plots; because of this it is possible to see which buildings are associated with which, and thus to get a clearer picture of the settlement's social and economic basis.

From the north of Norway and Sweden down to the south of Denmark there were some general similarities in the plan forms of houses built during the Viking Age, although the materials used to construct them varied to reflect the regional abundance of stone, turf or timber. Timber buildings had many different forms of wall construction; upright posts with their bases set in post-holes dug into the ground or, sometimes, set into a continuous foundation trench, provided a framework; walls were clad with upright planks (staves) or with a lattice of interwoven twigs and/or withies that was plastered over with mud in the wattle and daub tradition that has been recognized, for example, at Vorbasse. Roofing material also varied, with thatch, turf and shingles all employed according to regional custom.

A typical farmhouse in the pre-Viking period was what is known technically in Britain as a longhouse, a name that reflects its defining feature, which is that both humans and their livestock lived, albeit in separate compartments, under one long roof. The long walls of longhouses were often slightly curved, so that the widest part of the building was at its centre. Longhouses varied considerably in length but were normally about 5 m (16 ft) wide, and had their roofs supported internally by two rows of paired posts that divided the

Reconstruction of the village at Vorbasse, Jutland, Denmark, as it was in c. 900. Three farms, each arranged around a large main building, can be seen on each side of a trackway.

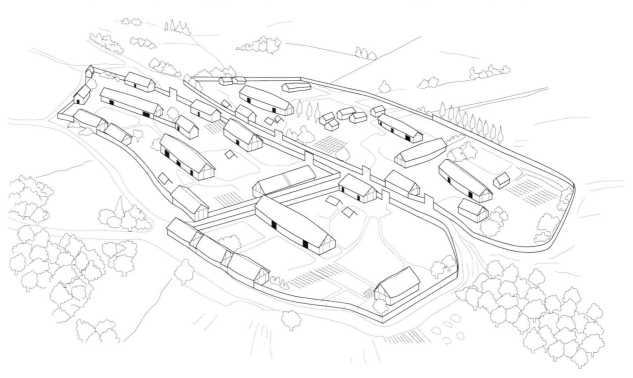

building lengthwise into three, creating the effect of a nave and aisles. There was usually an entrance in the centre of each of the long walls, leading into a narrow compartment that separated the humans (upslope) from the byre draining out through the downslope gable. Animals could be stalled inside during the winter, and let out to graze during the rest of the year.

There were examples of this longhouse with byre in the earlier Viking Age layers at Vorbasse. They were about 33 m (110 ft) long and up to 7.5 m (25 ft) wide, and had stalls for 20 or more beasts. They occupied fairly central positions in each of the six individual farmyards, defined by fenced boundaries, that adjoined each other, three on either side of a road that was 8–10 m (26–32 ft) wide. Within each of these 7,000 sq. m. (75,000 sq. ft) farmyards other buildings of several forms and functions were erected just inside the boundary fence. They included smaller (thought still quite substantial) aisled structures, and 'pit-huts', typically up to 6 m (20 ft) long and dug into the surface for up to 1 m (3ft 3 in). Most of these pit huts contained loomweights and they had clearly been used as weavers' workshops.

The longhouse with byre type of building fell out of favour during the Viking Age, even though examples were still in use into the tenth century at sites such as Lejre on Sjaelland and Borg in the Lofoten Islands (see box on p. 43) where the aristocracy may have wished to emphasize their traditional supremacy by retaining an otherwise outmoded form of dwelling.

A broadly similar form of structure, but without the byre component, is referred to in Scandinavia as either a longhouse or a hall-house, and remained one of the main house types of the Viking Age. By the end of the period, in the eleventh century, the tradition of having internal pairs of posts to support the roof, a custom that created the nave and aisles effect, had been superseded. Roofs were now supported on the side walls and this created a more open-plan effect in the interior, although it was normally sub-divided laterally into several rooms. One form, known as the 'Trelleborg-type' after its recognition at late tenth-century forts (see p. 186), had a large central chamber and a separate compartment at each end, while the walls were buttressed by an external set of angled posts. Within the dwelling, a large rectangular hearth occupied a central position, warming the house and heating the food. The inhabitants sat and slept on benches within the aisles, or on the floor. One key piece of furniture for every head of household may have been a 'high seat' which proclaimed his status. There are suggestions that such seats may have had high backs which were adorned with elaborately carved terminals, for instance in the form of animal heads. Otherwise, most furniture on the average farm was probably fairly utilitarian, including chests within which to store a variety of goods.

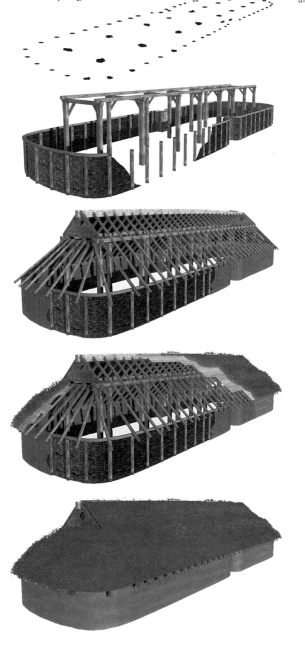

Stages in the construction of a hypothetical longhouse. After postholes were dug to hold the main upright timbers, the outer wall posts were positioned and had wattle woven around them. Roofing material, sometimes a twig or bark underlay with turf or thatch on top, was put in place and the walls might be insulated with turf. By the start of the Viking Age longhouse corners were no longer rounded, as shown in this pre-Viking example, but right-angled.

The trend towards undertaking particular activities in separate buildings is also exemplified by the farm excavated at Ytre Moa in Øvre Årdal, in the Sognefjord county of western Norway. Six small rectangular buildings were identified, measuring up to 6.5 m x 3.5 m (21 ft 6 in x 11 ft 6 in) internally. The walls, typically 3 m (10 ft) thick, were made of stone and turf, lined on the inside with wooden panelling. Built on a variety of different alignments, and each with a single entrance in one of the shorter walls, they were dispersed over an area measuring approximately 60 m (200 ft) square.

Within and around this area there were also about 20 circular stone cairns interpreted as burial mounds; at the edge of the settlement a single boat-shaped stone setting contained a woman's grave. It is thought that each of the buildings had one particular purpose, for example as a house, a byre, storage shed or workshop. The farm at Ytre Moa survived because its site, on a small terrace high above the valley floor, was not occupied by later, medieval farms; it is generally assumed that the rarity of excavated Viking Age farms in Norway is because generally their sites continued to be favoured in later periods. In some parts of the country there are characteristic 'farm mounds' that rise up above the surrounding landscape, crowned by a modern farm but incorporating the debris from centuries of occupation.

The village communities identified in Jutland were not a new phenomenon – their sites had often already been occupied for many hundreds of years. So this was a relatively stable society, with aspects of long-term continuity; but it was also one that was evolving, as can be seen from the growth in the size of both individual farmsteads and in village communities. At Vorbasse, for example, in c. 1000, the size of the individual farms dramatically increased yet again, to 25,000 sq. m (270,000 sq. ft), signalling a new emphasis on arable production.

The interior of a reconstructed tenth-century Viking longhouse at Trelleborg, Denmark, following the pattern of the post holes revealed when the site was excavated, and showing the wall benches and high, open roof. There were few sources of natural light, but the hearth and lamps or candles provided illumination. Textile wall hangings could have countered the bare, spartan appearance.

AN ARCTIC CHIEFTAIN

North of the Arctic Circle, a remarkable chieftain's residence, the largest single building known from Viking Age Scandinavia, has been excavated at Borg on Vestvågøy in the Lofoten Islands. It was erected in the seventh century, before the Viking Age began, but continued in use until the 950s or slightly later.

It measured about 80 m (260 ft) long and its curved, bow-shaped sides gave it a width of 7.5–9 m (24 ft 6 in – 29 ft 6 in). The external walls, erected to the inside of a drainage ditch, were built of turf sods. This sod wall was not load-bearing but acted as an insulating screen,

separated by an air gap from an inner wooden wall. This was constructed of vertical timber planks (staves) set at their base into a horizontal timber sill beam. Five entrances gave access, whilst 19 pairs of posts supported the roof.

Internally, the building was subdivided into five rooms, a more complex arrangement of space than was normal. Presumably this was a reflection both of the status of its owner and of the particular climatic conditions this far north.

The narrow entrance compartment with opposed doorways separated one room,

almost 20 m (65 ft) long, at the western end, and thought to be the main living room, from another slightly smaller space that may have functioned as a ceremonial hall. Both were entered from the vestibule rather than directly from the outside. Beyond the hall was another room, again slightly smaller, but of uncertain function; and beyond that, occupying over 30 m (100 ft), was the byre.

Imported luxury goods from the Rhineland confirm the status of residents here, but most of the objects found in and around the building were fairly mundane; they included

many soapstone items from north Norway and many whetstones from the country's Telemark area.

(Above) A reconstruction of the huge, 80-m (260-ft) long hall excavated at Borg. The plan (below) indicates possible uses for the individual rooms.

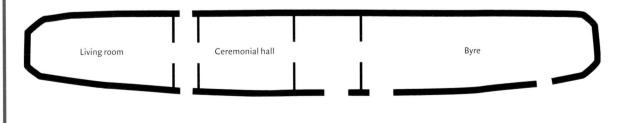

Living room   Ceremonial hall   Byre

CRAFTS AND TECHNOLOGY

The Viking Age was an era manufactured by iron and traversed by timber – the skills of working in wood and metal were fundamental, for Vikings built their houses and their ships with these two materials, and undertook many of their daily tasks using iron tools, utensils and weapons. Most of these items were made locally, for there was a long tradition of self-sufficiency and practical knowledge of how best to work raw materials.

Iron bloom from Øyane, Telemark, Norway, and iron bars or ingots (length c. 30 cm (12 in)), shaped for ease of transport, from Hverven, Buskerud, Norway.

Ironworking

The technology of iron production – smelting iron ores derived from bogs, ironstone and other deposits to create iron, and then fabricating products through the smithing process – was not an invention of the Viking Age. It had already been practised in Scandinavia for a millennium, and Viking Age smiths were heirs to generations of skilled predecessors. As iron ore was not available everywhere, there was a trade in blooms of smelted iron; in contrast, smithing was a widely spread skill. There was a difference, however, between the skill levels necessary to weld a simple repair to a plough-share, to forge a steel-edged knife or to create a finely balanced, pattern-welded sword (see pp. 69–71). Skilful smiths commanded a certain mystique through their ability to transmute dull iron bloom into shining prestigious weaponry, and this prestige is echoed in Scandinavian mythology

where Völund the Smith is portrayed as a master artificer and resourceful character whose products are coveted by kings.

Smithing itself is elusive in the archaeological record. The best evidence for ironworking often comes from visually unprepossessing waste products including slags and hearth bottoms, items normally overlooked or discarded by many archaeologists before about 1950. Nevertheless, it is metallographic analysis of these residues and of finished products that has provided detailed information about the techniques commonly available in the Viking Age. This supplements the pictorial evidence for metalworking found in a few contemporary manuscript illustrations or in slightly later Norwegian woodcarving (see illustration overleaf). The smith's tool kit consisted of hammers, tongs and bellows, and he worked at a forge, most conveniently built up to waist height but therefore prone to collapse and not often recognizable to archaeologists. Although bellows were made largely from organic materials and therefore do not survive, the other tools have been found, most often buried as grave goods. So too have perforated furnace stones that were positioned at the furnace flue; the bellow's nozzle was aimed through the hole while the stone protected the bellows and their operator from the intense heat – smithing required temperatures of over 1,000 °C (1,800 °F).

Woodworking

Woodworking was even more deeply ingrained than ironworking in the Scandinavian psyche, with not centuries but millennia of collective experience underpinning the use of timber. Knowledge of the properties of wood – which species to utilize for a particular purpose and how best to work it – was almost innate in the rural societies of most of Scandinavia, as indeed it was throughout the pre-industrial wooded world. Only in a relatively few places was timber a scarce resource; almost everywhere there was an abundance of forests and woodland. With a small kit of relatively simple tools, comprising only axe, hammer and wedges, one man could fell a large tree, lop off the branches, and split the trunk into manageable

(Below) A wooden chest with tools for woodworking and blacksmithing, together with unfinished and complete iron products, found at Mästermyr, Gotland, Sweden.

lengths that could be fashioned fairly easily into planks and beams. Requirements for smaller wood from which to make such things as knife handles and wooden vessels, or for the withies that could be woven to make fences or wattlework panels, could be met by managing or farming the woodland through cycles of pollarding or coppicing trees to ensure the regeneration of a renewable resource.

Wood was the material of choice to satisfy a range of needs that today are frequently filled by other materials. Wooden shingles, for example, were often the preferred form of roofing material. Spades had not only wooden handles but also wooden blades, albeit sometimes tipped with an iron rim, and shovels too could be wholly made of wood. Furniture, such as chairs, chests and (for the wealthy) beds, was made of wood, as were toilet seats. Such was their familiarity with wood that even coopering (the making of casks and barrels) may have been within the capabilities of the average Viking Age woodworker. Tableware too generally consisted of wooden items. Many of them were fashioned with the more specialized skills of the lathe-turner, who could take a block of wood and turn it on his rotary lathe, gouging out wooden cups and bowls. This was a simple and portable technology that could fashion basic everyday items.

Bone and Antler

One type of raw material that is not much used in the modern world but which was frequently employed in the Viking Age is bone and antler. Animal bone was available in every Viking-Age farmstead, and it took little skill and not much time to fashion such simple items as pins, needles, spindle whorls or bone skates. More care was sometimes lavished on playing pieces or on dress accessories such as strap-ends, which could be finely carved and quite elaborately decorated.

Antler, mainly from deer but sometimes, in northern Scandinavia, from reindeer or elk, was also commonplace. Its advantage over bone was that, if cut with the grain of the antler rather than across the grain, it could withstand much greater stresses. Experience taught craftsmen this fact, as can be seen from an analysis of the antler combs that are so commonly found. Although cutting the 'wrong' way along the length of the antler would have allowed the craftsman to fashion a comb's tooth-plate as one long piece, the craftsmen invariably cut with the grain, even though this automatically required them to make several small tooth-plates for each comb that all had to be riveted individually into place.

Wooden kitchen and other equipment from the Oseberg burial of 834, including stave-built pails/buckets, and hollowed troughs and ladles.

Whalebone was much less common, but invaluable on occasion because of its size and density. It was whale shoulder blades, for example, that were converted into the elegantly carved smoothing boards sometimes found in women's graves. Whalebone could also occasionally be utilized for other items such as sword pommels.

Archetypal of the Viking Age, but so vulnerable to decay that only one example survives, were drinking horns. In aristocratic households fine examples might have their rims and terminals decorated and protected by silver mounts. Some of these mounts survive – otherwise, we have to look to representations in Viking Age art to demonstrate the existence of such horns.

At the most expensive end of the boney spectrum was walrus ivory, a luxury item originating in north Norway and, later, Greenland, which was utilized for carving highly decorated items such as boxes. It was exported as a raw material to sites including Dublin and Gorodisce (in Russia).

Leatherworking

Leather goods were fundamentally important in the Viking Age; shoes, sheaths and scabbards for knives and swords, harness and other horse riding gear are just the most obvious requirements. As animal hides are organic materials they are only rarely preserved, and so our knowledge of Viking Age leatherwork is rather limited. Footwear, the commonest form of leatherwork, is

(Above) Whalebone smoothing board from Scar, Sanday, Orkney.

(Right) Antler combs and a bone comb-case (left), together with bone pins, spindle whorls and needles, and rectangular pieces of antler in which to saw comb teeth, all from Coppergate, York.

(Opposite) Door frame from Hylestad stave church, Setesdal, Aust Agder, Norway, decorated c. 1200 with scenes from the Sigurd saga. Below, a smith wields a hammer while holding tongs on an anvil; an assistant works a pair of bellows. While above, the sword blade is tested on the anvil.

A re-enactor demonstrating some of the techniques of Viking Age leatherworking.

A jug of eighth/ninth-century Tating ware, decorated with applied tin foil, found at Birka, Uppland, Sweden.

large Badorf ware jars, both produced in the wine-producing region of the Rhineland, were imported into Scandinavia; and in tenth-century England the production of well-made, fast-wheel-thrown pottery vessels flourished at several centres in the Danelaw, with Stamford in Lincolnshire famous for its glazed wares.

Non-ferrous Metalworking

Base metals including copper alloys, lead and tin were all easier to work than iron, for they required significantly lower temperatures to smelt the ores. Lead, which melts at a mere 327 °C (620 °F), was used for weights, in some cheap jewelry, and as the material that was shaped to impress the clay moulds for casting brooches in bronze or in precious metals. Brooches and, sometimes, dress-pins were fashioned from copper-alloys (bronze) which melt at about 1083 °C (1980 °F). Oval brooches in particular were complex castings that involved the craftsman in many stages of manufacture. Once cast and finished, items could be given a more shiny finish with a coating of tin, or a gilding with mercury.

Some more expensive items were made from silver and, exceptionally, from gold. Silver was the staple medium in which most Vikings expressed their wealth. Silver melts at 960 °C (1760 °F), gold at 1063 °C (1945 °F), so these two metals were also reasonably easy to work. The equipment used by non-ferrous metalworkers included pottery crucibles in which to melt the metal, tongs to hold the crucibles, bellows to heat the fire, tuyeres to protect the mouth of the bellows from the flame, hammers, wire-drawers and other tools, and polishing stones with which to give the finished objects a fine finish. The skill of the craftsmen came in the design of their products, in the production of the moulds to cast them, in the high quality of their finish and in the elaborate and delicate embellishment of the cast products with gilding and applied decoration such as twisted filigree wires or various inlays.

Glass working

Another form of high-temperature industry was that of the glassworker. Vikings, both male and female, had a liking for gaudy glass beads, which were made in the major trading places and aristocratic centres either by melting down shards of broken glass imported from the technically more

known principally from excavations in towns, where large quantities of finished articles and leatherworking debris have been found in places such as Hedeby and York. These are the products of specialist leatherworkers – but because very few leather items have been found in rural locations, the extent and skill level of home-based leatherworking throughout the countryside is not clear. Access to raw materials, particularly cow hide, was relatively easy; the requirements of the tanning process, where dog dung, bird droppings and urine were among the ingredients used to process the skins, were also easily met, although the foul smell of the lengthy process was 'lost' more readily on a farm than in the midst of a town.

Techniques and fashions in footwear varied across the Vikings' world; the range of styles included simple 'slip-ons' as well as boots and shoes that were either laced or fastened with a leather strap and toggle. Frugality generally dictated that when the one-piece sole was worn through it was stripped off and replaced with a new one; hence archaeologists find many more discarded soles that complete shoes. Most shoes were functional and plain, but knife sheaths in particular provided an opportunity for embellishment with elaborate tooled decoration, usually of interlace or geometric patterns.

Pottery

Although there was localized production of pottery vessels in the Viking Age Scandinavia, they were generally relatively simple forms such as bowls. Highly decorated jugs of Tating ware, and accomplished glass-producing sites in western Europe, or by making the glass from raw materials. Skilful combinations of contrasting colours at different stages in the production process allowed richly coloured and dexterously patterned beads to be produced. Glass vessels were not produced in the Viking lands, and had to be imported for those few who were wealthy enough to afford them.

Textiles

Making clothes was a never-ending part of the domestic routine for women in the Viking Age. Although few complete garments survive, there is a wealth of evidence that demonstrates the processes involved, and enough pieces of cloth to indicate the considerable expertise that had been developed. Wool and flax were the two raw materials that were prepared and then spun to make threads. The spinning was done by hand, feeding the fibres on to a wooden or bone spindle; this was weighted near its bottom with a stone, metal or fired clay spindle whorl which helped to maintain the momentum of the revolving spindle. These whorls are among the commonest objects found in the excavation of domestic sites.

The threads were woven into lengths of cloth on a loom. Rows of loom weights, made of clay or, less commonly, stone, which were fastened to the base of the vertical ('warp') threads on the loom to hold them in position, occasionally show where a wooden loom once stood. Weaving could produce cloth of many different patterns, including diagonal, chevron and diamond patterns, but the most obvious decorative effects came from dyeing. A range of natural dyestuffs, mainly derived from plants, was available, and was frequently employed; in terms of textiles this was by no means a 'dark age' but an era of vibrant colours and warm hues. Extra opulence could be displayed with the addition of elaborately decorated strips of braid, often only 5–10 cm (2–4 in) wide. These were produced by a technique known as tablet-weaving, in which vertical warp threads were passed through holes in the corners of small bone or wooden plates ('tablets'). The tablets were then twisted into different configurations as the weft (horizontal) threads were woven through them, thus creating the intricate designs.

(Above) Gold disc brooch made in Scandinavia under west European influence in c. 1000, one of two found together with a gold arm-ring at Hornelund, Horne, Jutland, Denmark. Techniques used in its manufacture include filigree twisted wires, granulation and, unusually, the insertion of settings (now missing).

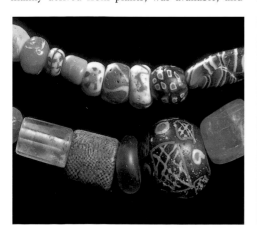

(Left) Some of the colours available from natural dye-stuffs to weavers in the Viking Age.

(Far left) Glassworkers fused rods or trails of different coloured glass to make multicoloured beads, such as these found at Birka, Uppland, Sweden.

SHIPS: CATALYST OF THE VIKING AGE

A picture stone from Smiss, När, Gotland, Sweden, shows some details of sail and rigging; when originally coloured, the details would have been more obvious.

Critical to Viking activities, and symbolic of the era, ships were the catalyst of the Viking Age. It was the development of the sailing ship in Scandinavia and the skills of the shipwright and the seaman that opened up possibilities for raiding, trading or settlement across the oceans. Yet, as with so many other aspects of the Viking Age, its ships were the descendants of centuries, indeed millennia, of nautical experience. Scandinavia's long coastlines and often impenetrable interiors made the sea the preferred pathway for anyone with an eye on the distant horizon. Norway took its name from this natural sea route, 'the north way', which gave access to communities up its deeply fjord-indented coast; Denmark was a patchwork of intervisible islands that beckoned the adventurous onwards; and Sweden too had its far-reaching inlets and outer islands, as well as nearby neighbours just across the Baltic Sea.

From early times both coastal trade and fishing encouraged the mastery of inshore waters in rowing boats. By the early centuries AD these were already constructed in the clinker-built method that was characteristic of Viking ships. In this technique, after the keel had been fixed to the stem- and stern-posts, the ship's sides were built up, plank by plank. These strakes each had a wedge-shaped cross-section which made it easier to overlap them vertically and hold them together with iron clench-nails or wooden trenails. Only when the entire hull was complete did the shipwright add the internal framing that finally held the vessel together.

In the pre-Viking era of the fourth to seventh centuries AD it was oar-power alone that propelled boats around Scandinavia and across the North Sea – in the fifth century the Anglo-Saxon invaders of England, who originated in northwest Germany and Scandinavia, rowed their way to Britain's shores. Of three ships discovered in a bog at Nydam in Nordslesvig, at the base of the Jutland peninsula, the most complete, which was built of oak, has been dated to around AD 310. Measuring 21.5 m (70 ft 6 in) long and 3.5 m (11 ft 6 in) wide, it could have transported about 45 warriors. It had a

The most complete of the Nydam boats, as depicted in the excavation report published in 1866.

keel that was no stouter than a plank, not capable of bearing the weight, stresses and strains of a mast; five very long planks, sturdy but heavy and rigid, made up either side of the vessel.

By about 700 the shipwrights' techniques had been refined. This is demonstrated by a boat discovered in a bog at Kvalsund in Sunnmøre, Norway and excavated in 1920. About 18 m (59 ft) long and 3 m (10 ft) wide, with 10 pairs of oars, its builders had amassed the confidence and experience to nail together shorter lengths of plank to make up the required length of each strake. Another improvement was that the keel was now rather more substantial, capable of bearing a mast. An equally important innovation was that the steering oar (rudder), instead of being loose, was now attached to the starboard side, and thus gave greater control. This is recognizably a Viking ship.

It is not known when exactly a mast and sail became the norm, but by the ninth century there is ample evidence from a range of excavated ships that sails were commonplace, even though few traces of them survive. There are, however, representations on the 'picture stones' from the island of Gotland, southeast of mainland Sweden, that show sails and rigging in enough detail to demonstrate the relative sophistication of Viking Age sailing. The importance of sails can hardly be over-emphasized for Viking activities; with their adoption the effort of travel was lessened, journey times decreased, and energy levels for an attack were sustained. Sails could be made with differently coloured strips of material (woollen sails seem to have been commonplace), and walrus hide was a favoured raw material for making ships' ropes.

The variety of craft plying Scandinavian waters is hinted at in Old Norse vocabulary. The word *skeið* means 'warship', as does the word *dreki*, which literally means 'dragon ship', and is presumably a reference to carvings on ships' stem- and stern-posts. Although the Vikings didn't invent such carvings and were not the only seafarers to have them, representations of dragon prows have been found on Viking Age sites such as Jarlshof in the Shetland Islands. Warships were narrow in relation to their length and had a shallow draught that allowed them to penetrate far up rivers or be easily run ashore at the outset of a raid. *Knarr* came to mean a merchant ship, a wider and deeper vessel, strongly built and able to transport substantial cargoes through the North Sea, Baltic and North Atlantic.

The Gokstad ship, perhaps the archetypal Viking vessel, was found during the excavation of a mound near Sandefjord, Norway, in 1880. It was

The Gokstad ship under excavation in 1880, looking towards the stern. The gable ends of the burial chamber can be seen behind the mast.

(Below) The Gokstad ship reconstructed; the three T-shaped uprights allowed oars to be stored above the deck when the ship was in port.

23.33 m (76 ft 6 in) long with a greatest width of 5.25 m (17 ft 6 in) and had 32 oars. Fashioned from oak, dendrochronology indicates that it was built c. 895–900. Its construction exhibits advances in ship-building technique over those seen in the earlier ninth-century vessel from Oseberg, on Oslo Fjord, which was unearthed in 1904. The sturdier Gokstad vessel would have been able to undertake voyages into the Atlantic or across the North Sea, and could have been used on voyages of raiding, trading or settlement.

The Skuldelev and Hedeby Ships

With the continuing discovery of more vessels it is becoming ever clearer that ships of the Viking Age varied considerably in size, draught and profile, although they were built to the same basic double-ended, clinker-built pattern which was handed down from generation to generation of shipwrights in communities all around the coasts of Scandinavia. Very few ships have been discovered with their timberwork preserved, but many more are known as stains in the soil. Altogether the archaeological evidence shows that Viking ships ranged from small, four-oared sailing vessels that might have been used for inshore fishing (although capable of crossing the North Sea, as modern experiments have shown) to warships some 30 m (100 ft) long, like the Skuldelev 2 ship raised from Roskilde Fjord in Sjaelland, Denmark, or the fire-damaged warship excavated within the palisaded harbour at Hedeby in Schleswig, a vessel constructed around 985. Another of the Skuldelev wrecks, number 1, is a

Reconstructions of the Skuldelev 1 cargo vessel (opposite), originally built in the Sognefjord region of western Norway in c. 1025, and the Skuldelev 2 longship (below), originally built in southeastern Ireland in c. 1042.

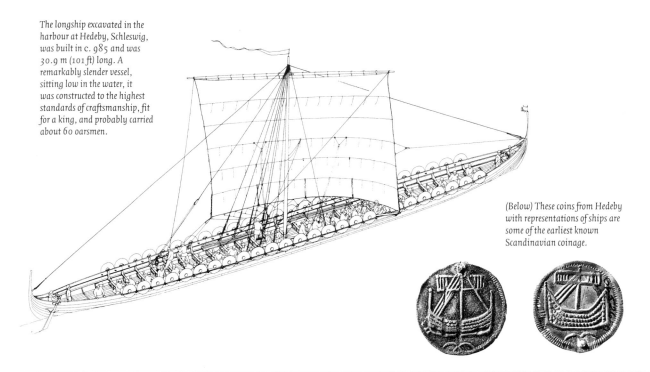

The longship excavated in the harbour at Hedeby, Schleswig, was built in c. 985 and was 30.9 m (101 ft) long. A remarkably slender vessel, sitting low in the water, it was constructed to the highest standards of craftsmanship, fit for a king, and probably carried about 60 oarsmen.

(Below) These coins from Hedeby with representations of ships are some of the earliest known Scandinavian coinage.

NAVIGATION

It was experience and knowledge of winds, tides, directions and sailing times, accumulated over generations, rather than instruments and calculations, that allowed Viking seafarers to find their way to and from their desired landfalls. Coasting along within sight of land whenever possible was one method of reaching a destination. Identifiable features along coastlines, for example in south Wales, are still known by Old Norse names, suggesting that they were important seamarks in the Viking Age. Close inshore, although their craft had shallow draughts, lead-weighted lines might be cast over the side to measure the depth of water, as shown in a scene on the Bayeux Tapestry. When venturing beyond the horizon, natural phenomena helped to indicate the way. Cloud formations, wave patterns and the presence of sea birds or whales could all suggest the proximity of land; the sun's daily course across the sky established an east-west datum, and the North Star could guide nocturnal navigation. There is no convincing evidence that the Vikings used any form of compass, and a supposed 'bearing dial' found in Greenland may in fact be a piece of ecclesiastical computational equipment.

This broken wooden disc, 7 cm (2¾ in) in diameter, with, originally, perhaps 32 triangular notches cut into its surface at the edges, was found at Narsarsuaq in Uunartoq Fjord in the eastern Greenland settlement. This site was believed to have been that of a medieval Benedictine convent, but the disc has generally been accepted as Viking Age; in fact, there is uncertainty about this early date.

Although widely accepted as a form of sun compass, the best parallels for its form are the rather later and larger so-called 'confession discs' known in

The wooden disc from Narsarsuaq, Greenland, shown life-size.

Iceland, and used by parish priests to count the number of people taking confession. Precisely what the Uunartoq disc was, and when it was used, remains uncertain.

broad-bellied vessel capable of carrying much cargo on long-distance trading voyages, while Skuldelev 3 is a smaller version measuring 13.8 m (45 ft) by 3.4 m (11 ft), suitable for coastal trade.

Insights into the building of ships are given in the sagas. Olaf Tryggvason's saga describes the building of the *Long Serpent* in c. 1000; a vessel with 34 rowing benches in a length of 74 ells, said to the the biggest and finest ship built in Norway. The reality of such a job has been measured in the building at Roskilde Ship Museum of a replica of the Skuldelev 2 warship, launched in 2004. The Museum's ship-builders, already experienced in making replica boats, took 10,000 hours over the basic boat building, after 14,000 hours had been spent in cutting, trimming and moving the timbers, and completed the operation in 27,000

hours. This means that a team consisting of a master boat-builder and ten shipwrights could have created this large vessel within about seven months. The natural resources consumed are vast; in addition to 150 cubic m (5,300 cubic ft) of oak, there were 7,000 nails made out of 400 kg (880 lb) of iron (a process that itself needed the production of large quantities of charcoal), 18 cubic m (635 cubic ft) of pine wood tar, 2,000 m (6,500 ft) of hand-made rope, and 120 sq. m (1,300 sq. ft) of sail. The result of all this effort and input is a vessel that can be propelled under oars at 5–6 knots, the equivalent of 10 km (6½ miles) per hour, while under sail it can reach 10 knots and average 7 knots. At this rate, a similar vessel could cross from Scandinavia to Britain in a couple of days.

Comparative profiles of the ships from Skuldelev, Roskilde Fjord, Denmark. Clockwise, from top left: coastal cargo boat; inshore fishing boat; small warship; large warship; deep-sea cargo boat.

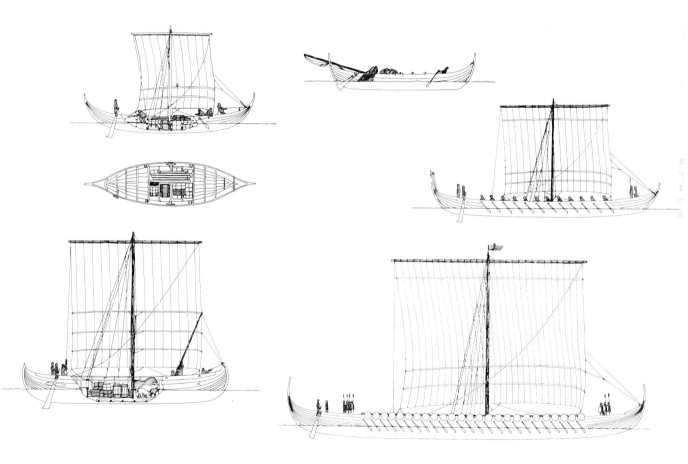

TRADE

(Opposite) Part of the silver hoard from Spillings, Othem, Gotland, Sweden, deposited in c. 867.

Inter-regional or international exchange of raw materials or products made by local specialists, in return for goods that were not readily available at home, had a long pedigree in Scandinavia. With the capability to build bigger and more seaworthy ships came opportunities for Scandinavians to venture further afield not only to raid but also to trade. Transactions carrying goods over very long distances might be conducted through a chain of middlemen; some items could be carried from one side of the Vikings' world to the other.

Treasure Island

The island of Gotland, off southeast Sweden, was a natural stepping-stone between Scandinavia, the Baltic seaboard and Russia. If measured by the quantity of silver that has been found there, Gotland was one of the wealthiest areas in the Viking world. Over 700 hoards of silver have been discovered, and more are still coming to light on a fairly regular basis. Some of Gotland's riches may have been collected through raiding and piracy, but the island was also an international market place, the base of many very successful merchants who exploited their homeland's location, making it a key point on the east-west axis from Scandinavia to Islamic lands. Altogether over 145,000 coins have been uncovered on Gotland, of which about 65,000 are Islamic dirhams and the remainder are mainly English and German pennies. Silver jewelry, hack-silver and ingots are also found in profusion, although there is nothing to match the two silver hoards found side by side at Othem in 1999. Between them they contained over 14,000 coins, over 500 rings of various shapes and sizes, and other items as well, and altogether they weighed more than 65 kg (143 lb), making this the world's largest deposit of Viking silver.

A NORWEGIAN AT THE COURT OF KING ALFRED

Living proof that Scandinavians were prepared to undertake long trading trips, even into places where Viking raiders were simultaneously active, comes in the person of Ottar, a chieftain from northern Norway. We know that at some time in the 870s to 890s he made a visit to the court of King Alfred in southern England, for his traveller's tales of life beyond the Arctic Circle were considered so remarkable by the king that some were written down and copied into an Anglo-Saxon manuscript that survives to this day. Ottar, whose home was probably near Tromsø – perhaps somewhere like Borg (see p. 43) – was a well-travelled man. He had ventured around North Cape into the White Sea; he had hunted whales and walrus, and had brought walrus ivory as a gift to Alfred. Back in Norway he collected animal skins – seal, walrus, marten, otter, reindeer, bear – as well as feathers, all of which would have been much coveted in markets further south. In pursuit of trade he had sailed south to a Norwegian trading settlement named *Sciringes heal* ('the shining hall'), thought to be a place now called Kaupang in Vestfold, and then on to the Danish town of *aet Haeþum* (Hedeby). Presumably, having entertained King Alfred with his stories and having sampled Anglo-Saxon hospitality, this 'non-Viking' returned to his reindeer herd in the far north of Scandinavia, to regale his neighbours with recollections of the way of life in England.

The voyage of Ottar, as visualised by the artist Karl Haar.

VIKING TOWNS

This was a time when towns – places, that is, where a relatively large permanent population made a living through fashioning and selling a variety of non-agricultural goods – were relatively rare throughout even the more civilized parts of Europe. There were a few foreign mercantile centres that offered rich pickings to Viking raiders, and these may have been the models which inspired the development of similar places in Scandinavia, where there were already a handful of settlements that showed some urban characteristics before 800. The Viking Age, however, was certainly a time when several new towns were founded and developed.

The foundation in the early eighth century of Ribe, in southwest Jutland, has already been described (see p. 23). By about 850 the limits of the settlement there were defined precisely for the first time by the digging of a small encircling ditch that served to emphasize that Ribe was a special place. This was soon replaced by a wide though shallow moat, inside which was a rampart faced with turf; a combination that provided a workmanlike defence.

The German missionary Ansgar, who had previously erected churches at Hedeby and Birka, two thriving trading ports, was allowed in 854–57 to build a church at Ribe; this too suggests that Ribe was still an important commercial centre. However, archaeological evidence for manufacturing of the types so common in the eighth-century phase of the site's development had dwindled and disappeared by Ansgar's time, and although Ribe was nominally a bishopric it may have been largely deserted between the late ninth and mid-eleventh centuries. The earliest description of Ribe, written by the German Adam of Bremen in about 1070, talks of 'a river which flows in from the Ocean, and by way of which ships sail out to Frisia, England and Saxony'; and these places had probably been the destinations of Ribe's Viking-Age traders as well.

Norway's First Town

Kaupang – a name which means 'market-place' – is today a small village ranged along the western side of a shallow tidal inlet by the Viksfjord in the district of Tjølling, at the southern end of

The site at Kaupang, Viksfjord, Vestfold, Norway, where a trading centre was founded in the early 800s.

Vestfold. Inland it is overlooked by the cliff edge of a rocky outcrop that leaves only a relatively narrow strip along the shore suitable for cultivation. It looks very different from how it would have appeared in the Viking Age, when the water line would have been over 3.5 m (11 ft 6 in) higher. This place has, however, been identified as the trading centre known as *Sciringes heal*, mentioned by the Norwegian merchant Ottar in his conversations at King Alfred's court in the late ninth century (see box on p. 56).

Clusters of Viking Age grave mounds at the head of the bay indicate occupation somewhere thereabouts, and rich dark-coloured soils in the fields between the modern houses and the bay provide a clue to the position of the former settlement. The soil derives its colour from the debris of human occupation, particularly powdered ash and charcoal as well as all forms of domestic waste, which has been thoroughly mixed into the earth by medieval and later ploughing. Not only famously tasty early potatoes but also a vast range and density of archaeological objects have been recovered from these soils, most importantly in a series of excavations and surveys undertaken from 2000 to 2002.

Excavation revealed that in about AD 800 craftsmen began to work at Kaupang, although perhaps only seasonally – no sign of permanent houses or workshops has been found. Their activities, close to the water's edge, took place within quite small but non-standard plots, variously measuring 8–10 m (20–33 ft) long by 6–8 m (20–26 ft) wide, which were defined by fences. Only a few years passed before a permanent settlement developed; it measured only about 750 m (2,450 ft) long by 20–90 m (65–300 ft) wide. A ten-minute walk would have taken a visitor from one side to the other. There were probably no more than 150 plots, suggesting a population of less than 1,000 people. They lived in rectangular houses built with post and wattle walls. Timber posts that supported the roof divided the building into a central space flanked by 'aisles'. Typically there was a hearth in the centre of the building. The 'aisles' appear to have had organic materials such as grass or heather laid in them, perhaps to make them more comfortable for sleeping.

How long this place flourished is unclear, for although the nearby cemeteries continued in use into the mid-tenth century, there is no discernible occupation evidence after about 850. Perhaps

An artist's impression of the appearance of part of Kaupang in the ninth century, based on the excavated evidence.

Kaupang reverted to being a seasonal market; perhaps the damage done by ploughing has removed some of the archaeological evidence for later buildings.

Kaupang's craftspeople made a wide variety of specialized products, among them glass beads; one telling discovery was a metal rod used by a

Finds from Kaupang:

(Above) Part of a jet bracelet from England, and beads made from carnelian and rock crystal from the Black Sea, and amethyst from continental Europe.

(Centre) Silver coins and fragments of jewelry fused together by the heat of a melting pot that has now disappeared.

(Below) Part of an Arab silver coin with a Thor's hammer symbol incised into it.

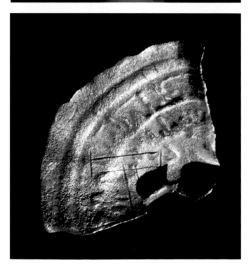

bead-maker, which was found with a blob of glass still fused to its tip. Equally unusual and revealing has been the recovery of several decorated lead models, used to impress the clay moulds in which brooches, strap-ends and other items were cast; jewelry of lead, bronze, silver and gold was made at Kaupang. The lead may have been imported from England, but a source for the silver is graphically illustrated by a clump of semi-melted Arab dirhams, fused to fragments of other silver items – a melting pot for the silversmith's work which was somehow left for posterity.

Kaupang's foreign contacts are also represented by drinking glasses, pottery jugs and lava quernstones from the Frankish Rhineland, by an Anglo-Saxon penny, by Slavonic and Jutlandic pottery, and by beads of carnelian, rock crystal, amethyst and intricately decorated glass, that may have come from places as widespread as Ireland, Ribe, Byzantium, the Black Sea/Caspian Sea region, and the Near and Middle East. Trading at Kaupang required silver for payment and lead weights to measure the bullion, and both have been found in abundance, with coins, jewelry and ingots all cut up into hacksilver to be weighed on the merchants' scales.

Hedeby in Jutland

Another early Viking Age trading centre is known on the Schlie Fjord at Hedeby (Haithabu), on the eastern side of Jutland's southern border, at one end of the Danevirke defensive rampart (see pp. 22–23). Hedeby is best known today for its own impressive semi-circular rampart, 10 m (32 ft) high and 1,300 m (4,250 ft) long, that was thrown up in the tenth century to enclose 24 ha (59 acres); but the settlement can be traced back to the later eighth century through the recovery of timber that is tree-ring dated to 787. Some piles from the harbour have been dated c. 725-50, suggesting that there was some activity hereabouts at this even earlier date.

A key event, however, is recorded in the *Royal Frankish Annals*, which tell how in 808, at the end of a military campaign against the Obodrites, a Slav people, a Danish King Godfred devastated a coastal marketplace known as Reric and transplanted the merchants from there to a port which is thought to be Hedeby. Reric has now been identified with Groß Strömkendorf, 150 km (90 miles)

to the southeast of Hedeby, near the German Baltic city of Wismar. This recently excavated site is notable for the range of Carolingian, Saxon, Frisian and Scandinavian objects found there; it was in existence by about 730, but seems to have grown and flourished c. 770–790, at a time when Franks and Obodrite Slavs were in league against the Danes. Attacking the town and removing its merchants to a site with development potential that was under his own direct control was an effective means for Godfred simultaneously to stifle this opposition and gain market share – an excellent takeover strategy.

Excavation at Hedeby has shown a densely occupied settlement which was carefully laid out on either side of a canalized stream which flowed through the centre of the town. The stream was bridged over in places; a timber date of 811 confirms that there was indeed building work shortly after the historically-attested enlargement of the town. The plan of the settlement was based on an irregular rectilinear grid of streets and lanes. A street of wooden plank construction was laid out approximately parallel to the shore line, and lanes ran at right-angles to either side of it, down to the

water and inland up to and beyond a second, approximately parallel, street. Fenced plots were entered from the streets and lanes, and within the plots were houses of varying size, built of posts and wattle daubed over with clay. These buildings had an average life span of 10–30 years before they had to be rebuilt.

Geophysical prospection has shown that the entire area enclosed by the rampart contains archaeological features, amongst which are plots with what are interpreted as 'pit-houses'; a new exploration of some of these began in 2005. Metal-detecting in the ploughsoil that surrounds the disturbed layers relating to the later phases of Hedeby's existence, in the tenth and eleventh centuries, has brought to light several thousand Viking Age objects including Carolingian disc brooches, evidence for jewelry production, and German and other coins. Mapping the incidence of smithing slag suggests that some metalworkers were concentrated in the northwest part of the settlement.

In the western part of the walled town there is a cemetery in which 350 burials have been archaeologically examined; the rites and orientations of

Hedeby, near Schleswig; tenth-century ramparts enclose the area of the manufacturing and trading centre that existed here since the late eighth century.

(Opposite above) Artist's reconstruction of part of the Hedeby settlement on either side of the brook running down towards the harbour.

(Opposite below) Recreating one of the buildings excavated at Hedeby; this view shows the structure before wall cladding and roofing material is added.

(Below) Original plans of the excavated grave chamber at Hedeby and (at a smaller scale) the remains of the ship that covered the grave chamber, and the three horse skeletons.

the burials vary, although the majority of the simple inhumations, including some in coffins, are aligned west-northwest/east-southeast. The southern part of this cemetery area is taken up by burials inside wooden chambers, typically measuring 2.5 x 1.5 m (6 ft 6 in x 4 ft 6 in). Of the ten chamber graves excavated in 1930, nine could be assigned to men on the basis of the associated gravegoods, and one belonged to a woman.

About 100 m (330 ft) north of the ramparts, besides a separate, smaller, undated defended enclosure called Hochburg ('hillfort'), lies a small cemetery of coffined burials, perhaps dated to the ninth century; an eighth- or ninth-century cemetery, incorporating some cremation burials as well

as inhumation graves aligned north-south, lies just outside the rampart to the south. Altogether it is estimated that there were 10,000–12,000 burials at Hedeby and, on the basis of burial rites and grave goods, it is suggested that the people buried here included Danes, Saxons, Slavs and Swedes.

The single most prestigious burial found so far is a unique fusion of chamber and ship-burial rites, found about 200 m (650 ft) south of the rampart and excavated in 1908. A chamber grave measuring 3.7 x 2.4 m (12 ft x 7 ft 9 in) had been sub-divided into two compartments. The slightly smaller, western part held the finest grave goods that included a richly ornamented sword, remains of two shields, arrows, spurs and riding equipment, a glass cone beaker, a bronze bowl and an elaborately made piece of silver filigree jewelry. The eastern part of the chamber contained two swords, two shields and horse-riding gear. A separate pit next to the chamber contained the skeletons of three horses; but no human remains have survived.

Above the chamber a ship, perhaps 20 m (65 ft) long, had been positioned, and then a mound thrown up. Of the ship, only nails and soil-staining survived. It has been suggested, on the basis of the grave goods, that this is the grave of a prince or king, buried in c. 840–50, who was in close contact with his Frankish neighbours; whether the triple swords, shields and horses suggest that he was accompanied in death by a pair of retainers has

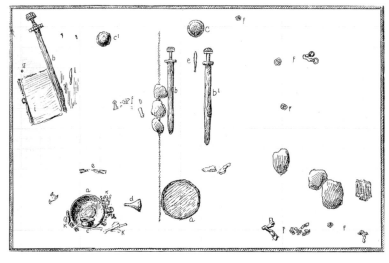

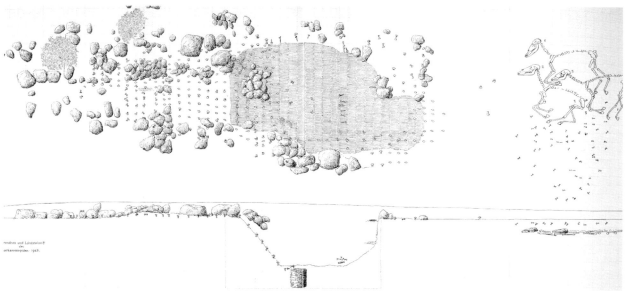

been debated but not proved. Conceivably, this was the person who, in c. 825, initiated the striking of coins at Hedeby, some of which had a ship motif on one side.

Survey and excavations in the bay that fronts Hedeby have demonstrated that the harbour was defended by a semicircular piled timber palisade, which may have had further structures (defensive towers?) associated with it. Jetties, constructed in incremental stages during the ninth and tenth centuries, ran out into the water. Remains of three ships and several logboats have been identified, and the Hedeby 1 wreck of a longship approximately 30 m (100 ft) long, built c. 985 and ultimately destroyed by fire, has been excavated. Hedeby 2 seems to be a modest cargo boat, but Hedeby 3, about 22 m (72 ft) long and built in c. 1025, is the largest cargo ship known from the Viking world, capable of transporting about 60 tons. Yet, shortly after this ship's construction, at a date that is probably in the mid-eleventh century, Hedeby was deserted and a new town created at nearby Schleswig.

Birka in Sweden

The Swedish equivalent of Hedeby or Kaupang was at Birka, on the island of Björkö in Lake Mälaren, near modern Stockholm in eastern central Sweden. A focus for international contacts had long been established at Helgö, nearer the seaward end of the lake (see pp. 21–22), but from the later eighth century Birka became the focus for manufacturing and trading activities. The settlement, defined by what is known as 'black earth', which contains much occupation debris, eventually covered about 7 ha (17.3 acres).

Relatively late in Birka's occupation a defensive rampart, still visible in part, was thrown up around it, just as had been done at Hedeby. Another parallel with Hedeby is the presence of an adjacent hillfort which, in this case, seems to be contemporary with the urban settlement, although its precise function is not yet properly understood. At some time in the 960s or 970s Birka seems to have been largely abandoned in favour of Sigtuna, but by that time several thousand burials had taken place around the settled area, distributed among several distinct cemeteries. Most of the graves were marked by mounds. Over 1,100 burials were excavated in the later nineteenth century; the drawings and records from these investigations show that about half of them were cremations, and the other half included burials in coffins as well as some chamber graves.

To the thousands of objects dug out of its 'black earth' layers and from its associated cemeteries in the nineteenth century can now be added the results from excavations in 1990–95. These suggest that the earliest settlement radiated around the edge of a small inlet, and that over the next two centuries extra plots were laid out both upslope

The island of Björkö in Lake Mälaren, Uppland, Sweden. The manufacturing and trading settlement of Birka was in the front part of the grassed area behind the bay at the bottom right of the island; the hillfort rampart can be seen just to the right of this.

(Right) An oval ('tortoise') brooch and fragments of the clay moulds used in casting brooches of this type, found at Birka.

and also downslope, encroaching over the former shore line.

At first, up to about 850, the majority of Birka's foreign contacts were with western Europe, but thenceforth eastern contacts became more important, going beyond the Baltic to Russia, Byzantium and points even further east. Pottery from the Khazar kingdom, which lay between the Black Sea and the Caspian Sea, provides a tangible link to the Arab world which, as elsewhere, is also represented by finds of silver coins.

Birka is notable for the enormous numbers of broken clay moulds for making oval brooches and other items of jewelry that have been recovered – some 20,000 pieces. Together with a large quantity of hacksilver, crucibles for melting it, and a selection of metalworkers' tools, they demonstrate one important mass production industry. Amber working to fashion beads, pendants and amulets, and making beads from glass and semi-precious stones, were also significant industries.

(Top left) A pale green glass beaker of eighth/ninth-century date imported from the Rhineland and buried in a grave at Birka.

(Above left) Grave mounds in the Hemlanden cemetery beside Birka.

(Above right) Thor's hammer symbol from Birka, made of amber.

III • RAIDERS AND INVADERS

Although their victims treated the earliest Viking raids as a bolt from the blue, the Viking voyagers were not embarking upon a foolhardy venture into the unknown. For centuries before the raids started, Scandinavian traders had presumably brought home critical information about conditions and prospects in foreign lands. The Viking raiders simply followed in their wake, sometimes enticed by the very same markets where the merchants had done business, but intent on making a profit in a totally different manner. Raiding sometimes led, sooner or later, to full-blooded invasion and on to the founding of a settlement, and from there either more raids or trading activities could be mounted – these activities were closely intertwined.

What caused the Viking Age to start when it did? What inspired or necessitated the raiding? These are enduring questions about the Vikings, and many different answers have been put forward. One view – perhaps the most pragmatic – is that the ever-growing political power of Scandinavian kings encouraged chieftains to bolster their waning status in the homeland by seeking the large and instant rewards that could be gained in lucrative overseas ventures. A further pragmatic consideration may have been the state reached in the development of ship-building and an advance in the capabilities of sailing vessels, although more discoveries of eighth- and ninth-century ships are needed to support this contention. Another suggestion is that the raids on Europe were a calculated political response by Scandinavian rulers, counter-attacking against the growing military power of the Frankish emperor Charlemagne and his successors. This explanation cannot apply to the British Isles, however.

An allied interpretation is that raids on churches and monasteries were not merely a result of selecting easy targets with rich pickings; instead, it is claimed, this was a deliberate targeting of the sites which provided the religious and ideological underpinning of west European Christianity. An attempt, in other words, at a form of psychological warfare, with the aims of undermining the west European belief system and showing that the Christians' god was not omnipotent but vulnerable, and not superior to the gods of Scandinavia. Whatever the truth of these suggestions, it seems most likely that rank and file Vikings probably set out simply to better their standard of living, through harvesting the riches of foreign lands.

Viking raiders, as depicted in the Life of St Aubin, written and illuminated in c. 1100 for the abbey at Angers, Maine-et-Loire, France. The illuminator depicted the armour of his own time, most noticeably the kite-shaped shields that were not used by Vikings. Although St Aubin was bishop of Angers in the sixth century and the area was raided by Vikings in the ninth century, in the medieval period St Aubin was identified as offering protection against pirate raids.

THE VIKING WARRIOR

A viking warrior was a well-armed and formidable opponent, but he had no particular technical superiority in his kit; broadly similar weapons equipped fighting men across much of Europe. Vikings were foot soldiers; they might use horses to travel across country, but they didn't customarily fight from the saddle. Nor did Vikings wear any particular uniform – although there was a basic uniformity to their weaponry. Protective gear might have included a leather body-protector, and for those who could afford much greater expense, additional protection from the knees to the neck

Eleventh-century warrior's head carved from the tip of a 22.4-cm (8³/₄-in) long elk antler tine and found at Sigtuna, Uppland, Sweden. The conical, pointed helmet has a nose-guard, an integral strip that protected the nose. This was also a feature of mid-eleventh-century Norman and Anglo-Saxon helmets, as can be seen on the Bayeux Tapestry (see p.201).

was available in the form of a shirt of chain mail, sometimes called a byrnie. It is possible that hard leather skull caps were worn by some Vikings, although such things don't survive in the archaeological record. Iron helmets, either hemispherical or conical in shape, and with some form of simple bar projecting down from the forehead to protect the nose, are very rarely found, and are more likely to have been worn by the rich and powerful or the hardened Viking than by the occasional fighter.

A large round shield, averaging about 1 m (3 ft 3 in) in diameter and made from parallel wooden boards, provided protection for most of the warrior's body. An iron grip in the centre was held fast in one hand, protected by a hemispherical iron boss that protruded from the outer face. Because the boss is usually the only part to survive, we know little about how often the shields were strengthened by a leather cover, or about the coloured decorative designs and devices, fragmentary traces of which adorn just a few surviving examples.

Spears and axes, both of which had a variety of different shapes and sizes, were the commonest offensive weapons. Bows and arrows were also deployed; sharply pointed, narrow and relatively heavy bolt-like arrowheads were particularly effective against mail-shirted opponents. A moderately sized but relatively wide single-bladed knife, known in Old English as a seax, was carried in a leather sheath which was sometimes worn horizontally across the waist, attached to a belt – a weapon, perhaps, of last resort. In contrast, the favoured offensive weapon was the sword. At the beginning of the Viking Age some were single-sided, but double-edged blades eventually became universal. All their war gear could be acquired from weaponsmiths back home in Scandinavia, but some foreign swords were considered especially good and were eagerly sought after, perhaps for reasons of prestige as much as for practicality.

Where did the first Vikings to raid in the British Isles come from? The documentary sources provide only a little precise information, such as that the early attackers on Portland in Dorset were from Hordaland on the west coast of Norway, according to the *Anglo-Saxon Chronicle*. If the distribution of insular material in Norway is a guide, it was northwest Vestfold, in the Vik area, that provided many of the early ninth-century raiders, whereas Rogaland in southwest Norway assumed that prominence in the mid-ninth century. When Iceland was settled, traditionally slightly later in that century, the documentary sources suggest that it was people from the Sognefjord area, just north of Rogaland, who were prominent among the first arrivals. These concentrations of movement, as raiders or migrants, hint at a changing pattern of political ferment across those particular regions; a pattern that still requires further elucidation.

Swords

Swords were prized above all other weapons, for they were the most technically accomplished and most elaborately decorated items in the Vikings' armament. The ideal sword had a strong but flexible iron blade that would not shatter under an enemy's blows, and sharp edges to give maximum

WARRIORS IN STONE

Figures carved on a series of tenth-century grave markers from northern England present a vision of Viking Age warriors as they wished themselves to be remembered. Horsemen portrayed at Sockburn, County Durham, wear helmets, carry spears and sit on high-backed saddles. A standing figure on another stone from Sockburn wears a garment, presumed to be a kirtle, that comes down to his knees; he too is equipped with helmet and spear and he also, unusually, carries a round shield. The so-called 'Weston warrior', named after its findspot in North Yorkshire, again shows its hero clad in a knee-length kirtle, but this time clutching a sword and a battle-axe.

Best known and most fully equipped are the figures on several stones from the church at Middleton, North Yorkshire. Their pointed heads indicate the representation of helmets, and each has a seax or large knife slung across his waist in a sheath that is suspended from a belt. One, who is posed as if sitting in a high-backed chair, has a range of weaponry disposed about him – a spear, point upwards, to one side, balanced on the other by a circular shield, its boss visible, above a sword and an axe. Although the added details that would have been visible when the stone was originally painted have been lost, these sculptures provide vivid portraits of the might of Viking raiders and invaders.

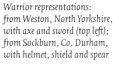

Warrior representations: from Weston, North Yorkshire, with axe and sword (top left); from Sockburn, Co. Durham, with helmet, shield and spear (above left); and from Middleton, North Yorkshire (above right) with (clockwise, from left) a spear, shield, sword and axe. He wears a helmet, and has a knife slung horizontally below a belt. Originally the details would have been coloured (the other side of the cross is illustrated on p.106).

penetration. Swordsmiths sometimes used a technique known as pattern welding for the blades, either in an attempt to give them added resilience or in order to make them look impressive.

Rods of iron, usually three in number, were twisted and forged before being hammer-welded together to form the central core of the blade. Sometimes rods with a low or high carbon content were deliberately placed alternately, and the twisting gives rise to the plaited patterns which were visible when the blade was finally etched with a weak acid, and which can be revealed today using X-rays. Steeled iron strips were then welded on to

form the cutting edges, which were forged, ground sharp and polished. The blade's centre strip was also ground out on both faces to create slightly hollowed fullers along its length, lightening the blade without reducing its effectiveness.

Other weaponsmiths produced blades of pure steel, and sometimes 'signed' their work by inlays in the blade. Two famous workshops that adopted this practice are known by the inlaid names Ulfberht and Ingelrii; they probably operated originally in the middle Rhineland, but it seems that their trademark was pirated by other smiths throughout western Europe.

BERSERK WARRIORS?

The English adjective 'berserk', meaning 'violently frenzied', derives from a word used in the Icelandic sagas for a stereotypically ferocious warrior. One saga describes them being 'as mad as dogs or wolves, they bit into their shields and were as strong as bears or bulls'. Two explanations of their name have

been put forward. One derives it from words meaning 'bare shirt', and thus describing someone who fought naked; the other, more likely, origin derives from 'bear shirt', meaning someone who wore a bearskin. There are representations in pre-Viking Scandinavian art of people

dressed in a bearskin and carrying weapons, but they probably depict a ritual relating to the 'shape-changer' aspect of Germanic religions rather than a functional warrior. The portrayal of berserk warriors in the sagas probably reflects medieval literary conventions rather than fact.

Three chess pieces, warders or rooks, made of walrus ivory 1150–1200 in Norway and found with many others buried in sandhills at Uig, Lewis, Outer Hebrides, Scotland in 1831. The warders bite their Norman-style kite-shaped shields in a manner also associated with berserk warriors of the Viking Age. Height 8–9 cm (3–3½ in).

The top of the sword blade ended in a tang on to which the horizontal bars of the upper and lower guard and the crowning pommel knop could be fixed. The smiths could lavish elaborate decoration on these components of the hilt, and a wide variety of inlays or cast plate embellishments have been found. The sword grip was usually made of an organic material such as wood or horn or antler which does not often survive, and may well have been wound around with textile. The sword was housed in a wooden scabbard case which could have a textile and wool inner lining – the natural oil in the wool helped to prevent the blade from rusting. The wooden scabbard case was itself protected by a leather scabbard. At the tip of the scabbard was a metal chape, often elaborately decorated, which protected the sword point.

(Above) Re-enacting an assault by a particularly well-helmeted Viking war band.

(Below) A sword from Visnes, Stryn, Nordfjord, Norway, its blade inlaid with iron billets forming the name or trademark Ulfberht.

TARGETS AND TACTICS

'Here terrible portents came about in the land of the Northumbrians, and miserably afflicted the people; there were immense flashes of lightning and fiery dragons were seen flying in the air, and there immediately followed a great famine, and after that in the same year the heathen miserably devastated God's church in Lindisfarne island by looting and slaughter.'

Anglo-Saxon Chronicle, 793

(Below) Map of the sites mentioned in this chapter.

The serendipity of documentary survival over the last millennium and more means that details of the first Viking raids do not survive, and we know about them only by inference. Yet it appears that raids were taking place on both sides of the English Channel in the late eighth century. In 792 the monasteries of Kent in southeast England were required to contribute to raising defences against 'pagan seamen' who were, presumably, Vikings; across the water, in 800, the Frankish emperor Charlemagne organized coastal defences against 'pirates' who were also, presumably, Vikings.

The very first well-documented Viking raid took place on the northeast coast of England in 793. The target was an important monastery on the tidal island of Lindisfarne. Its attraction was the expectation of loot – church plate, ecclesiastical fittings, anything easily portable that contained gold, silver, or precious inlays. The site's royal endowments and its associations with two important saints, the Irishman Columba and the Northumbrian Cuthbert, ensured that news of the event was spread widely, not only in Britain but also to Europe. Its prime victims, the religious community, perceived it as an attack by foreign infidels on a Christian shrine, the desecration of a sacred Christian site – the work of the devil.

Alcuin, a Northumbrian churchman, described the events in a letter written to King Aethelred of Northumbria, sent from the continent in 793: '...never before has such an atrocity been seen in Britain as we have now suffered at the hands of a pagan people. Such a voyage was not thought possible. The church of St Cuthbert is spattered with the blood of the priests of God, stripped of all its furnishings, exposed to the plundering of the pagans.'

In the early days of raiding in Britain, in the late eighth and early ninth centuries, Viking attacks were completely unexpected. The experience of the King's representative in Dorchester, near the south coast of England, at some time between 789 and 802, illustrates this well. When told of the approach of ships, he assumed that traders were coming and rode with a few men to the landing place at Portland to meet them – and was promptly killed. The shipmen were not the peaceful merchants he had anticipated but three Viking crews.

Coastal or riverine trading centres such as Portland (in Dorset) or Hamwic (Anglo-Saxon Southampton), Dorestad on the River Rhine in Holland or Quentovic on the River Canche in the Pas de Calais, France, were potentially lucrative targets for Viking raiders. But Europe had a limited number of these secular emporia, and in places such as Scotland and Ireland there were none. In contrast, significant ecclesiastical sites adorned with precious altar vessels and richly ornamented religious furnishings with a high bullion value were ubiquitous throughout much of western Europe.

Major ecclesiastical sites were also foci for the exchange of imported goods; they were in the market for such things as wine to celebrate Mass and

high-quality textiles, such as silk, for making priestly robes and church vestments. Additionally, their own farms and estates provided surplus agricultural produce and raw materials for the religious community, and these could be equally attractive pickings for Vikings on the lookout for supplies. On top of all this, secular magnates sometimes used major churches as safe deposits for their own portable wealth. To sack a major monastery was thus to hit the financial jackpot. And since coastal headlands and islands were favoured locations for these wealthy and undefended monasteries, their accessibility and vulnerability to shipborne attack made them a natural magnet for Viking raids. The trademark smash-and-grab, hit-and-run tactics of the Lindisfarne raid in 793, singling out a 'soft' target for a brutally efficient intervention, set the pattern for many other attacks around Europe over the next century and more.

The Vikings soon recognized how to increase still further the profits to be made from raiding churches. Bibles, gospels and other religious books probably first came to the attention of Viking marauders because of gold or silver embellishments on their outer covers, but some raiders soon realized that the pages within also had a value. Lavishly illuminated manuscripts were treasured by the church; they were both the embodiment of the Christian faith, and the products of many painstaking hours of careful design, scribing and decoration. Religious communities or their benefactors were therefore prepared to buy back such books from Viking thieves. Notes added to a page of the *Codex Aureus* ('the Golden Book'), a copy of the four gospels, record how the Anglo-Saxon aristocrat Ealdorman Aelfred and his wife paid pure gold to Vikings to ensure the book's safe return to Christ Church, Canterbury, perhaps after the Viking attacks on Canterbury in 851.

(Above) Lindisfarne, Northumberland, looking landwards across its east coast. The monastery was at the far side of the bay on the south side of the island.

(Below) 'The Warrior Stone', a fragmentary grave-marker from Lindisfarne. Dated to around 875–900, it may depict the famous raid of 793, or perhaps some other historic incident or hypothetical catastrophe.

Abbots and the monastic community were themselves a source of potential profit to Vikings; many leading churchmen came from aristocratic families who might be prepared to pay a ransom to get them back from the hands of the heathens. In the aftermath of the Lindisfarne raid, for example, Alcuin promised to do his best for the boys who had been carried off as prisoners. These early abductions set a precedent which later raiders followed religiously. In 914, for example, Vikings raiding along the coast of south Wales kidnapped the bishop of Archenfield (in modern Herefordshire) and took him to their ships. In what was probably a political as well as a religious gesture, the Anglo-Saxon King Edward 'the Elder' paid the substantial ransom of £40.

Vikings could be thwarted, however. On their approach, valuables could be hidden. Frustration might then prompt the killing of monks, as on Iona in 806 (see box opposite), or the burning of the monastery, as happened at Landevennec in Brittany in 913. Kidnapping, too, was not assured of success. When, in 1011, a Danish army captured Archbishop Aelfheah of Canterbury, he refused to allow a ransom of £3000 to be paid; in a drunken fury some of his captors pelted him with bones and ox-heads until one of them put him out of his misery with an axe-blow to the head.

The Codex Aureus (the 'Golden Book'), a mid-eighth-century copy of the Gospels from Canterbury, Kent. Above and below the gospel text is a mid-ninth-century inscription describing how the book was ransomed back from marauding Vikings who had stolen it.

TARGET IONA

Iona, a small island off the west coast of Scotland, was the site of one of the most important and wealthy monasteries of the Irish church. First plundered by Vikings in 795. It may have been on the Hebridean itinerary of a raid in 798, and was certainly struck again in 802. In 804 the monks were already thinking of providing an alternative, more secure haven for the community and its treasures when they acquired land in Ireland at Kells, County Meath. However, they were still resident on Iona in 806 when 68 monks were killed during yet another attack; thwarted by the monk Blathmac,

who had managed to hide the important relic shrine of St Columba and then refused to reveal its whereabouts, the Vikings massacred him and his companions.

The new monastery at Kells was completed by 814, but part of the community stayed on in their original home. Although Iona suffered further despoliation at the hands of Vikings in 825, the monks seem to have maintained a permanent presence there through successive centuries. The pre-Viking expertise in creating elaborately carved stone crosses was not lost, for there were

sufficient resources to underwrite the creation of the monument known as St Matthew's Cross in the ninth or early tenth century. In 980 the former king of Viking Dublin Olaf Cuaran Sihtricsson, retired to the monastery 'in penitence' at the end of his long reign, and gravestones, including one with a runic inscription and scenes from Scandinavian mythology, testify to the presence of other Scandinavian converts. Even so, the abbot and 15 monks were killed in yet another raid in 986.

Iona, Hebrides, Scotland, looking northeast. The sandy bay at bottom left is, traditionally, where St Columba landed in 563; Martyrs Bay, where monks were allegedly killed in the raid of 806, is just south of the village. Beyond this, the monastery and later abbey are towards the top right hand corner of the island, just below 'The White Strand of the Monks' at the north tip, allegedly the site of the massacre by Viking raiders in 986. The island is a little over 3½ miles (5.6 km) long from north to south.

VIKINGS IN FRISIA

Map of Frisia and Carolingia.

Gold brooch elaborately inlaid with glass, almandine (red stones) and pearls along the rim, made in Carolingia c. 800. Found in 1969 during excavation of a well at Dorestad, on the River Rhine in Holland, it reflects the considerable booty available to raiders at this important international trading centre.

At the time of the first Viking raids, Charlemagne (742–814) held sway over an enormous territory which embraced most of present-day France, Belgium, Holland and western Germany. His realm, Francia, had an extensive North Sea coastline and its northern border was at the foot of the Jutland peninsula. Although he prepared defences against their incursions, there are no contemporary records of Viking raids into Charlemagne's domain. Yet they must have been tempted!

As Viking raiders sailed south from Denmark along the coast of Europe they passed first the territory between the rivers Scheldt and Weser known as Frisia. This area of modern Holland and Germany had lost its independence between the 680s and 730s as the Franks gradually extended their power northwards. The landscape which they took over was very different from today, for there have been enormous changes in the coast line and the inland waterways. Geographically, Frisia was a highly fragmented area, but it did include the rich, internationally known trading centre of Dorestad on the River Rhine, a focus of commerce between the Rhine/Meuse region, Scandinavia and England. Dorestad inexorably attracted Viking interest; it was first raided by Vikings in 834 and was finally destroyed in 863. The island of Walcheren, with the trading centre of Domburg, was also a favourite target.

Frankish kings, more concerned with defending their heartlands than the farther flung parts of their territories, granted parts of Frisia to a number of Viking leaders during the ninth century. Most of them were members of a Danish royal family, utilized on the 'poacher turned gamekeeper' principle, and several of them faithfully carried out their obligations. In 885, however, the over-greedy and treacherous attitude of the Viking warlord Godfrid resulted in his overthrow and death; with his demise any possibility of a permanent Scandinavian settlement of the area disappeared.

Viking Camps

Frankish documents record many places where Vikings made bases in the ninth century, but none of these camps have yet been located and identified archaeologically. Place names provide other possible clues. On the Dutch island of Texel is Den Burg ('the fortress'), a double-ditched, circular enclosure with a diameter of 200 m (650 ft). Other sites with names that include the burg place-name element once existed on the nearby former island of Wieringen, and also on Kennmerland, the mainland coastal strip south of Texel. These burg names, recorded first in the ninth to eleventh centuries, may indicate a set of anti-Viking fortifications; but this suggestion remains speculative as the sites have not yet been investigated. If these forts were one outcome of Viking raids in North Holland, another seems to have been the strangulation of settlement in the area. There had been an expansion in the density of settlements in the eighth and early ninth centuries, but the Viking disruptions coincide with stagnation or even regression for about a century.

Further south, a series of circular earthworks in Flanders and Zeeland (modern Belgium and Holland) which all had a timber-faced earth rampart surrounded by a wide ditch, has excited interest

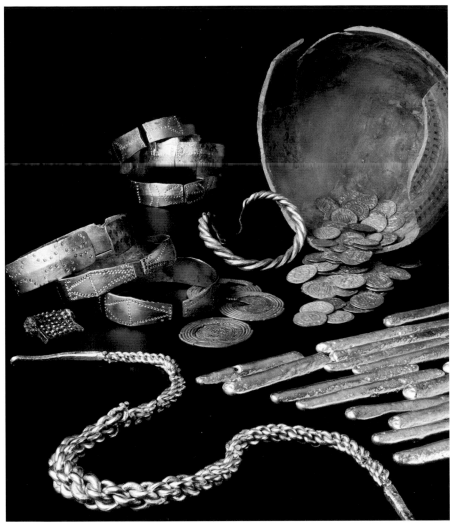

Silver armrings, a neckring, a belt mount, Arab dirhams mounted as pendants, silver ingots and Carolingian coins, all buried in a Badorf ware Rhenish pot around the year 850 at Westerklief, Wieringen, North Holland.

VIKING SILVER FROM HOLLAND

In 1996 a silver hoard was found at Westerklief, on the former island of Wieringen, now in the Dutch province of North Holland, a coastal area where the IJsselmeer meets the Waddensea. The hoard, which had been buried in about 850 within a pottery vessel made in the Rhineland, contains 1.7 kg (3 lb 12 oz) of silver. It includes six silver armbands of Danish type, a plaited silver neckring of 'West Scandinavian' type, a twisted armring, three coin brooches incorporating Arab dirhams, 16 silver ingots, and 78 Carolingian coins which indicate a date of about 850.

Remarkably, in 1999 and 2001 parts of what is probably another hoard of silver were found in the same field as the 1996 hoard. This second hoard was also of Scandinavian origin, for it contains many of the same forms of silver. In this instance, however, Carolingian coins indicate that the hoard was hidden in or after the late 870s. Why should two Viking hoards have been buried here?

Wieringen was an island of workable agricultural land, and was probably the base for a high ranking member of the Frisian regional aristocracy. It continued as a royal property in Frankish times, when a trading centre was founded to the south at Medemblik. Wieringen was therefore a likely target both for Viking attack (although there is no documentary record of one), and for settlement during the time when Viking leaders were granted lands in Frisia. It would also have offered a good base for controlling the important water route along the Vlie, the large tidal inlet between the islands of Vlieland and Terschelling. The hoards present new and important tangible evidence for Viking activities in this area, even if the precise reason for their deposition remains elusive.

because of their similarity to the famous, but rather later, series of Danish circular camps (see pp. 186–187). Excavations from 1969 to 1971 at Souburg in Zeeland revealed that this camp was originally built in about 900. The interior was divided into four quarters, with timber-surfaced roads leading to the four gates and out over bridges crossing the ditch. This regular layout looks as if it was the product of a powerful central authority. In contrast, the rather irregular layout of the timber buildings inside the camp, on either side of the roads, may indicate re-use in the eleventh to twelfth century, long after the fort was originally constructed. It is believed that not only Souburg but also the similar forts at Domburg, Middelburg and Burg date from the time of the ninth-century Viking raids; but the favoured interpretation is that they were built as refuges, fortified to defend the local population *against* Vikings. They are probably the camps which we know that Count Baldwin II of Flanders constructed in about 890.

CARNAGE IN ZUTPHEN

Zutphen, a medieval town 25 km (15 miles) northeast of Arnhem in Holland, was laid out in the neck of land between the rivers Berkel and IJssel, the latter a tributary of the lower Rhine. Excavations in 1997 on the site of a new town hall revealed a scene of carnage buried about 2 m (6 ft 6 in) below the modern ground level. Covered by a layer of charcoal that represents a major fire were remains of two timber buildings, together with four adjacent huts which had originally had their floors about 50 cm (20 in) below the contemporary ground surface.

Human skeletons – a child aged 12 years and an adult aged 30–40 – were found in two of these semi-subterranean huts. The bones from the child's skeleton were scattered, and many were missing entirely. The adult's skeleton was fairly complete, although both hands and one foot were detached; the foot was found separately, in a corner of the hut.

Carrion?

The grisly explanation for this may be that the corpses had been left unburied in the huts for some time, and dogs, wolves or other carnivorous beasts had taken advantage of this carrion. They might also have feasted upon the remains of slaughtered farm animals, mainly cattle, which were found in the soil that eventually infilled and covered both the sunken huts and the human corpses within them. All of this looks like the aftermath of a horrific catastrophe, which can be dated to some time after the early 840s by the discovery of an Anglo-Saxon coin in close association with one of the skeletons. Other strands of evidence, including pottery and radiocarbon dating, point to the late ninth century, a time when there is documentary and archaeological evidence for a destructive Viking raid in 882 on the ecclesiastical and trading centre at Deventer, just 16 km (10 miles) to the north. It is highly unlikely that the Vikings would have ignored Zutphen, a place which seems to have already been a centre for royal administration and, perhaps, the collecting of taxes in the form of agricultural produce; it was a ready-made supply centre for hungry Vikings (similarly to Croydon, see p. 82).

So it is reasonable to suggest that these remains provide a graphic and ghastly insight into the terrible outcome of Viking raiding. Another outcome was that within a few years a fortification was built to protect Zutphen from suffering similar devastation; another anti-Viking defence in the series noted above.

Adult skeleton found within the remains of a building at Zutphen, Holland.

THE CAROLINGIAN HEARTLANDS

Like his father, Charlemagne's sole surviving son and successor, Louis the Pious, also seems to have been relatively untroubled by Viking attacks, although around the year 820 pirates (Vikings?) were reported on the lower River Seine. But in the years after Louis's death in 840 the Vikings increased their impact.

In 841 it was recorded in the *Annals of St-Bertin* that Rouen was burnt by Vikings: 'Danish pirates sailed down the Channel and attacked Rouen, plundered the town with pillage, fire and sword....' Archaeological evidence for a major fire at and around Rouen Cathedral in the mid-ninth century adds physical reality to the dry textual record. Rich churches on the River Seine, including Jumièges and Saint-Wandrille, were also ransacked at this time, and in 845 a Viking fleet went up the Seine as far as Paris. Charles the Bald paid them a bribe of £7000 in gold and silver to go away.

Rival Frankish kingdoms, squabbling Frankish royal dynasties and pretenders to the royal thrones all enlisted Viking forces in their struggles, and rulers were also tempted to employ one Viking force to defeat another within their territory. In 860 Charles the Bald hired the Viking leader Weland and his army based in the Somme to attack Vikings operating along the River Seine. Weland duly besieged them on the island of Oissel, but lived up to his role of mercenary by accepting a bribe of £6000 of silver to let the Seine Vikings escape.

It was a sign of the times in 864 when, in the *Edict of Pîtres*, Charles the Bald tried to limit the Vikings' fighting capability by prohibiting, on pain of death, both the sale and the giving in ransom to Vikings of Frankish mailcoats, weapons and horses: 'Anyone who should give a coat of mail, or any sort of arms, or a horse to the Northmen, for any reason or for any ransom, shall forfeit his life without any chance of reprieve or redemption, as a traitor to his country.'

Pont de l'Arche

From the mid-ninth century Vikings established winter camps on islands in the River Loire and River Seine. One counter-measure deployed against the Vikings by Carolingian rulers was to build bridges across rivers in order to bar the passage of Viking ships. The *Annals of St-Bertin* record that such a bridgework was begun at Pistis in 862, and this site has convincingly been

Silver gilt cup, highlighted with black niello (sulphide of silver), made in Carolingia in c. 800 but found in 1872 on the island of Fejø, between Lolland and Sjaelland, Denmark. A product of trade or loot?

(Opposite) A silver coin, a so-called, 'St Peter's Penny', struck at York in the early tenth century but found at Camp de Péran, Brittany.

equated with Pont de l'Arche, 5 km (3 miles) downstream from Pîtres on the River Seine, close to its confluence with the River Eure. Here the two rivers run parallel for a short distance and, including the sliver of land between them, have a combined width of 300 m (1,000 ft). A roughly square enclosure defined by an earthen rampart with sides 270 m (890 ft) long, enclosing an area of 6.5 ha (16 acres), has been identified at Igoville on the north bank of the Seine, opposite Pont de l'Arche. The fort, presumably designed to house a force which would defend the bridgehead, was apparently finished but ungarrisoned when a Viking attack in 865 captured it.

The Vikings held the fort for a year while Paris was besieged, leaving only when they were given a substantial pay-off of 4,000 pounds of silver. After this there was a hiatus in Viking attacks, and the Franks quickly took this opportunity to strengthen the fort. Documents record their use of wood and stone, and archaeologists have discovered evidence for just such a refortification. The front of the original and relatively simple clay rampart was removed, interleaved clay and horizontal timbers were inserted to provide extra strength and stability, and then a stone wall was erected as a new and more impressive facade. All this effort was to little effect, however; in 885 a Viking fleet, reported to consist of 700 ships, neutralized the fort and slighted its defences before going on to besiege Paris.

BURNT IN BRITTANY: THE ÎLE DE GROIX BURIAL

The most spectacular Viking burial in continental Europe took place on an island called Île de Groix, 6 km (3¾ miles) off the southwest coast of Brittany, 14 km (8¾ miles) from Lorient. Towards the southeastern end of the island, near the village of Locmaria, was a promontory with schist cliffs 5 m (16 ft 6 in) high.

This was neither the tallest nor the longest of the nearby promontories, but it was the one closest to a modern harbour which may also have been a Viking Age landing place. On the promontory, at the eroding cliff edge, stood a mound which was investigated in 1906 by two amateur archaeologists. They found an extensive cremation deposit containing about 1,000 iron rivets – the remains of a cremated ship.

The vessel, which seems to have been about 11–13 m (36–42 ft) long, had contained the remains of two people, one adult and one adolescent.

Weapons buried with them included two swords, arrowheads, four spearheads, two axeheads, buckles and spurs, and between 15 and 24 shield bosses. In addition there were items of jewelry and clothing; feasting equipment in the form of bowls, buckets and a cauldron; tools including an anvil, hammer, tongs and drills; 19 bone gaming pieces, and two dice.

Pilfering by night during the investigation removed who knows what else, but the surviving items leave no doubt that this was the grave of a tenth-century Viking war leader.

(Below left) Buckles, a gold finger-ring and other small objects from the burial.

(Below) The site of the Île de Groix cremation burial, Brittany, France.

Camp de Péran

One circular fortress in France that does have demonstrable links with Vikings is Camp de Péran, 5 km (3 miles) south of Saint-Brieuc and close to the north coast of Brittany. This circular fortification, 140 m (460 ft) in diameter, is defended by a single, 3-m (10-ft) high stone wall which stands on a clay bank that was braced with vertical and horizontal timbers. These defences perhaps originally stood 4 m (13 ft) tall and were 5 m (16 ft 6 in) thick, but eventually they succumbed to a fire which had, apparently, destroyed the entire site.

Excavations on a modest scale within the ramparts have uncovered traces of internal structures and a wide range of artifacts. Some are purely domestic or agricultural in character, including a wool comb, a two-pronged cooking fork, the iron tip of a spade, an adze or pick, pottery jugs, bowls and cooking pots, and an iron cauldron. None of these is specifically Scandinavian in character; but there are weapons that could have been owned by Vikings – a sword of Scandinavian style, spearheads, a shield boss, and stirrups. Another discovery was a silver 'St Peter's Penny' minted by Viking rulers of York in c. 905–19. Although there are many means by which this coin could have arrived in Brittany, it could well have been carried to Camp de Péran by a Viking warrior.

Vikings virtually controlled Brittany for 30 years after the death of the Breton Count Alan in 907. A Viking fleet sailed from the Severn Estuary in southwest England in 914 and attacked Brittany, where they campaigned for the next four years; the Camp de Péran coin could, for example, have been brought to the continent by one of those Vikings. Camp de Péran may not have been built by Vikings – it could be a product of the wars between Franks and Bretons, or indeed be an anti-Viking measure – but it does look as if Vikings occupied the site during the heyday of their attacks.

(Above) Viking swords, spearheads, a broken shield boss, fragments of stirrups and other objects found at Camp de Péran.

(Top) Camp de Péran, near Saint-Brieuc, Brittany, France; the field divisions inside the 140-m (460-ft) wide circular earthwork are later.

In 850 there was a change to the normal pattern of Viking activity in England. Instead of leaving the country after their summer raids, a Viking warband settled down to spend the winter rather than sailing back to Scandinavia. The same tactic was followed again in 855, but a more profound change of strategy came 10 years later with the campaigns of what was described as a 'great heathen army'.

This force landed in the kingdom of East Anglia in 865 and spent the winter there. In 866 they rode north to the kingdom of Northumbria where, on All Saints' Day, 1 November, they attacked and captured York, the most prestigious settlement in the region. York provided a base for them over the winter; in spring 867 they strengthened their grip in the face of a Northumbrian counter-attack, and killed the two most important Northumbrian leaders. Thereafter, for 13 years, they ranged across England, defeating local militias and royal armies alike, and capturing key strategic centres. Each winter they established a base in some impregnable spot, often utilizing pre-existing defences. In this way they conquered the kingdoms of Northumbria, Mercia and East Anglia, deposing or killing the defeated Anglo-Saxon kings. Only Wessex, in southern England, under the leadership of King Alfred, managed to hold out against them.

The 'great heathen army' probably maintained contacts with the homelands, but supply lines could not stretch to Scandinavia, and there was a continual need to forage for provisions. Although this could have been done opportunistically, there is evidence that the Vikings went about it in a more systematic fashion. The *Anglo-Saxon Chronicle* records that the 'great heathen army' overwintered in London in 871–72; a hoard of silver found at Croydon, 16 km (10 miles) south of London, can be dated by the coins it contains to c. 872. Furthermore, fragments of silver jewelry and foreign coins reveal that it belonged to a Viking. Croydon at this time was a residence of the archbishops of Canterbury, a place where the church's tithes and the farm produce from its own estates would be assembled to feed the clergy and their staff. Taken together, the archaeological and documentary evidence suggest that the hoard's owner was a member of the 'great heathen army'; and the most likely reason for him to be at Croydon was that the Vikings simply plugged into the archbishops' ready-made supply chain, and harvested the rewards.

The Viking Camp at Repton

The *Anglo-Saxon Chronicle* records where the 'great heathen army' established its winter camps, but until the 1970s no tangible trace of any such *winter-setl* had been positively identified. Repton in Derbyshire, the site of an important Anglo-Saxon monastery patronized by Mercian kings, was

Viking invaders, as pictured in The Life, Passion and Miracles of St Edmund, King and Martyr, an illuminated manuscript produced around 1130 in the monastery at Bury St Edmunds, Suffolk, burial place of Edmund, the East Anglian king killed by Vikings in 870. The artist pictures them with weapons, such as kite-shaped shields, more appropriate to his own times (see p.66).

where the Vikings chose to overwinter in 873–74. A campaign of excavations there, begun 1,100 years later around the crypt at the east end of the Anglo-Saxon church, revealed human skeletons; some of the bones bore the marks of fatal wounds (see box on p. 38). Weapons, jewelry, coins and other items found with the skeletons clearly indicated that these were Vikings.

Next to be identified was the butt-end of a large V-shaped ditch, 4 m (13 ft) deep and 9 m (30 ft) wide at its top, dug against the east end of the church. A geophysical survey traced its course as it arced away to the cliff edge marking the old course of the River Trent, and then located a matching ditch running from the west end of the church. Traces of an earthen rampart, formed from the soil thrown up from the ditch, were found on the inner side of the ditch. This D-shaped enclosure of 1.46 ha (3.6 acres) is surely the Viking army's *wintersetl* of 873–74. The Vikings had simply incorporated

Excavation of the mausoleum at Repton, Derbyshire. The scale rod lies in the western room; human bones and skulls are in situ in the eastern room. The stone kerb which marked the edge of the overlying cairn is visible.

The 'Warrior's Tomb', a hogback tomb-stone from Gosforth, Cumbria. Below the shingled roof, two armed bands face each other, their circular shields prominent.

the church into their defensive scheme, probably using its north and south doors as the entrance into their camp. Whether it was at this stage, or later, that the upper parts of the church's walls were dismantled, is uncertain.

An early eighteenth-century account of the local history of Repton contains an unlikely story of discoveries made in the vicarage garden in about 1686, when a stone coffin containing 'a Humane skeleton of an extraordinary size' was uncovered within the remains of a stone building. Even more unbelievably, this central burial was reportedly surrounded by 100 skeletons, arranged with their feet pointing towards it. Incredible though these details seemed, the site of these findings was still recognizable in the 1980s, some 60 m (200 ft) west of the church.

A meticulous excavation of the site laid bare a remarkable story. An Anglo-Saxon two-roomed building of high quality, perhaps a royal mortuary chapel, had been dismantled almost to ground level, and its western room had been used as a smiths' workshop. Within the truncated eastern room, on a deliberately laid floor of red marl, the disarticulated longbones and skulls of some 264 individuals had been stacked up – just as had been reported. Originally buried somewhere else, their bones had been exhumed and brought here for ceremonial re-interment. There was no trace of the central stone coffin mentioned in the original account, but a small number of objects among the bones include five coins which were probably deposited in 873 or 874 – the date of the Vikings' overwintering. A low stone cairn had been piled over the bones, its edge defined by a stone kerb, and this was capped by a pebble mound.

Just southwest of the mound a pit had been dug in which four young people had been buried simultaneously. One child, aged 8–12, lay on its back, faced by a 17-year-old lying in a crouched position. At their legs, two children aged 8–11 had been laid, crouched and back to back. This carefully orchestrated arrangement could well represent the culmination of a series of ritual acts, a sacrificial dedication to the gods in a ceremony marking the closure of the mass grave.

Who exactly was buried in the mass grave has been much discussed, for radiocarbon dating of the charnel bones suggested that some of these people died in the period c. 700–750, and that others may have died c. 800–850. Osteological studies of the bones show that 82 per cent were male and 18 per cent female, a higher percentage of men than might have been expected in an average

Four children/youths, laid out in a carefully choreographed ritual position close to the mass grave at Repton, Derbyshire. The white labels mark individual archaeological features; the significance of the square stone setting towards the top of the picture is uncertain, but it could have held a substantial grave marker. A narrow strip of soil running from it directly across the burials has been deliberately left unexcavated at this stage of the investigation. The scale is in 10 cm (4 in) units.

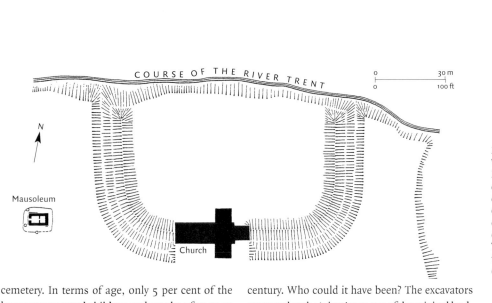

Plan of the main features of the Viking camp and burials at Repton, Derbyshire. Vikings, among others, were buried around the east end of the church; the D-shaped Viking ditch ran from either end of the church to the cliff above the River Trent. The mass burial utilized the Anglo-Saxon mausoleum outside the ditched enclosure.

cemetery. In terms of age, only 5 per cent of the bones represented children and youths of up to 17 years; 68 per cent were aged 17–35, 25 per cent were aged 36–45, and 3 per cent were older than 45. The absence of children and youths is atypical, although their bones, being smaller and less robust, would have been least likely to survive the exhumation from wherever each had been originally buried which preceded re-interment in the charnel deposit. Examination of the skulls has revealed that 45 per cent of the men and 30 per cent of the women had suffered cuts to the head, an extraordinarily high number.

The radiocarbon dates have led some commentators to suggest that the bones represent earlier Anglo-Saxon burials in monastic and aristocratic cemeteries at Repton, where men might have predominated, and that these were accidentally or deliberately disturbed during the Vikings' overwintering. They may have been piled up in the mass grave as symbolic retainers or slaves of whoever was originally buried in the centre of the deposit. However, there are particular methodological problems with radiocarbon dates in the period c. 700–900, well illustrated by the fact that the dates for the four children buried together, who surely died virtually simultaneously, range over a 200 year period.

Given the high incidence of wounds, it can be suggested that most of the charnel represents the bones of Viking warriors who had died earlier in the 'great heathen' campaign, and who were brought to Repton for some major ceremonial purpose. Wherever the charnel originated, its presence emphasizes the importance of the central burial reportedly seen in the eighteenth century. Who could it have been? The excavators suggest that the 'giant' was one of the original leaders of the great heathen army, Ivar 'the boneless'.

The Ingleby Cemetery

A second but very different Viking cemetery lies just 4 km (2½ miles) southeast of Repton, at Ingleby. There, on a prominent ridge overlooking the River Trent and clearly visible from Repton, are 59 mounds, clustered into four main groups. In a rite unique within the British Isles, cremated human remains were interred in the mounds, together with personal possessions including costume fittings, weapons, and animal remains which may represent funeral feasting. Although there is no precise dating evidence such as that provided by the coins found at Repton, it is very likely that this cemetery, which is distinctly pagan and Viking, also dates to the overwintering of 873–74. Not all the dead were warriors, however; one mound contained the remains of both a woman and a child or juvenile.

Why were there two separate Viking cemeteries in the vicinity of Repton? They seem to represent two ideological factions within the 'great heathen army' who remained distinct from each other in death as, perhaps, they had been in life. These differences may have directly contributed to the subsequent history of the army, for it split into two units that pursued separate objectives in the years after 874. Within a few years, however, some detachments of the 'great heathen army' decided to turn from fighting to farming, and returned to the Anglo-Saxon kingdoms which they had already subdued. The Danelaw was in the making.

SHIP-BASES IN IRELAND

Contemporary Irish annals provide the fullest documentation for Viking activities available from any part of the British Isles. They first record a Viking raid in 795, on Rathlin Island, off Ireland's northeast coast. Thenceforth, until the 820s, raids in Ireland occurred sporadically; indeed, in the years 813–21 there is no mention of Viking raids at all. Particular events in these early raids were sometimes briefly described, giving an insight into the Vikings' modus operandi. In 798 there is a reference to the breaking of a shrine or reliquary, and also to the seizing of cattle, while in 823 or 824 Comgall's relics were scattered from his shrine. On other occasions churchmen were taken captive, either to hold for ransom or to sell as slaves. Perhaps these were the types of deeds, inflicted by attackers who were referred to by the Irish as *genti*, 'heathens', which inspired a short verse, penned by an anonymous Irish monk, in the margin of a ninth-century manuscript copy of a book of grammar:

> *Bitter is the wind tonight*
> *It tosses the white-waved sea*
> *I do not fear the coursing of the great sea*
> *By the fierce warriors from Lothlind.*

From the 830s Vikings began to sail further up the rivers and into the great lakes of Ireland, raiding deeper inland. They also began to establish *long-phoirt*, literally 'ship-bases', along the east coast. This enabled them to spend the winter in Ireland and to extend the terror season – to demonstrate their new-found tactic, Clonmore, County Carlow,

THE DONNYBROOK GRAVE

In 1879 workmen levelling a slight mound on a ridge above the River Dodder at Donnybrook, about 5 km (3 miles) southeast of the Viking-Age city of Dublin, uncovered the burial of a Viking, as well as hundreds of other skeletons. The man lay on his back, his head to the north and his feet to the south. Death had apparently been caused by a blow that pierced his forehead. Tools of the warrior's trade had been placed with him – a sword to one side, a spearhead to the other, and three arrowheads close by.

The contemporary report of this discovery suggests that two skeletons at the warrior's feet represent women sacrificed to accompany their lord in the afterlife, but this cannot be verified. It does, however, seem likely that the Viking had been interred in a pre-existing Irish cemetery – an act that could be interpreted as symbolic of his supremacy.

The sword is particularly magnificent although now somewhat damaged, with an elaborately decorated hilt. On the side faces of the guards, a brass plate had been hammered into a decorative network which had been forged into the guards' iron cores, thus forming a design with raised and lowered elements. This created the effect of a row of equal-armed crosses lying along each side's central ridge, with similar but truncated remains above and below; smaller equal-armed crosses occupy the depressions between

their larger counterparts. Ring and dot motifs made from silver wire were hammered into position within both the large and small crosses. The sword handle was made from the wood of a conifer, and was bound around with linen to ensure a better grip in the heat of battle.

The sword blade had been protected by a wooden scabbard lined with sheepskin. The double-edged blade bore traces of an inlay in which one element had been a trellis pattern, but overall it was indecipherable. Removal of a thin slice at the

blade's broken tip, extending from the edge to the centre, took four hours using a hand saw – a striking testimony to the blade's resilience. Analysis confirmed that this was a tough, flexible sword with a keen cutting edge. Altogether, this is one of the finest products of Viking Age weaponry yet found in the British Isles, exhibiting technical virtuosity of a high standard.

The elaborately decorated guard of the sword buried at Donnybrook, Dublin.

THE SCOTTISH ENIGMA

Although parts of modern Scotland, including the Orkney and Shetland Isles, lie closer to Scandinavia than any other part of Britain, no records written in Scotland survive to report Viking activity before the mid-ninth century. Instead, we must rely on Irish sources, and not surprisingly, the view of the Irish annalists was focussed on the territory occupied by their kinsmen the Scotti, in Argyll and the inner Hebrides, and they ignored the areas of northern and eastern Scotland that were under the control of the native people, the Picts. Presumably, a Pictish monastery was as tempting a target as any other major church, but only archaeology is going to elucidate the fate of such sites.

Excavation at Portmahomack, Tarbat, in the Moray Firth area of northeast Scotland, has demonstrated this difficulty. Over a monastic workshop was a layer of burnt debris incorporating freshly fractured decorated stone monuments. The layer must have formed in the period from c. 800–1100, but, in the absence of written records, its cause is ambiguous. Does it reflect the intolerance of fundamentalist native religious reformers in the eleventh and twelfth centuries, or some local political rivalry played out on an ecclesiastical stage; or was it the work of Vikings who, according to saga, conquered this area in the later ninth century? Vikings are, indeed, the prime suspects – but the case isn't proven.

The same uncertainty surrounds a hoard of silver objects, perhaps the possessions of a Pictish aristocrat, which was buried in the decades around 800 at an early church site on St Ninian's Isle in the Shetlands. It may perhaps have been hidden when Vikings were sighted on the horizon or, alternatively, be buried Viking loot – but, as with much else in a consideration of early Viking contacts in Scotland, this is only speculation.

One intriguing hypothesis, albeit wholly speculative, is that the size and ferocity of Viking attacks on Ireland in the mid-ninth century are best explained by the presence of Viking bases relatively close at hand. It has also been suggested that such bases could have housed the enigmatic Gall-Gaedhil, the 'foreign-Irish' or 'Viking-Irish', who appear occasionally in the Irish annals at exactly this time. Such Viking bases may have been established in the Scottish isles and coastal areas, and the Isle of Man, in the first half of the ninth century. A key argument has been that when Irish annals for the years 848 and 853 mention a region called Lothlend or Laithlinn, from which Vikings came to raid in Ireland, they are referring to parts of Scotland. This, however, has been hotly contested.

The hoard of silver from St Ninian's Isle, Shetland. It includes bowls, brooches, sword trappings, a spoon and a 'pick', silver cones of uncertain function, and the jawbone of a porpoise. Its hiding in c. 800 may have been prompted by Vikings.

UNINVITING WALES?

Despite its long Irish Sea coastline, according to documentary sources the petty kingdoms in the area now united as Wales did not suffer a Viking raid until as late as 852. That is not to say that ninth-century Wales was a haven of internal peace; as in Ireland, neighbouring kingdoms were often at war, and Anglo-Saxons also harried the Welsh. In these circumstances sporadic Viking raids probably made no lasting impression, and a specifically Viking menace cannot be proposed as the reason for the concealment of most of the eleven silver hoards known from mid-ninth to early eleventh century Wales.

A Viking army overwintered in Dyfed, southwest Wales, in 878, but there is no indication that this was a frequent occurrence. Asser's *Life of King Alfred*, 878, records the expedition: '...the brother of Ivar and Halfdan sailed with 23 ships from Dyfed, where he had spent the winter, after slaughtering many of the Christians there, came to Devon, and met an unhappy death there with 1,200 men....'

Viking raids on Wales were usually made by war-bands or armies based elsewhere in Britain or Ireland. When the Viking leader Ingimund was expelled from Dublin in 902 he is thought to have landed first on the island of Anglesey, off the northwest cost of Wales, but he was forced to move on, eventually settling on the mainland near Chester, in England.

Welsh kings could sometimes count on political and military support from the English in pursuit of their joint enemy; but for some of the Welsh, Vikings were not a problem but a potential solution to their very real problems with the English. In *c.* 930 a Welsh monk wrote a poem expressing the hope that the Dublin Vikings would join with the Welsh and other Britons to expel the Anglo-Saxons: '...there will be reconciliation between the Welsh and the Dubliners, the Irish of Ireland and Anglesey and Scotland, the men of Cornwall and of Strathclyde will be welcomed among us...' (*Armes Prydein*, The Prophecy of Britain).

Wishful thinking, poetic licence – or a welcome reminder that contemporary perceptions of Vikings were by no means uniform?

Arab silver coins called dirhams, found with the slightly smaller Anglo-Saxon and Anglo-Viking coins of the period, in a hoard buried c. 925 near St Deiniol's monastery, Bangor, Wales.

IBERIA, NORTH AFRICA AND THE MEDITERRANEAN

The great majority of the Vikings' activities in Francia have not yet been detected archaeologically. So it is hardly surprising that there is no excavated proof that Vikings sailed further south, along the Atlantic coast of Spain and Portugal and into the Mediterranean Sea. Yet there are documentary references which report Viking raids not only on modern Spain but also on both the European and African coasts of the Mediterranean. In 844 a fleet left the River Loire and sailed south. On the Spanish north coast, in the kingdom of Galicia, they were driven off and suffered heavy losses. Undeterred, they rounded Cape Finisterre and headed on south to reach the coasts under the control of the Arab Emir of Cordoba. They sacked Lisbon, Seville, Cadiz and other sites before being heavily defeated by a Muslim army. They even sailed across the Straits of Gibraltar and ransacked Asilah on the Atlantic coast of modern Morocco before returning home.

There is no record of more Viking raids on Spain until 859 when another Loire fleet of 62 ships, led by Hastein and Bjorn Ironside, sailed southwards. After defeats during their raiding voyage down the Iberian peninsula they turned into the Straits of Gibraltar and attacked sites on both the European and North African sides before sailing on into the Mediterranean. Turning northwards they attacked the Balearic Islands, southeast France and Roussillon before overwintering in the Camargue at the mouth of the River Rhône.

The next year, 860, they ventured further east, attacking sites in northwest Italy. Where they overwintered is not known, but in 861 they were again defeated off Spain; the sacking of Pamplona, over 60 km (37 miles) inland in the Basque country of northeast Spain, was their final act before returning home. This is all documentary history – to date there are no archaeological discoveries which can illuminate the written record.

One small item now in the treasury of Léon cathedral, in north-central Spain, may reflect somewhat later contacts with Scandinavia. It is a cylindrical box, only 4.5 cm (1³/₄ in) tall and 3.3 cm (1¹/₄ in) in diameter, made of an as yet unidentified boney material and decorated with an openwork bird motif carved in the Mammen style (see p. 178). This suggests that it was made in the later tenth century; its original purpose is unknown, although after its gilt bronze lid had been altered it may have served as the reliquary container for a holy relic. Léon was the capital of an independent kingdom at this time, and the monastery, attested since 1063, was already an important, royally supported religious foundation in earlier centuries. When and why the box arrived in Spain is not recorded; perhaps it was a diplomatic gift to the king of Léon, who in turn gave it to the monastery.

(Above) The Léon box.
(Below) A map of the region.

IV · INVADERS AND SETTLERS

Viking raiding voyages contributed to a growing pool of geographical and political intelligence, identifying the resources and possibilities of different overseas areas, and ultimately paving the way for permanent settlements. The time lag between raiding and settlement varied from place to place. Well-documented parts of the Viking world, such as England, Ireland and Carolingia, seem to have endured several decades of attack before there was any attempt by Vikings to settle permanently. In the Scottish isles and in places around the Baltic Sea, by contrast, there may have been an influx of colonists relatively soon after the first contacts.

Land could be acquired either by dispossessing the previous owner or by reaching agreement with him; the most compelling way in which Vikings acquired land abroad was through the sustained and strategic deployment of substantial military force. A good example was the takeover of England by the 'great heathen army' in the 860s and 870s. The culmination of this type of attack, when royal authority and national resources were thrown into the fray, was King Svein Forkbeard of Denmark's campaigns against England in the early eleventh century.

The reasons *why* Scandinavians left their homelands permanently to settle abroad have also been hotly debated. There is no evidence to support the idea that it was necessary to find new land abroad to support the growing size of the population; studies have shown that there was sufficient productive farmland available in Scandinavia. It is more likely that chieftains and local aristocrats who felt themselves squeezed by powerful neighbours, or by rulers bent on strengthening their grip and uniting their territory more firmly into one kingdom, opted to look for new pastures across the seas.

New lands were also the arenas where ambitious and successful warriors with only a relatively low social standing in their homeland could escape those constraints, dramatically improve their fortunes and become their own masters. The careers of some leaders suggest that they were not mere opportunists, but were prepared to assault target after target in dogged pursuit of a territory over which they could exert control.

Scenes on the picture stone from St Hammars Daggäng, Lärbro,
Gotland remind us that Viking invaders seized land at sword point;
and that some, at least, brought beliefs, practices and traditions
that were anathema to the Christians of western Europe

VIKINGS IN THE EAST

Although the start of the Viking Age is defined by the documentary records of raids westwards from Scandinavia on the British Isles and the coast of northwest Europe, Scandinavians were just as active at about this time in lands to the east as traders, raiders and, in some cases, settlers.

History and Legend

There are no contemporary writings from the illiterate societies around the Baltic Sea that chart the course of Viking contacts there, although further east and south we do occasionally see them through the eyes of Arabs and Byzantines. Remarkably, there is one important western European source. In 839, at Ingelheim (near Mainz, on the River Rhine), the Frankish emperor Louis the Pious received envoys sent to him from Constantinople by the Byzantine emperor Theophilus. With them came some men who had been sent by their king on a diplomatic mission to Constantinople. Theophilus had been loath to send these men back by the route along which they had come to him because it had taken them among 'primitive tribes who were fierce and savage'; so he had sent them with his own envoys to Louis and expressed the hope that Louis would be able to despatch them homewards by a safer route. These men called themselves *Rus*, the first reference to the people whose identity is perpetuated in the name Russia. Louis, however, identified them as Swedes, and thereby set running a question that was to be politically vexatious over a millennium later – the degree of Swedish Viking influence in the creation of the Slavic Russian state.

The *Chronicle of Past Years*, compiled in Kiev in the early twelfth century, and known to modern scholars as the *Russian Primary Chronicle*, is the most important indigenous source for the early history of Russia. It recounts that in 862 Slavs and other tribes went across the sea to a group called *Rus* and invited them to become their rulers. Rurik, the eldest of the three brothers who accepted the invitation, reportedly settled in Novgorod (more probably in Gorodisce – see below) and founded the Ryurik dynasty, which ruled Russia until 1598. Although the story of Rurik is at best semi-legendary, the region's links with Scandinavia are confirmed by archaeological evidence.

Around 882, Oleg, Rurik's kinsman and successor, captured Kiev and made it the *Rus* capital; by the reign of Igor (913–45) the *Rus* state (with a predominantly Slav population) stretched from the Gulf of Finland to the lower River Dniepr. These early rulers had Norse names, albeit rendered in Slav form, but Svyatoslav, Igor's son, had a Slav name, as did all his successors, and by the later tenth century the Slav identity had become totally dominant.

Map of the eastern Viking world, stretching from St Petersburg to Istanbul and Baghdad.

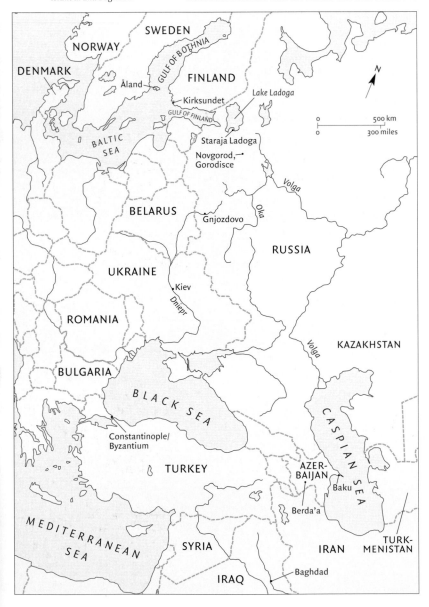

Staging Posts to the Sun

A short voyage of 240 km (150 miles) eastwards across the Baltic Sea from Sweden, perhaps with a stop midway on the Åland Islands, brought traders into the Gulf of Finland. In southwest Finland, finds of Scandinavian-style jewelry and even of a fragmentary rune stone – the only one from Finland – have recently been reported from Kirksundet in Hitis; perhaps this was a stopping point for traders on their way eastwards. Scandinavians had certainly penetrated beyond the Gulf of Finland into Russia by the late eighth century. Sailing up the River Neva into Lake Ladoga, they could turn south and continue up the River Volkhov to Staraja Ladoga. Founded as a craftworking and trading settlement in about 750, Ladoga was a gateway community linking the Baltic to Eastern Europe. Scandinavians were certainly present there, either in transit, seasonally, or perhaps resident for longer periods; their cemetery, with burials of men and women in boats, has been identified directly across the river at Plakun.

Some 200 km (125 miles) up the River Volkhov from Ladoga stands the important medieval town of Novgorod ('the new town'). Excavations have revealed that it was founded in the 950s, and have uncovered some Scandinavian objects. In the late 1970s, however, investigation at the nearby site of Ryurikovo Gorodisce ('Ryurik's deserted town') showed that there had been a settlement there with Scandinavian connections in the ninth century, well before Novgorod existed. This small defended hilltop was a key strategic position from which to control the surrounding area, and a focus for craftwork and long-distance commerce.

The Viking presence is reflected in a wide variety of artifacts. For example, there is typically Scandinavian jewelry, including women's oval brooches, equal-armed brooches and pendants (one of them of 'Valkyrie' form), and a large group of cult and magic objects, among them two runic amulets and several Thor's hammer amulets. In contrast, the pottery is of local types, the building traditions are Eastern European, and there is a range of Slavic, Baltic and Finnish artifacts. The Viking immigrants, particularly from Sweden, were a significant element in Gorodisce's population, but their identity was transmuted as they mingled with the locals; by the end of the tenth century, Scandinavian-style objects had virtually disappeared.

Infiltrating southwards from Gorodisce or approaching by an alternative route from the Baltic along the River Dvina, and journeying on foot between rivers, Vikings could penetrate the catchment of the River Dniepr and reach the settlement of Gnjozdovo, approximately halfway down the

(Above) Toy wooden swords from ninth-century Staraja Ladoga mimic west European/Scandinavian types.

(Below) Mounds in the Velema cemetery at Staraja Ladoga.

THE VARANGIAN GUARD

Just as their distant ancestors had served as auxiliary mercenaries in the Roman army (see p. 14), so Viking warriors are known to have enrolled in the armies of the Byzantine emperor as early as the mid-ninth century. In the late tenth century the emperor formed a new, elite corps among the imperial bodyguards known as the Varangian Guard because in addition to other foreigners it included a large Scandinavian contingent. The name echoes Slavic and Greek words meaning 'Scandinavians and/or Franks'.

The deeds of individual Varangians were included in several Icelandic sagas, but contemporary evidence comes from a handful of rune stones; one in Uppland, Sweden, records a man who was a commander in the imperial army. The most famous Varangian of them all was Harald Hardraada (see pp. 200–201) – although a Byzantine source suggests that he was not so important a figure in Byzantium as his saga suggests.

Illustration from the Chronicle compiled by the Byzantine historian John Scylitzes in the mid-eleventh century, showing the emperor Theophilus (829–42) with his bodyguard, which Scylitzes perhaps modelled on the contemporary Varangian Guard.

Gnjozdovo, near Smolensk, Belarus: extensive cemeteries contain over 4,000 mounds.

Part of a large hoard discovered in 1868 at Gnjozdovo. The human mask pendant (bottom centre) is of Scandinavian appearance.

route to Kiev; it also gave access to the River Oka and thence to the River Volga. Fortified in the early tenth century, and with 16 ha (39.5 acres) of suburbs where traders and craftsmen lived, the best-known archaeological evidence comes from a vast series of cemeteries. Some mounds contained the cremated remains of warriors who had been buried in boats with their weapons; several were also accompanied by females, perhaps sacrificial victims. Much of the detail of these discoveries has yet to be analyzed and published, and the indigenous contribution to these rites needs further exploration. Nonetheless, there is certainly evidence for a Viking presence, with Scandinavian jewelry and amulets of the types found at Gorodisce.

Despite the documentary evidence of its importance, there is little archaeological evidence for Kiev at this crucial period. Byzantine documents fill in the story, even though a journey from Kiev to Byzantium involved travelling 800 km (500 miles) down the River Dniepr and then sailing 640 km (400 miles) across the Black Sea. Whatever the friendly protestations of the Rus envoys to Emperor Theophilus in 839, Constantinople was attacked in 860 by a Rus fleet said to be 200 ships strong. Perhaps Kiev had a hand in this raid, although this was over 20 years before the Rus are known to have been in control there. It certainly was the Kievan Rus who attacked Byzantium again in 907, after which a trading treaty in 911–12 heralded 30 years of peace before a new round of hostilities in the 940s and a new treaty of 945. This agreement shows what the Rus were after, for it included regulations about how much silk they could buy.

The emperor of the day, Constantine Porphyrogenitos, recorded how in late spring each year Rus boats from Gorodisce, Gnjozdovo and other settlements came to Kiev. The Kievans too had prepared their cargoes of furs and slaves, and made ready their dugout logboats for the hazardous trip to Constantinople. Constantine successfully ensured that the Rus could not use their trading voyages as a pretext to attack Constantinople, and thereafter Rus-Byzantine relations generally improved. It helped no little when the Kievan ruler Vladimir adopted Greek Orthodox Christianity in 988, and married the Emperor's sister into the bargain. By this time, however, the Rus state was essentially Slavic, not Scandinavian, and at the time of the final raid on Constantinople, in 1043, the true Viking warrior's

The so-called Radziwil Chronicle is a history of Russia and its dealings with its neighbours in the ninth-early thirteenth centuries. It survives

in a fifteenth-century manuscript with illustrations that are believed faithfully to copy those of the early thirteenth-century original (now lost).

(Top) Oleg unleashes his Rus forces against Constantinople in 907.
(Centre) The Byzantines repulse the Rus.
(Bottom) Vladimir is baptized in 988.

The Byzantine church of Hagia Sophia, Istanbul; a runic inscription was recognised in 1964, carved into the marble balustrade on the south side of the gallery. It is just a graffito, which probably read 'Halfdan carved these runes', and is thought to be eleventh century in date.

interest was more in joining the emperor's Varangian Guard (see box on p. 98) than in joining with the attackers.

Rus Trade with the Arab World

Numerous Byzantine and Arab coins found in *Rus* settlements, as well as scales and weights, testify to trade, and emphasize how the *Rus* thrived through exploiting two complementary trade routes. A north–south axis linked the east Mediterranean world of Constantinople with the Baltic; and an east–west route was profitable for any Viking or

Rus merchants willing to venture eastwards to the markets of the Volga Bulgars, who in turn controlled much of the trade between Europe and the East.

The Islamic Samanid state that occupied modern Turkmenistan, Uzbekistan and Kazakhstan was one economically important contact, but the intrepid trader could also reach Baghdad. Indeed, it was the Arab Ibn Fadlan, sent in 921 on a mission from the Caliph in Baghdad to the King of the Volga Bulgars, who recorded his impressions of the *Rus* whom he encountered: 'I have never seen more perfect physical specimens, tall as date palms, blond and ruddy.... Each man has an axe, a sword and a knife and keeps each by him at all times. The swords are broad and grooved, of Frankish sort...'.

Other comments, for example about their cleanliness, were not so complimentary. His relatively detailed description of funeral ceremonies for an important Rus has them culminating in the sacrifice of a slave girl and her cremation alongside her lord within a ship, together with weapons and animals, and the subsequent raising of a mound marked by a wooden post. The question of how much this and other Rus customs was the product of an amalgamation of Scandinavian, Slavic and other east European traditions is still under discussion.

The Arab geographer Ibn Khordadbeh, writing in the 840s, described Rus merchants as 'a sort of European, bringing beaver skins and black fox fur and swords from the furthest part of their land.... They reach the Caspian Sea and sail out, putting in wherever they want. Often they bring their wares by camel... to Baghdad, where Slavonic eunuchs interpret for them'.

Not all Rus incursions across the Caspian were so peaceful. Al Mas'udi, writing in the mid-tenth century, reports how in 910 a fleet of 16 ships crossed the Caspian and attacked Baku and Azerbaijan. Another attack on the same area in 943 was initially successful but, after capturing the town of Berda'a, counter-attacks and disease took their toll on the Rus and they were eventually forced to retreat. The Muslims promptly opened the graves of the dead Rus and took the swords that had been buried in them – swords that reportedly were still prized half a century later.

The eleventh century saw continued Viking interest in the east. In 1041 Swedish Vikings under the leadership of Ingvar the Far-Travelled undertook an expedition to Serkland, 'the Saracens' land', which probably refers to the territory controlled by the Caliph of Baghdad.

The events became the theme of an Icelandic saga, and perhaps would have been dismissed as wholly fictional were it not that nearly 30 rune stones, mostly in the Mälaren region of Sweden, commemorate lost members of the expedition. Most evocative is the stone at Gripsholm: 'Tola raised this stone to her son Harald, Ingvar's brother. They journeyed like men far after gold and in the east gave the eagle food. They died southward in Serkland.'

DIRHAMS: ARAB SILVER

The importance of trade with the east is represented by the large numbers of Arab silver coins – dirhams which arc found in Europe. Two characteristics make dirhams easily recognizable – they have a larger diameter than contemporary European coins, and they bear a distinctive style of lettering. The script, also employed for the Koran, takes its name from the city of Kufah in Iraq; dirhams have been known generically as Kufic coins.

Dirhams are archaeologically invaluable, for the coins proclaim the ruler for whom they were minted, the minting place and the date of striking. They can thus act as chronological markers, as well as subtle indicators of the direction, extent and fluctuating patterns of economic contact. Over 1,000 hoards of these coins have been found in Europe. They show that the eastern trade had started by the 780s, increased in the 860s–880s and grew dramatically to a peak in the 910s–950s. Thereafter decline set in as the central Asian silver mines were shut off. Before that happened, however, dirhams were shipped back in huge quantities to the island of Gotland and mainland Sweden, with just a few reaching Norway and a modest number in Denmark; and some were carried westwards to Britain and Ireland.

Part of a huge hoard of 2,270 Arab dirhams found at Ralswiek, on the island of Rügen, Germany.

'In that year Healfdan shared out the land of the Northumbrians, and they proceeded to plough and to support themselves'
Anglo-Saxon Chronicle, 876

One part of the 'great heathen army' had gone north to the River Tyne after leaving Repton in 874, but after a year ravaging the Picts and the Britons of Strathclyde they shared out the land of the Northumbrians and settled there permanently in 876. In 877 a contingent from the other part of the 'great heathen army' returned to the midland kingdom of Mercia and settled in the eastern half of it. Viking settlers now controlled a large swathe of eastern England.

The only Anglo-Saxon royal dynasty to have survived the onslaught was that of King Alfred in the southern English kingdom of Wessex. In 878 he defeated the remaining active but depleted section of the 'great heathen army' in battle at Edington in Wiltshire, and made the Viking King Guthrum and 30 of his leading men accept baptism. Guthrum also swore to leave Alfred's kingdom; he kept his

word, and settled in East Anglia in 879. Shortly afterwards, Alfred and Guthrum drew up a treaty which defined the boundary between them, and the agreement seems to have been kept until Guthrum's death in 890. Alfred defeated other Viking incursions in the 880s and 890s, but Vikings continued to be a threat. When Alfred died in 899, Scandinavian rulers were still in control of all or part of three formerly independent Anglo-Saxon kingdoms.

Vikings and Place names

When Halfdan shared out the lands of the Northumbrians' in 876, he was overseeing a huge change in land ownership, and the same was true in the settlements of the east Midlands and East Anglia in 877 and 879 respectively. The losers were the defeated Anglo-Saxon aristocrats and

WARRIOR, TRADER, MERCHANT, FARMER?

An unusual group of objects that may represent one of the earliest Viking burials from the settlement period was uncovered in 2003 at Ainsbrook in Yorkshire when metal detectorists dug up a remarkable clutch of objects that may represent a grave. They included weapons, a whetstone, clothing accessories such as a ringed pin, weights and parts of a pair of folding scales. A few clench

nails, of the type that Viking shipwrights used, initially tempted speculation that this was a ship burial, but we now know that was not the case; perhaps the nails held together a chest or even a bier of some sort.

There was also a small quantity of silver items, including an ingot and fragments of others, hacksilver fragments and, most importantly, a group of coins.

Apart from a fragment of an Arab dirham, these were English issues, two struck for King Alfred of Wessex and seven for his ally and father-in-law, King Burgred of Mercia. Fortunately it is possible to date the minting of Burgred's coins quite precisely to 871–74; they indicate that the objects were placed in the ground in the period 875–900.

Of the skeleton itself, however, there was no sign;

soil conditions were such that all bone had completely decayed. Research on this unusual group of objects is in its early stages, but it may represent an important addition to the small number of Viking burials known from northeast England, and its peculiarities may contribute to our understanding of the early days of the Vikings' takeover in this region.

Parts of two swords and a whetstone from Ainsbrook, Yorkshire.

churchmen, many of whom had profited from vast landholdings. The winners were the Viking warriors who were awarded campaign spoils, and who took over their allotted portions of those rural estates. Some of these Vikings' names may have come down to us, preserved in the names by which the individual *vills* were known when they were recorded two centuries later in William the Conqueror's *Domesday Book*. Many of these names have a distinctively Scandinavian form.

A good example is Brandsby: the *-by* element is an Old Norse word for a settlement, while the first element is a Scandinavian personal name. *Brandr* may have been a Viking who fought in the 'great heathen army'; but he may alternatively have been a descendant of such a Viking, or indeed an Englishman or an Anglo-Scandinavian who later acquired the *vill* or parish which now bears his name. Many other place names in England also echo Scandinavian name-giving habits. They include names ending in *-thorpe* or *-thwaite*, or names like Grimston which combine a Scandinavian personal name (in this case *Grimr*)

with an English word for a settlement (ton), or even simple one-syllable names like Lund, which is the Old Norse word for a grove of trees. Whatever their precise form, the distribution of these names is almost exclusively to the north and east of the border between the kingdoms of Alfred and Guthrum.

Viking Age Villages

One of the most coherent and consistent sets of evidence for changes in settlement patterns in the century or so after the Vikings' land grabbing comes from the rolling chalk hills of the Wolds in east Yorkshire. Excavations at three sites there have yielded complementary stories which together point in a single direction.

The best evidence has come from excavations at the deserted village of Wharram Percy. Below a few of the visible humps and bumps in the landscape that mark the site of the houses and small-holdings of the later medieval village, traces of pre-Viking houses have been discovered, showing that some people were living hereabouts from the eighth century. But there is reason to think that

Earthworks mark the site of the deserted medieval village at Wharram Percy, Yorkshire, where excavation of the church has shown that it originated in the Viking Age together, perhaps, with parts of the village's plan.

(Above) Cast copper-alloy belt slide from Wharram Percy, a characteristically Scandinavian item of high quality, decorated with a Borre-style ring knot of mid-ninth to early tenth century date. Height 3.5 cm (1⅜ in).

(Below) Tenth-century grave covers and headstones found in the cemetery below York Minster.

key elements in the earthwork boundaries of the regularly organized medieval village were first laid out in the late ninth or early tenth century. A fine strap-end and belt-slide, decorated in the Scandinavian Borre style, have been interpreted as the possessions of a new Scandinavian landlord at that time. In addition, excavation of the ruined medieval parish church at Wharram Percy has demonstrated that it too was first erected in the tenth century – presumably by a lord of the manor (the one who lost his strap-end?) who wanted to proclaim his status.

At a site in the parish of Cottam, a pre-Viking settlement has been revealed, but here it seems to have been abandoned in the mid- to late ninth century, when a new farmstead was built higher up the valley, in a more visible and dominating position. This repositioned farm stood within an enclosure which boasted an imposing although indefensible gateway – perhaps the work of new (Viking?) owners proclaiming their recently acquired social status. This new settlement lasted for only 30 to 50 years before it was abandoned, and the settlement was moved again, perhaps to the nearby sites of either Cottam or Cowlam village, which were to endure into the later medieval period.

A broadly similar picture has emerged from extensive excavations in the parish of West Heslerton. Today the site in question is an agricultural landscape of large fields, but in the centuries before the Vikings conquered Northumbria this was the site of a thriving village. At some time in the mid- to late ninth century, just when Halfdan's men were settling in Yorkshire, this long-established settlement was abandoned. The best guess is that the population was relocated by a new Viking landlord to the medieval village site of Heslerton.

Together, these Yorkshire sites suggest fundamental changes in the landscape that coincide with the aftermath of Viking takeover. The redistribution of estates among the Viking invaders allowed opportunities for new experiments in agricultural practices and social organization. Bringing the population together into carefully laid out villages may have been one means of assuring more productive use of available land; perhaps the origins of the classic later medieval three-field agricultural pattern lie in this tenurial revolution. It would indeed be a paradox if the archetypal English village, so obviously a product of the medieval period, turns out to owe its origins to invading Vikings.

Monuments to Migration

The church at Wharram Percy provides an important clue to the aspirations of the new lords of the manor in the tenth-century Danelaw, but this is a relatively rare form of evidence, for very few churches have been excavated in England. However, a substantial number of churches and churchyards retain fragments of tenth-century gravestones, memorials to the new Anglo-Scandinavian elite. This widespread distribution of stone sculpture contrasts starkly with its very restricted use in the pre-Viking period, when commemoration in carved stone was the preserve of major religious houses and the very highest-ranking figures in secular society. It is thus another indicator of a new social order in Viking Age England. Usually there is only one, or perhaps two or three, of these

Westness — Scar
Skaill — ORKNEY IS.
Cape Wrath
Pentland Firth
LEWIS
Jarlshof
SHETLAND IS.
NORTH UIST
SOUTH UIST
COLONSAY
ORONSAY
ARRAN
Firth of Clyde
Cumwhitton
Gainford on Tees
Brompton
Flusco Pike
West Heslerton
Wharram Percy
Strangford Lough
ISLE OF MAN
Ripon
Middleton
York
Cottam
Carlingford Lough
Red Wharf Bay
Penmon
Cuerdale
Dublin
Derby
Lincoln
ANGLESEY
The Wirral
Nottingham
Talacre
Leicester
Limerick
Northampton
Cambridge
Dunmore Cave
Bedford
Cloghermore Cave
London

— Danelaw boundary

0   100 km
0   80 miles

Map showing the extent of the Danelaw and the distribution of Viking sites throughout the United Kingdom.

DANELAW

'Up the Thames, and then up the Lea, and along the Lea to its source, then in a straight line to Bedford, then up the Ouse to the Watling Street.'
Treaty between King Alfred and King Guthrum, c. 880.

In these words the two principal kings of England south of the Humber, one a Viking, the other a native English man, defined the mutual boundary of their kingdoms. Although military success eventually passed from the invaders to the defenders, and this boundary was quickly

superseded, there remained political and social differences between 'English' England and the land settled by Scandinavian émigrés.

Constitutionally, this is well seen in the nuances of the various Codes of Law that successive English kings issued to the different constituencies among their subjects; rulers were careful to recognize that Codes applicable in Anglo-Scandinavian areas might differ subtly from those governing conduct elsewhere.

In the opening years of the eleventh century Archbishop Wulfstan of York described areas of England in which aspects of Danish legal procedures were maintained as the 'Danelaw'. Unfortunately he didn't define the geographical location of these areas, but they were presumably in the eastern and northern parts of the country. It is in those regions, which the Vikings had taken over in the 870s, that we might expect to find evidence for the impact of Viking settlers on the landscape.

We should beware, however, of simply attributing changes to Viking influences: social, economic or environmental changes across the whole of England might alternatively account for innovations.

(Right) The shaft of the ring-headed cross from Middleton, North Yorkshire, was carved with poorly executed animal ornament in c. 925–50. (The other side of the cross is illustrated on p.69.)

(Below) House-shaped 'hogback' grave markers, carved in the tenth century, are particularly characteristic of North Yorkshire, and may be monuments commissioned for Hiberno-Viking immigrants. The triangular shapes just below the ridge represent a shingled roof, like those on the simulation of the Fyrkat, Denmark, building on p.186; the significance of the bears is uncertain. This group is at Brompton in Allertonshire, North Yorkshire; their average length is c. 130 cm (50 in).

monuments at any given church, a distribution which suggests that the monuments had a particular vogue, perhaps commemorating the church's founder and his immediate family.

Some of the monuments are crosses, others recumbent slabs with or without head- and foot-stones. They take a variety of forms and bear a range of decorative motifs, reflecting an interplay between established local tastes, the idiosyncrasies of individual schools of carvers, and the regional affiliations of the patrons. Just occasionally the non-local geology of a monument or a characteristic form of decoration identify a sculpture that has been transported some distance from its point of origin, but most originated in the immediate region. There was, for example, a York 'metropolitan' group of carvers whose products, often carved on re-used Roman building stones, are found in the Viking Age cemetery around York Minster and in several of the city's parish churches, with a distant outlier at Gainford on Tees. Another school of carvers was centred on Ryedale in north Yorkshire, and was responsible for a distinctive group of representations of seated lordly figures such as that at Middleton (see box on p. 69), as well as for some ludicrously crude depictions of beasts. Their crosses typically employed a characteristically short shaft surmounted by a form of ring-headed cross which originated in Ireland, and

FASHION STATEMENTS

An explosion in the number of pieces of decorated metalwork discovered below the fields of rural England by metal detectorists in recent years has allowed archaeologists to reappraise the fashions that were popular in Anglo-Scandinavian England. What has emerged is that decorative styles and some jewelry types generally thought of as typically Scandinavian were favoured in the 'Danelaw' area.

Surveys in both Norfolk and Lincolnshire have demonstrated regional variations on this same theme – a proliferation of cheap jewelry which shows how Danish tastes were adopted or blended with English designs. Additionally, pure Scandinavian imports or faithful, high-quality copies of such items are beginning to provide a new picture of the depth of Scandinavian influence in the century after the Viking invasion and settlement.

A single example to demonstrate this is a small 'Valkyrie' figure, the fearsome female of Norse mythology, found at Cawthorpe, near Bourne, Lincolnshire. Several silver amulets in the shape of Thor's hammers from Norfolk, although much simpler, also testify to this Scandinavian tendency. Yet the very volume of the new discoveries reinforces continuing significant absences, most notably the scarcity of women's oval 'tortoise' brooches which are so typical of ninth- and tenth-century Norway and Sweden (albeit they perhaps went out of fashion earlier in the Viking Age in Denmark).

In short, jewelry was yet another medium through which new, Anglo-Scandinavian, regional identities were being created in late ninth- and tenth-century England; you were what you wore.

(Above) Copper-alloy pendant from Cawthorpe, a warrior figure with spear, shield and sword; the long clothing suggests a female, perhaps a Valkyrie.

Thor's hammers found in Norfolk, worn as pendants around the neck.

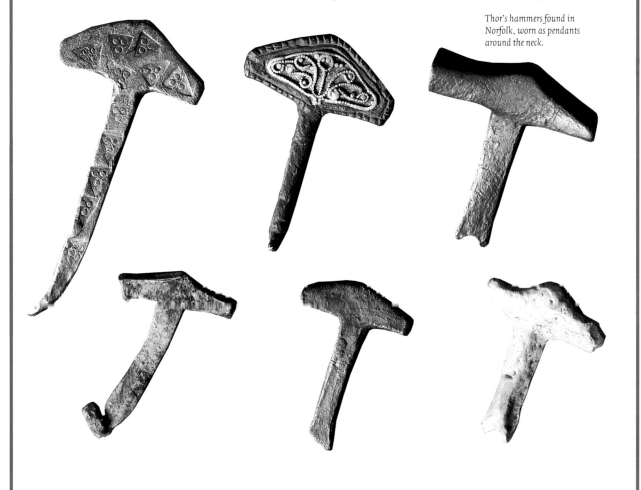

*'In this year King Edmund,
lord of the English, protector
of men, the beloved performer
of mighty deeds, overran
Mercia as bounded by Dore,
Whitwell gate and the broad
stream, the River Humber;
and five burhs, Leicester and
Lincoln, Nottingham and
likewise Stamford, and also
Derby. The Danes were
previously subjected by force
under the Norsemen, for a
long time in bonds of
captivity to the heathens,
until the defender of warriors,
the son of Edward, King
Edmund, redeemed them,
to his glory.'*
Anglo-Saxon
Chronicle, 942.

which reflects the contribution which Vikings coming via Ireland made to the settlement of this part of Yorkshire.

Most innovative of all the Viking Age sculpture in England is the series of house-shaped monuments, usually about 1.5 m (5 ft) long, and with a bowed top like a pig's back which has resulted in their popular name, 'hogbacks'. Their inspiration may have come from the shrine tombs or house-shaped reliquaries that were found throughout the British Isles, and some of them are ornamented in a way which echoes house construction, with panelled sides and shingled roofs.

They are most frequent in the Allertonshire area of north Yorkshire, where Brompton church alone has produced eleven examples. These Allertonshire examples are notable for having a large muzzled quadruped, identified as a bear, clasping the gable ends of the monuments, perhaps as a symbol of conversion from paganism to Christianity. Although essentially undated, hogbacks are generally thought to be yet another outcome of the influx of Hiberno-Vikings into this area from around 920 to 950 (discussed in the next section).

Forts and Towns

The principal means used by both the English and the Vikings in the struggle to consolidate power in England was the building of defensible bases at strategic points. These could act as refuges for the rural population in times of attack, and as platforms from which to invade enemy territory. Known to the English as *burhs*, and recorded in a variety of documentary sources, they were often erected by royal command at sites that already had a long history and prehistory as foci for occupation. Some had their brief period of importance in the Viking wars and then were abandoned, but others were developed during the tenth century and became important towns that figure in *Domesday Book's* description of England in 1066. Other places, although not mentioned explicitly in connection with the Scandinavian settlement and the English resurgence, are referred to as fully-fledged towns in *Domesday Book*. Archaeology is the sole means of investigating their origins and the role they played during these crucial years.

The early tenth-century *Anglo-Saxon Chronicle* talks about individual Viking armies based at or around places including Northampton, Leicester,

Bedford, Huntingdon, Tempsford, Cambridge, Stamford, and Nottingham – places which almost all gave their names to English counties. Slightly later, in 942, after a notable Anglo-Saxon reconsolidation in the east Midlands, the *Chronicle* recorded five burhs in that region – Derby, Leicester, Lincoln, Nottingham and Stamford (see margin). And north of the Humber Estuary was York, the only town in the region. It is certain that by the late tenth century these were all significant places of manufacture and trade, administrative and commercial centres. Much earlier, however, while still under Viking rule, some of them had probably been the sites of local administrative centres and of coin mints.

Striking New Identities

Only in recent years has it has become apparent that by the 880s Viking rulers in East Anglia and the east Midlands were issuing silver pennies which copied contemporary issues struck for King Alfred of Wessex. Having disrupted the previous Anglo-Saxon administrations, and without experience themselves of coin production, they imported continental moneyers, whose names are recorded on the coins, to oversee the minting. Unfortunately, only Leicester, Lincoln and Shelford (Cambridgeshire or Nottinghamshire) are named as minting places on these coins, but there must have been other sites where currency was struck.

By about 895, after the death of the Viking King Guthrum whose baptism Alfred had sponsored, the Viking ruler(s) of East Anglia and the east Midlands had begun to strike a novel series of coins in the name of St Edmund – the very same king of East Anglia whom their invading forebears had defeated and killed a quarter century earlier. Shortly after, in *c.* 905, York adopted a coinage in the name of St Peter, the patron saint of the cathedral church

(Right) Silver penny of King Guthrum of East Anglia, with his baptismal name Aethelstan, copying the design of coins struck for his godfather, King Alfred.

Few things are so evocative of the Viking ability to adapt to circumstances as the coins struck in the late ninth and early tenth century for Viking rulers in parts of England that invoke the names of Christian saints – St Edmund of East Anglia (above, killed by Vikings in 870!), St Martin of Lincoln (below) and St Peter of York (above right). The St Peter coin die (the image here deliberately reversed), found in excavations at Coppergate, York (see pp.114–117) combines the saint's name with a Viking sword and, at bottom centre, a Thor's hammer.

there; and later still, in the 920s, the authorities at Lincoln issued coins in the name of St Martin, presumably a dedication of local significance. All these coin designs give a fascinating insight into the way in which Scandinavian political dominance was maintained and made palatable through recognizing and respecting the traditions and susceptibilities of the Anglo-Saxon population. Indeed, the coins may represent deliberate attempts to create regional power blocks in which the children of Viking invaders and the children of the conquered Anglo-Saxons were bound together into carefully manufactured and unique identities, distinct from that of the increasingly powerful and predatory West Saxon dynasty of King Alfred. If that was the intention, it failed.

From Viking Victory to the Creation of England

For more than a decade after Alfred's death the Viking settlers maintained the territorial status quo, raiding with varying success from East Anglia and Northumbria. It was only from about 910 onwards that Alfred's son and successor, King Edward 'the Elder' (899–924), and his sister, the redoubtable Aethelflaeda, gradually put a stranglehold on many of the Viking-dominated areas.

At first the advances were minimal, but in 917 East Anglia capitulated, and the following year it was the turn of the east Midlands. By 920 only York and its ambit remained outside English control;

Northumbria proved a hard nut to crack. The Viking kings of York and the Archbishops of York had come to appreciate that it was in their selfish mutual interests to support each other, and this alliance also fostered the Northumbrian spirit of independence.

Alfred's grandson, King Athelstan (924–39) managed in 927 to displace the Hiberno-Viking dynasty of Dublin origin which had been in control of York, and he maintained his rule in Northumbria throughout the remainder of his reign. He won a notable victory in 937 over a Hiberno-Viking/Scottish coalition at a site known only by its contemporary name, *Brunanburh* (see margin), but his death offered the invaders another opportunity. The 940s and 950s saw frequent changes of control, with further attempts to resurrect Hiberno-Viking power in York.

The kings of Wessex countered with northern campaigns and, to encourage the Archbishop of York to respect his power, the English King Eadred reportedly burned down the important church at Ripon, north of York, in 948. It was not until the death of the exiled Norwegian interloper Erik Bloodaxe in 954 that the Wessex dynasty finally assumed what turned out in the medium term to be unassailable power over a newly united kingdom – England.

'King Athelstan, lord of nobles, dispenser of treasure to men, and his brother Edmund, won by the sword's edge undying glory in battle round Brunanburh. Edward's sons clove the shield-wall, hewed the linden-wood shields with hammered swords... their enemies perished; the Scots and the pirates fell doomed.... Then the Norsemen, the sorry survivors from the spears, put out in their ships to make for Dublin... they left behind the black raven with its horned beak to share the corpses....'
Anglo-Saxon
Chronicle, 937.

IRISH VIKINGS IN NORTHWEST ENGLAND

Although their coming was unrecorded in any surviving Anglo-Saxon annals, Vikings also settled in the northwest of modern England. An Irish source records the movements of a Viking leader named Ingimund in the opening years of the tenth century; expelled from Dublin, he attempted first to invade the island of Anglesey in north Wales, but was driven off and ultimately settled near Chester, on the English side of the Welsh border. Ingimund's adventures have received a lot of attention, for this is the only documentary account to complement other evidence which suggests extensive Viking settlement along the coastal plains from the River Dee northwards to the Solway Firth. Archaeological evidence for Scandinavian settlement and influence in the northwest of England includes burials with Scandinavian affinities, some individual objects of Scandinavian form, a series of silver hoards, and some distinctive stone carvings, such as that from Bidstone in the Wirral which came to attention in 2004.

Viking Burials in the Northwest

Three Viking burials in mounds can be identified with certainty in northwest England. With one exception, their discovery is known exclusively from eighteenth- or nineteenth-century antiquarian accounts rather than through modern archaeological investigation.

The grave on the locally prominent site at Beacon Hill, Aspatria, in Cumbria, which came to light in 1789, has several of the key features. The corpse was that of a male, who had been interred in a mound and accompanied by weapons

'Miniature hogback' grave marker with stylized beast embracing both ends, from Bidstone, Wirral, Cheshire. Compare with the Brompton hogbacks on p.106.

CHANGING PLACES, CHANGING NAMES

A series of place names containing Old Norse and Old Irish elements is one indicator of immigrants to this area who had previously lived in Ireland or, perhaps, the Scottish isles. The Wirral peninsula of Cheshire, which may have been the area of Ingimund's settlement, provides some good examples. Irby ('settlement of the Irish'), Meols ('sandbank'), where coastal erosion has exposed artifacts that suggest a beach-market flourished there in many eras including the Viking Age, Thingwall ('field where the thing meets') and Tranmere ('sandbank where the cranes gather') are Old Norse forms, while Noctorum ('dry hillock') is from the Irish.

Other name forms of Scandinavian or Irish/Scandinavian ancestry include those containing the elements *buð* meaning 'booth', and *aergi*, *skali* and *saetr*, all of which denote shielings, the seasonal huts occupied by graziers tending their flocks and herds in upland areas during the summer months. And in addition to all of these there are other names, comparable to those found on the other side of the Pennine mountains in Yorkshire, which suggest that Viking settlers were pushing westwards from there.

(a sword, axehead and spearhead), a horse's bridle-bit and spur, and a Carolingian gold buckle and strap-end. All of these objects have been lost over the centuries, but re-excavation of the site in 1997, before a telecommunication mast was erected, recovered more objects from the burial. These included a copper-alloy ringed pin, a folding knife, an iron buckle, part of a tin-plated iron spur, and fragments of iron vessels.

Broadly similar groups of objects are also known from graves in mounds at Hesket-in-the-Forest, near Carlisle, and at Claughton, near Garstang in Lancashire. This last site also yielded two oval brooches, typical Scandinavian women's dress jewelry, but reportedly found back to back, 'forming a kind of box', and containing two beads, one red and one blue, and a molar tooth. The Claughton grave may have contained a double burial of a man and woman, and a decorated Carolingian silver-gilt mount from the grave implies a degree of wealth and status, like the gold items from Aspatria. It is clear from the range and quality of the objects found in these graves that they contained local aristocrats, and that these people had some links with Hiberno-Viking Ireland; it is most likely that the burials date to the period c. 900–950.

The most recent, spectacular and unexpected discovery is that of a cemetery of at least six individuals, initially located by a metal detectorist searching near Cumwhitton in Cumbria in 2004. Two copper-alloy oval brooches, tell-tale signs of a female Viking burial, first indicated that this was an important site, and led to a scientific examination of the area. This identified that five other graves were present, all of which were archaeologically excavated. The woman who had been buried with the brooches also had a wooden chest close to where her feet would have been; but her bones, like those of all the other skeletons, had completely decayed. A second woman had been buried with several items of personal jewelry, including a jet bracelet on her left wrist. The four other burials were all of males, who were accompanied by an assortment of weapons, horse riding gear and other items that are still being identified. This cemetery, provisionally dated to the early tenth century, is highly unusual in the British Isles; when fully studied, it will make an exciting addition to knowledge of the Vikings' customs in this area.

Viking burials have also been found in several northwestern churchyards. In 1898 a gravedigger at Ormside churchyard in Cumbria uncovered a skeleton associated with a shield boss, knife and sword. Here, many years earlier, a magnificently decorated gilt-bronze and silver-gilt bowl, made in Northumbria in c. 750–800 and later repaired, had been dug up; quite possibly it too came from the Viking grave. Whether or not this is the case, the warrior's burial is another example of the

Oval brooches from a woman's grave at Cumwhitton, Cumbria.

(Below left) Excavating the small, previously unknown cemetery at Cumwhitton, Cumbria.

(Below right) Soil conditions at Cumwhitton had dissolved almost all traces of the skeleton, leaving only the grave goods.

Silver 'thistle brooch' found in 1785. This huge brooch has a diameter of 19 cm (7½ in) and the pin, now broken, was originally 56 cm (22 in) long; it was made to show off the wealth of its wearer. Found near Flusco Pike, New Biggin Moor, Dacre, Cumbria.

well-attested phenomenon of Vikings being interred in churchyards accompanied by traditional grave goods. These are Vikings whose nearest and dearest, whether minglers or musclers-in, were demonstrating through their orchestration of the funeral rites that they were part – a dominant part – of the local community.

Silver Hoards

The northwest of England also has its share of silver hoards in which distinctive types of jewelry or combinations of coins point to contacts with the Hiberno-Viking world. Silver penannular brooches, which have a ring that is almost (Latin *pene*) circular (Latin *annulus*), have a great variety of forms which have been intensely studied, categorized, dated and assigned to particular places of manufacture. Thus it is possible to say that a brooch found in 1785 on a hill called Flusco Pike, west of Penrith, is a 'ball-type' penannular brooch,

named after the spherical protrusions at its terminals. This brooch type, of Irish origin, was used as a cloak-pin and seems to have been particularly attractive to Vikings. This is an extraordinarily ostentatious example, with a ring just under 20 cm (8 in) in diameter and a pin over 50 cm (20 in) long.

Remarkably, parts of at least six more silver penannular brooches of the same or related types were discovered at approximately the same spot in 1989, although none is as large as the first. They include examples with what is called 'brambling' as a decoration on the 'ball' – known as 'thistle brooches'. Although we can only guess why the brooches were hidden on Flusco Pike, there is no doubt that they, and an array of similar discoveries, indicate tenth-century contact between the northwest of England and Vikings from Ireland.

The 40 kg (88 lb) of silver and coins in a hoard discovered at Cuerdale, Lancashire, in 1840 give the best impression of the riches to be won in Viking Age Britain and Ireland. Some 1,100 items of bullion comprise ingots, together with jewelry from the Baltic and Scandinavia as well as Irish and other insular and continental pieces. About 5,000 of the 7,500 or so coins were struck for Viking kings in East Anglia and York; about 1,000 are Anglo-Saxon and most of the remainder are

A small selection of jewelry, ingots and hacksilver from the enormous hoard buried in c. 905 and found at Cuerdale, Lancashire in 1840.

continental, probably loot from Viking raids on the Loire in the 890s and the Rhine/Meuse area in 902. Altogether this treasure looks like the war chest of a Viking army associated with both Dublin and York, hidden c. 905 and abandoned for reasons unknown, even though it was worth something like £500,000 ($875,000) by today's standards.

Sculpture

It is some of the sculptured stones, found in the region's churchyards, which demonstrate physically the presence of patrons who needed their monuments to display carved scenes drawn from Scandinavian mythology.

Gosforth (Cumbria) provides the most striking example of this eclectic taste, with two important monuments probably made by the same tenth-century craftsman. The so-called 'fishing stone' inside the church may have been part of a decorative frieze. It depicts the god Thor and the giant Hymir on their epic fishing expedition, a story recorded in later Icelandic documentary sources (see p. 167).

Outside in the churchyard at Gosforth, still in its original stepped socket, stands the most graceful and tallest of all crosses from pre-Norman England. Carved from a single block of red sandstone, it rises 4.42 m (14 ft 6 in), merging from a circular lower shaft on which are interlaced designs into a squared upper shaft decorated with a complex series of scenes and patterns, and culminating in a ringed cross-head of Irish derivation. A crucifixion scene is the only overtly Christian motif on the shaft; otherwise, the iconography concentrates on scenes associated with the Scandinavian concept of the end of the world at Ragnarök. A figure with a horn, for example, is Heimdall, the watchman

god; a pigtailed, manacled figure is Loki, leader of the forces of evil at the last day.

The juxtapositioning of the Christian and the mythological can be interpreted as a sophisticated expression of parallels between the two cultures in, for example, the recognition of a common Doomsday; the cross evokes an integration of an incoming, heroic Viking belief system with a pre-existing Anglo-Saxon Christian heroic tradition. Together with a series of (mostly fragmentary) sculptures found elsewhere in the region, these stones testify to Hiberno-Viking settlers taking root in the region during the period c. 900–950.

(Below left) The 'fishing stone' from Gosforth, Cumbria, a representation of the god Thor catching the world serpent.

(Below right) The Gosforth cross in Cumbria stands 4.42 m (14 ft 6 in) tall; scenes from the Bible and from Scandinavian mythology are separated by panels of Borre-style ring-chain ornament. It was carved in around 900–950.

JORVIK: THE VIKING AGE CITY OF YORK

(Opposite) Excavations in 'The Viking Dig,' Coppergate, York, looking towards the street Coppergate and the church of All Saints, Pavement, which was founded in Viking Age. The site covered some 1,000 sq. m (11,000 sq. ft). Viking Age buildings stood at the street frontage within each of the four excavated building plots, with rubbish pits and toilet pits in the large backyard area behind.

York – Jorvik as they called it – attracted Vikings because it was already a well-established political, religious and commercial centre, defended by Roman walls. Although about 60 km (37 miles) from the coast, York was accessible from the North Sea via the Humber Estuary and the River Ouse, and was an inland port with long-standing links to continental Europe. By modern standards, however, its population on the eve of the Viking invasions was tiny, probably numbering no more than one or two thousand. After its initial capture on 1 November 866 it was either under Viking control or firmly in their sights for almost a century; its take over by a second wave of Viking invaders, from Ireland in c. 917, bolstered the anti-Wessex stance of the city and its region, and strengthened its links with Dublin.

It was the principal and longest-lasting bastion of independent Viking power in England. Excavations by York Archaeological Trust have demonstrated that its historical significance is matched by the importance of its archaeological remains. Parts of the modern city are built on deeply stratified archaeological deposits of the Viking Age and medieval periods. The oxygen-free conditions allow the survival of organic remains of wood, textiles and leather which normally rot to dust, and thereby present a much more complete picture than is usual about the range of objects which the

townsfolk used in their daily lives. These soils also preserve biological data, such as seeds and insects, which can inform us about the ancient environment, climate, diet, and health.

Much of the detail in our picture of Jorvik comes from a single investigation of four Viking Age house plots at 'The Viking Dig' in the street of Coppergate, excavated in 1976–81. Overall, however, the picture is consistent – York was transformed in size, in appearance and in its economic role when under Viking control. At Coppergate, an area that had been unoccupied for hundreds of years since the Roman period was intensively built up by the early tenth century. Property divisions were demarcated with fences, dividing the site into long, narrow building plots. This act of Viking urban development, identified also at other sites across the city, had a profound impact on the appearance of York, for these land units were fossilized over the next one thousand years. Some of them are still recognizable in today's townscape, as are the streets that developed at the same time. Many of the city's medieval churches also had their foundation in the tenth or eleventh century, when Anglo-Scandinavian men of property sought immortal salvation, public recognition and the financial benefits of church dues. By 1066 York probably had 15,000 or more inhabitants, making it the second city in England in terms of both population and wealth.

(Below) An impression of how the Viking Age city of York may have looked in the later tenth century, based on evidence excavated in 'The Viking Dig' in Coppergate.

Jorvik's wealth was derived from two commercial sources. On the one hand it was a focus for long-distance trade in luxury goods such as Byzantine silks, German wines and Baltic amber. The Vikings had a more extensive range of overseas contacts than their Anglo-Saxon predecessors in Northumbria, and York benefited accordingly. But even more important was an entirely new function for York that developed under the new regime – as a manufacturing centre which supplied a wide hinterland with a range of everyday items.

Raw materials flowed into Jorvik from estates in the surrounding countryside, and specialist craftsmen fabricated them into necessities for sale in their street-front shops and market places. For example, the name Coppergate comes from Old Norse words signifying 'street of the cupmakers'; the excavation duly exposed hundreds of wooden cores, the characteristic debris of turning wooden cups and bowls on a rotary pole-lathe. Such vessels were the normal tablewares of the period, and it is clear that the cupmakers of Coppergate were mass-producing these items on a commercial scale.

However, this was not the only trade being practised on the four plots at Coppergate in the tenth century. Metalworkers produced iron objects such as knives, dress accessories, tools and a host of other items, as well working in gold and silver and making

(Above) Folding scales, scale pans and weights from Coppergate, York, a testimony to trade and commerce.

(Right) Viking Age town life in York as recreated at the Jorvik Centre, York.

Disc brooches and other items of mass-produced jewelry, mostly of lead alloy, made at 16–22 Coppergate in the tenth century. The largest brooch has a diameter of 7 cm (2³/₄ in).

cheap fashion jewelry in lead- or copper-alloy. Shoe-makers and shoe-repairers plied their trade, specialist carvers of bone and antler made combs and other items, and occasionally craftsmen had a bout of making beads, pendants and rings from amber or, less often, from jet.

All of these industries were carried out in and around the houses-cum-workshops which stood at the street frontage of each plot. Up to the mid-tenth century these buildings were single storey structures, typically at least 5 m (c. 5 ft) long by about 4.5 m (14 ft 9 in) wide. They are reminiscent of Anglo-Saxon buildings and have nothing particularly Scandinavian about them. Upright posts set into the ground at fairly short intervals along the wall lines supported the thatch roof; the walls themselves were made of wattle withies woven horizontally in and out of stakes set between these posts. Earth benches contained within a revetment of wattle-work sometimes ran along the side walls. The only other identifiable fixture in each building was a very large rectangular central hearth, its edges defined by reused Roman tiles or building stones, or by lengths

of wood. The floors were simply earth, onto which debris accumulated and into which objects were trampled, thus making them a rich source for the archaeologists. The disposal of rubbish around the houses, and the need to repair and replace the structures every few decades, with consequent dumping of building debris, caused the ground level to rise at the rate of about 1–2 cm (¹/₂–1 in) each year – more good news for the archaeologists.

Later, in the 960s and 970s, these post and wattle buildings fell out of favour and were replaced by two-storey structures in which a semi-basement was perhaps used mainly for storage. This type of structure is well known from other towns in England, and seems a favoured urban building form. Once again, it is not a Viking importation. Not only did these new buildings increase the amount of usable space, but on several of the Coppergate plots they were erected in two ranks. It seems as if Jorvik was a boom town in which space was at a premium, and it is quite likely that much of the area of the later medieval city had already been occupied by the time of the Norman conquest in 1066.

Lead pendant, 5.5 cm (2¹/₈ in) high, with an incised design of two human figures, a mast and waves; 'home-made' jewelry of the tenth century found at Coppergate, York.

THE WELSH EXPERIENCE

After a relatively peaceful interlude in the first half of the tenth century, Vikings from Ireland, the Isle of Man and the Hebrides again began intermittently to harry Wales, particularly coastal monasteries, from the 950s. However, there is no evidence for any Viking immigration and land-taking, as there was in England, nor for any long lasting independent Viking power base such as Dublin or the other Irish coastal settlements. There are no richly accompanied Viking graves like those from other parts of Britain and Ireland – a burial on the coast at Talacre, Flintshire, in north Wales, which lay within a stone cist and was accompanied by a spearhead and knife, is the most convincing discovery among just a handful of possibilities.

Nevertheless, Wales was part of the trading network that turned the Irish Sea into a Viking lake. Anglesey, off the north Welsh coast, seems to have been a favoured port of call, and the natural haven of Red Wharf Bay in particular attracted traders. Archaeological evidence for contacts with Viking Age Ireland first came in the form of a hoard of five Hiberno-Viking armrings (see pp. 125–126) found there.

Recently, excavations at nearby Llanbedrgoch have shown how a pre-Viking native settlement was strongly re-fortified in the Viking Age and how it developed its craft and commercial aspects. There is evidence that at one stage it may have been captured by Vikings.

Five human skeletons including that of a child, found in shallow graves dug into the settlement's defensive ditch and aligned north-south, appear to have been buried quite hastily and in an irregular fashion. Initial analysis suggests that some of these people had their hands tied together. This is a scenario that would fit the 'disposal' of native corpses by marauding Vikings – an attractive but unproven hypothesis. So, too, is the speculation that Llanbedrgoch may have been taken over as a base of operations and occupied for a short while by Manx Vikings in the 970s–980s.

However, the quantity of artifacts of Scandinavian type found on the site – hacksilver, weights, decorated dress accessories and personal jewelry – leave no room for doubt that Llanbedrgoch and the surrounding area of Anglesey were well integrated, in one way or another, with

(Above) Copper alloy buckles of tenth-century type from the Llanbedrgoch settlement.

Hiberno-Viking stamped silver armrings from Red Wharf Bay, Anglesey, Wales.

(Left) Excavations at Llanbedrgoch, near Red Wharf Bay, Anglesey, in 1998–99 revealed human skeletons buried unceremoniously in the ditch outside a native settlement, and possibly victims of Viking violence in the ninth or tenth century.

the Scandinavian influences that flourished in the later tenth century around the Irish Sea.

This is further confirmed by some of the decorated stone crosses surviving from important church sites. One is at Penmon on Anglesey, a site first mentioned when it was raided by Vikings in 971, and which lies relatively close to Red Wharf Bay and Llanbedrgoch. The cross shaft is decorated with Scandinavian-inspired Borre-style ring-chain interlace, perhaps of the mid-tenth century. It, along with others in Anglesey and along the north Welsh coast, may reflect the presence of Scandinavian settlers; it certainly emphasizes that north Wales lay within the orbit of Irish Sea Vikings.

PHASE TWO IN IRELAND

(Below right) Hacksilver Hiberno-Viking armrings from a small hoard found at Cloghermore Cave, deposited in c. 900–950.

(Below left) Torso of a man aged 30–40 buried in Cloghermore Cave, in c. 900; his head had been removed relatively soon after burial. Associated objects comprise personal jewelry including a ringed pin, and other items such as a shield boss, knife and whetstone; these indicate that this is a Viking rather than a native Irish burial.

Hiberno-Norse kings of Dublin maintained at least some sort of nominal independence from the time that the *Annals of Ulster* report the Vikings return to the City in 917 until the city was captured by advancing Anglo-Norman invaders in 1170. The ninth to twelfth centuries are known in Ireland as the Hiberno-Norse or Hiberno-Viking period, and this was a time of substantial changes in the political and economic sphere.

In the early and middle decades of the tenth century the dominant Viking dynasty in Dublin was that founded two generations earlier by Ivar/Imar and known as the *dubh gall* (see pp. 89–90). In 917

Sihtric 'the one-eyed' was ensconced in Dublin; an attempt to expel him by the king of Tara ended in an Irish defeat in battle at Islandbridge, just outside Dublin, in 919. Meanwhile Sihtric's kinsman Ragnall, who had seized control of Waterford in 917, had successfully installed himself across the Irish Sea in York. On Ragnall's death in 920 Sihtric moved from Dublin to York, thus continuing a link between the two Viking towns that the Dublin rulers pursued, persistently but with no long-lasting success, over the next 30 years.

Dublin Vikings also attempted to extend their sphere of control within Ireland. In the 920s they tried to establish outposts in Carlingford Lough ('the fjord of the hags') and Strangford Lough ('the swift-running fjord') in east Ulster, but they were diverted by the need to confront the ambitions of the Vikings of Limerick, who posed a significant threat.

**Cloghermore and Dunmore Caves:
Vikings Underground?**
According to the *Annals of the Four Masters*, a compilation made in the 1630s from earlier writings that have now mostly disappeared, in 928 the Dubliners demolished and plundered *Dearc Fearna*, where a thousand people were killed. *Dearc Fearna*, 'the Cave of the Alders', is thought to be Dunmore Cave in County Kilkenny, a place where human bones from at least 19 adults (mostly women) and 25 children have been found. Ten silver coins, including two dirhams and Anglo-Saxon pennies, suggest a Viking

hoard deposited in the mid-920s or thereabouts, and it is tempting to interpret these remains as representing the victims of the reported killings, and the possessions of one of their attackers.

However, excavations in 1999–2000 within Cloghermore Cave, County Kerry, which also recovered an early tenth-century Hiberno-Scandinavian silver hoard, have suggested that native Irish, albeit nominally Christian, may have used that cave as an ossuary in the fifth to ninth centuries, before a small group of interments accompanied by Scandinavian-style grave goods was placed there, perhaps in the late ninth century. This raises the possibility that the Dunmore Cave skeletal remains might also represent an Irish burial place rather than massacred victims of the Vikings.

Another remarkable discovery was made in Dunmore Cave when a group of 43 items of silver or copper-alloy was found hidden in a crevice in the rock. They include coins that suggest the group was lost in c.970, and can therefore have nothing to do with the events reported in the *Annals*. Much more unusual is the presence among them of 16 conical buttons of three sizes, made of interwoven silver wire. They would have formed an ostentatious embellishment to a tunic or some similar item of clothing; indeed, the suggestion is that the entire collection of objects was either on or within a garment that was stuffed into the crevice and then, for whatever reason, not reclaimed. Broadly similar, although not identical, items have been found on just a very few other Viking Age garments, for example at Dublin and at Peel Castle on the Isle of Man; the Dunmore Cave examples are a precious insight into the fashionable clothing of the very wealthy.

Plunder, Prosperity and Politics

Various Irish kings also pitted themselves against the Dubliners (and other Vikings in Ireland); Dublin was sacked by an Irish alliance in 944, recorded in the *Annals of Ulster*: 'Congalach son of Mael Mithig and Braen son of Mael Mórda, king of Laigin, plundered Dublin and took away valuables, and treasure, and much booty.'

This reverse for the Dubliners occurred a year after Olaf Cuaran Sihtricsson started a remarkably long reign there which came to an end after another major defeat for the Dubliners, at the Battle of Tara, in 980. Yet archaeological discoveries clearly demonstrate that this was a time when Dublin was becoming increasingly densely occupied. Prosperity now was not based primarily upon raiding; the last great raid by the Dublin Vikings, against the important monastery of Kells, County Meath, was in 951. It was also recorded in the *Annals of Ulster*: 'Guthfrith Sihtricsson and the foreigners of Dublin plundered Kells... 3,000 men or more were taken captive and a great spoil of cattle and horses and gold and silver was taken away.'

Payments for military services provided to ambitious kings both within Ireland and beyond also contributed to Dublin's wealth, but manufacture and commerce were becoming increasingly important. Although bracketed by military/political defeats, Olaf Cuaran's reign seems to have been a period of great prosperity for the Dubliners.

Nevertheless, this was still an era when military effectiveness was of key importance. In the 990s, early in the long reign of Olaf's nephew, Sihtric 'Silkbeard' (989–1036), the Dubliners were once again fighting the Vikings of Limerick. A more dangerous opponent was the increasingly powerful king of Munster, Brian Boru, who sacked and burned Dublin in 999 after it had sided with his Irish rivals. A further bout of inter-dynastic conflict culminated, in 1014, in the Battle of Clontarf, just north of Dublin. There Brian's Munster men overcame a coalition of Vikings and other Irish, although Brian himself was killed while the canny 'Silkbeard' avoided the great slaughter by remaining within the city's defences.

(Below) *Silver wire buttons from Dunmore Cave, Co. Kilkenny, Ireland, originally part of luxury clothing of a style favoured among Viking settlers in the Irish Sea region.*

(Above) *Copper-alloy buckle and strap-end, belt fittings decorated in Hiberno-Viking style, found in Dunmore Cave, Co. Kilkenny, Ireland, in 1999, together with 16 silver wire buttons (shown left) and other items including coins which date the deposit to c. 970.*

THE VIKING AGE CITY OF DUBLIN

When Vikings regained control of Dublin in 917, the new focus of their occupation was on the south bank of the River Liffey, immediately west of the River Poddle and *dubh linn*, 'the black pool' for which the settlement was named, and including the high ground where later the Anglo-Normans built Dublin castle. Excavations in this vicinity, at Temple Bar West, have brought to light traces of ninth-century buildings which show that this location had already been occupied by Vikings in the pre-expulsion period.

Tenth- and eleventh-century Dublin provides one of the most detailed and most comprehensive pictures of town life in the Viking Age. None of the other *longphort* sites which developed from raiding bases to towns – Limerick, Cork, Waterford, Wexford – has yet yielded archaeological traces of the tenth century. How their plans and layout evolved, and how they developed their roles as commercial and manufacturing centres, remain questions that will be answered only with further excavation.

Some aspects of Viking Age Dublin are known through the study of old maps and drawings, place names and documentary records. It is from these, for example, that we know of the existence of an earthen mound on Hoggen Green ('the green with mounds'), some 350 m (1,150 ft) to the east of the town's defences, which has been equated with the place name called *Thengmotha* in various Anglo-Norman documents. The name indicates the site of a place of assembly and discussion, a *thing*, of the type best known in Iceland at Thingvellir, in the Isle of Man at Tynwald, and at sites such as Dingwall in Scotland. The Dublin mound, about 73 m (240 ft) in circumference and some 12 m (40 ft) high, was removed in 1683. Across the River Liffey, the name Oxmantown provides an indication of the area where the *Ostmen*, the Hiberno-Norse Dubliners, lived after the arrival of the Anglo-Normans in 1169.

It is archaeology, however, that has made the most dramatic contributions to our understanding of the Viking Age city. The archaeological exploration of pre-Norman Dublin began, by accident rather than design, in 1961–62, in excavations at Dublin Castle. Since then, as central Dublin has been redeveloped, there have been opportunities to explore the city's origins and evolution. The National Museum of Ireland made the first, fundamental discoveries in a series of large-scale excavations at High Street, Christchurch Place and Winetavern Street in the 1960s and 1970s, culminating in

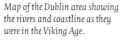

Map of the Dublin area showing the rivers and coastline as they were in the Viking Age.

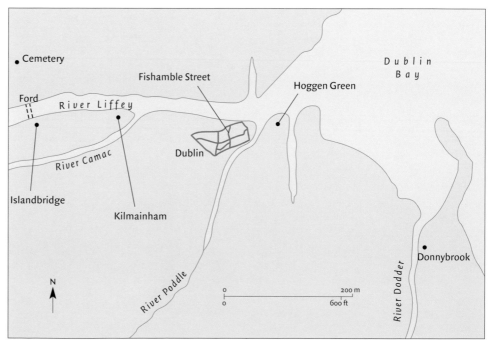

Excavations at Temple Bar West, Dublin, revealed sub-rectangular Viking Age buildings. Lines of white labels mark individual posts in the wall lines or the fences that formed boundaries to the plots.

A typical Viking Age house in Dublin with wattlework walls, a thatch-covered roof supported by four large internal posts, a central hearth and raised benches/beds along the walls. Based on evidence from Temple Bar West.

the remarkable discoveries at Wood Quay and Fishamble Street. Other sites investigated more recently have added significantly to the picture, particularly at Temple Bar West, a complex of sites which extends up to Fishamble Street.

Fishamble Street

Archaeologists have been able to show that Fishamble Street, which curves down to the River Liffey from the bluff on which Christ Church Cathedral stands, was first defined in the Viking Age. Two distinct campaigns of excavation, the first on the west side of the street in the 1970s and the second to the east in the 1990s, combine to reveal a story of Viking Age urban development unparalleled elsewhere in western Europe in its scale and chronological depth. This road, the medieval 'fish-market street', is perhaps the most exhaustively investigated streetscape anywhere in the Viking world.

Above layers which may relate to the ninth-century *longphort* phase of Dublin's existence there is evidence for a major redevelopment campaign. Earlier fence lines, which had divided up this area into three plots of land, were reinstated as part of an intensification of occupation; but now the land was subdivided between six properties. Houses were built in a distinctive technique and to a standardized form similar to that found in the ninth-century *longphort*. Presumably they fronted on to a curving street which is now lost, but which in the tenth century joined on to the upper end of the straight stretch of Fishamble Street. Within the backyards were pathways, initially made of wattlework hurdles, later of stone, which led

to and past smaller wattlework buildings.

Once these six plots had been defined, they were maintained with little change in their layout through a further eight successive rebuildings of the houses, extending over several centuries. The best indication of when they were created came from a coin associated with the first phase of rebuilding; it had been minted in the reign of the Anglo-Saxon king Edmund (939–46), and its presence here hints at an original laying out date of around 900–925.

Contemporary developments on the western side of Fishamble Street form an interesting comparison and contrast. There, parts of 14 property plots were excavated, and up to 13 phases of building and rebuilding were identified on some of the plots, spread over a period which extends for about 200 years from their laying out in the early tenth century. The earliest indication of dating is a coin of the Anglo-Saxon king Athelstan, minted in about 935, which was found in the second phase of buildings. It doesn't seem, however, that all the plots were laid out in a single operation; instead, it looks as if occupation gradually spread up the hill, and it may not have been until around the mid-tenth century that buildings stood on virtually all the plots.

Tenth- and eleventh-century Dublin, a substantial settlement of some 21 ha (52 acres), was protected

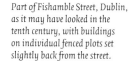

Part of Fishamble Street, Dublin, as it may have looked in the tenth century, with buildings on individual fenced plots set slightly back from the street.

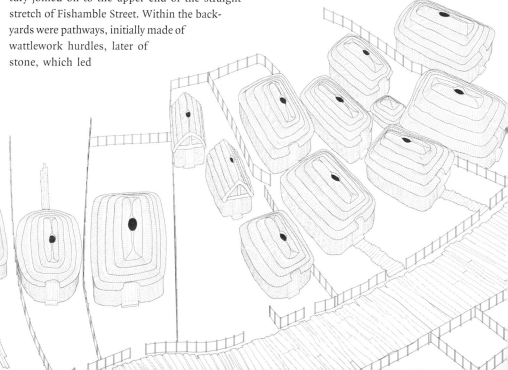

appears in both Orkney and Shetland, indicating the presence of *thing* assemblies of Scandinavian inspiration.

Jarlshof

The most famous Viking settlement site in the Northern Isles – indeed in the whole of Scotland – is on the southern tip of Mainland, Shetland. Here

stand the ruins of a sixteenth-century residence given the 'vikingized' name 'Jarlshof' in the early nineteenth century by Sir Walter Scott in his novel *The Pirate*. Later in that century coastal erosion at the site exposed massive stone walls from a prehistoric settlement, and excavations since then have revealed a succession of buildings spanning 6,000 years of occupation, including a series of Viking

Jarlshof contains traces of buildings from the Bronze Age onwards. Prehistoric houses, partially eroded by the sea, are now protected by a wall; Viking Age and Norse period buildings are rectangular and further from the sea. The earliest, now floored with white stone, runs parallel to the sea wall.

Age and later Norse houses, barns, stables and a smithy, occupied over several centuries.

The overall picture is of a series of long rectangular farmhouses built with earth-cored drystone walls. The earliest was about 21.5 m (70 ft) long and 6 m (20 ft) at its widest, with bow-shaped side walls. The roof, covered with thatch or turf, was supported on two rows of timber posts, creating a central space with a rectangular hearth and two 'aisles' with raised platforms, usable as benches or beds. A kitchen with a hearth and oven was divided by a partition at one end. Over time, two other large farmhouses were

built, and the settlement may have been occupied by several interrelated families. Line-sinkers (stones grooved so that fishing lines or nets could be tied to them) and spindle-whorls indicate that fish and sheep were important resources. A variety of bird bones, particularly sea birds, reveals an important dietary adjunct, but apart from miniature (toy?) querns found in later levels, there is no clear evidence for the growing of grain.

Analysis of Viking artifacts from Jarlshof, mostly found in the rubbish dumps ('middens') where they had been discarded, suggest that the earliest Viking houses were not built before about 850. The objects that survive are, with few exceptions, utilitarian – functional items made of bone or stone. There wasn't even any pottery in the earliest levels, its place taken by vessels carved from soapstone (see box on p. 127). Wood too was at a premium and, for example, when it came to fashioning a gaming board, it was a slate slab with lines scored across it that served the purpose.

Just a handful of pieces of decorated metalwork have been recovered, among them two fragments of horse harness, a gilt bronze strap-end decorated with Ringerike-style ornament, and a ringed pin, the cloak fastener characteristic of the Viking west. Some of the most attractive items from Jarlshof are bone dress pins, some of which have their tops carved into animal heads.

Island Burials – Rousay and Scar

No graveyard has been found at Jarlshof, presumably because it has been destroyed by coastal erosion over more recent centuries. Until quite recently, however, it was burials that provided the clearest evidence of Viking settlements in the Northern Isles. There are only about ten Viking graves from the Shetlands, but the Orkney Isles have many more, including some that have been carefully excavated.

At Westness, on Rousay, Viking graves were apparently inserted into a pre-existing Pictish cemetery. The Viking burials stood out because of their grave goods, the form of the graves and, sometimes, the arrangement of the corpse. The cemetery came to light in 1963 when a farmer dug a pit to bury a cow – and came upon the grave of a young woman and her newborn child. She had been buried wearing jewelry which proclaimed her importance: a pair of oval brooches, a splendid eighth-century Irish silver-gilt brooch-pin ornamented with gold

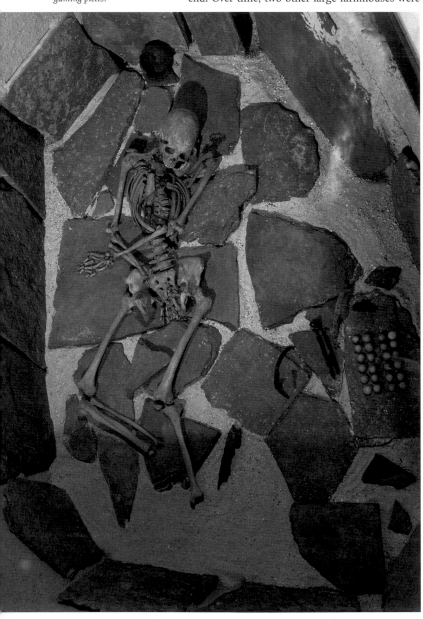

A man's grave from Westness, Rousay, Orkney, was lined and paved with stone slabs. Behind his head was his shield, of which only the iron boss survives. Other grave goods include arrows, a sickle, shears, a ringed pin, a strike-a-light and a set of gaming pieces.

THE SKAILL OF WEALTH

The most substantial Viking hoard from Scotland was found in 1858 near the shore in the Bay of Skaill, Mainland, Orkney.

Although some of the treasure was probably spirited away, never to reach public notice, 115 silver items have been recorded as well as 21 coins, with a total weight of 8.05 kg (17 lb 14 oz). The coins – mostly Arab dirhams – indicate that the hoard was concealed in c. 950–70. Outstanding among the mass of 'ring-money' and other armrings, neckrings and ingots is a group of 'ball-type' penannular brooches (see p. 112), four of which are decorated with animal ornament in Mammen style (see p. 178).

Comparison with a group of stone memorial crosses erected in the Isle of Man shows marked stylistic similarities, and suggest that the craftsman who made the brooches came from the Irish Sea area, perhaps from Man itself. Most probably this hoard was the family fortune of a leading Scandinavian settler, consigned to the earth in anticipation of a peril which indeed materialized and led to the non-recovery of this great wealth. The owner's house probably stood quite close by, but has likely been lost to coastal erosion.

Silver penannular brooches and a stamped silver armring from the Skaill hoard. The brooches are decorated with brambling and with Mammen-style ornament. The larger has a diameter of 16 cm (6¼ in), its pin is 38 cm (15 in) long, and it weighs 46.65 g (1⅝ oz).

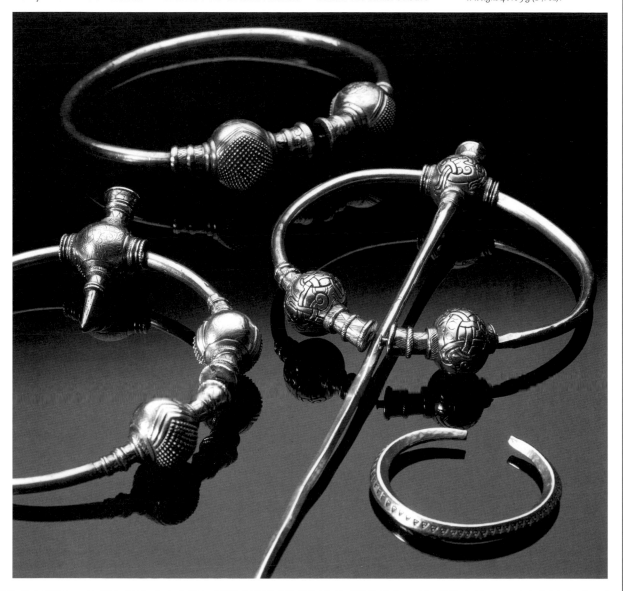

filigree and inlaid amber, a string of some 40 beads, and a pair of Anglo-Saxon copper-alloy strap-ends. Other grave goods included a weaving batten and a pair of heckles, shears, a sickle, a bronze vessel, a comb, and an insular mount that may have come from a box.

Nearby were two boat graves, each containing a man buried with warrior's gear, one with four arrowheads among his bones, presumably indicating the cause of his demise. The boats were *faerings* – four-oared rowing boats, 4.5 m (15 ft) and 5.5 m (18 ft) long – but their timberwork had decayed and only iron boat-rivets survived. Burial chambers had been defined amidships between stone slabs placed in the stem and stern. Other burials in the graveyard were laid in oval graves defined by stone slabs; these settings may also represent boats, for they had a higher 'prow-stone' at the head, pointing towards the sea. All of the graves have been provisionally attributed to the ninth century, but the contemporary farmstead occupied by the dead of the Westness cemetery awaits discovery.

A dramatic excavation of a remarkable Viking grave took place in winter 1991 at Scar on the island of Sanday, after human bones and iron rivets were exposed by coastal erosion. Half the grave had already been washed away, and the rest of the site disappeared through erosion just two days after excavation finished. Three people – an old woman aged about 70, a man probably in his 30s, and a child of about 10 or 11 – had been laid out in a rowing boat 7.15 m (23 ft 6 in) long. Sand grains trapped in the caulking between the boat's planks were geologically foreign to the British Isles, and probably Scandinavian – a pointer to the boat's place of origin. The woman and boy lay side by side amidships, but the man's body was crammed into the stern, his foot broken in the process. Their relationships with each other, in terms of both blood and status, are not clear.

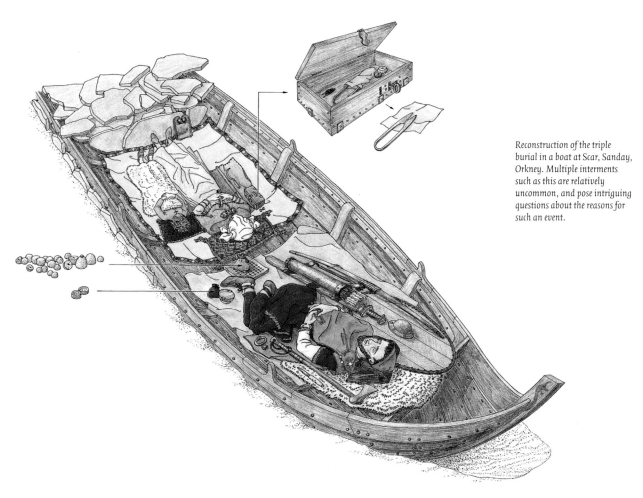

Reconstruction of the triple burial in a boat at Scar, Sanday, Orkney. Multiple interments such as this are relatively uncommon, and pose intriguing questions about the reasons for such an event.

The woman had been laid out with a fine collection of grave goods. A magnificent gilt-bronze equal-armed brooch of 'Troms' type and a whalebone 'plaque', functionally a smoothing board for 'ironing' linen garments but more probably a status symbol, are clear signals both of her high standing and of her links with northwest Norway. The plaque may also signal a reverence for Freyja, the fertility goddess, who was sometimes associated with flax, the source of linen. The man had weapons including a sword in its scabbard and a quiver of arrows, as well as a set of 22 whalebone gaming pieces. Anything buried with the child had been swept away by the sea. The grave cannot be dated very precisely – it falls sometime in the period 875–950 – but it may represent a final expression of old Scandinavian traditions in the face of encroaching Christian custom.

Mingle or Massacre?

The evidence of the Pictish to Viking transition, at Westness, Jarlshof and other sites, raises a series of important questions about Viking settlement throughout Scotland. Was there a massive invasion by Vikings? Were the natives slaughtered or expelled? Was there a substantial migration of Scandinavians from Norway?

Experts are divided, but there is no doubt that documentary sources make it clear that the Northern Isles were politically under Scandinavian control by the later ninth century. The Picts were the losers; or, at least, the Pictish ruling class in the islands. Perhaps they were overawed by Viking might, and quickly and quietly shipped out; perhaps some saw sufficient advantages to ally themselves with the new rulers, as some royal and aristocratic Anglo-Saxons did in England. Others may have put up a fight for their patrimony, but the archaeological evidence for any such encounters is non-existent – as it usually is in such circumstances. Whatever happened to the native ruling class, the bulk of the population may have remained, to be incorporated within a generation or so into the new Viking order, alongside new Scandinavian landlords and immigrants.

Viking Silver

Bullion hoards of silver and, very occasionally, gold, are found in both the Northern and Western Isles (see box on p. 131). They contain purely Scandinavian objects and their insular equivalents – personal jewelry including finger-rings, armrings and

Gilt silver annular brooch from Hunterston, ornamented with elaborate filigree panels and amber studs. Made in Ireland about 700, it has tenth-century runes on its inner face recording that Melbrigda owned it; he was perhaps an Irishman of Viking descent. Diameter 12.2 cm.

neck-rings, costume jewelry such as penannular brooches and ringed pins, and also ingots.

One distinctive form of jewelry characteristic of Viking Age Scotland is so-called 'ring-money', simple penannular arm-rings made from a rod of lozenge, multangular or circular cross-section, sometimes with a flattened or pointed end. Most examples have been found in Scotland, and discoveries in coin-dated hoards indicate that they were current in the tenth and eleventh centuries, mainly in the period 950–1050. Like the rather earlier Hiberno-Viking armlets (see pp. 125–126), ring-money was a convenient way to carry and display wealth, but so simple to make that no-one would have qualms about cutting one into bits of hacksilver in order to make small payments.

None of the peoples living in Viking Age Scotland issued coinage, and there are relatively few finds of coins, either in hoards or as single losses. The coins themselves are predominantly Anglo-Saxon issues; a few Arab dirhams and, later, some Norman deniers also occur. The relative economic inactivity indicated by the small number of silver hoards when compared to England or Ireland is mirrored in the absence from Viking Age Scotland of any urban settlement comparable to Dublin or York.

INNSE GALL: VIKINGS IN THE WESTERN ISLES

'Having landed in the west, Ketil fought a number of battles and won them all. He conquered and took charge of the Hebrides, making peace and alliances with all the leading men there in the west.'
Eyrbrygga Saga

Despite a resurgence of Gaelic speech and naming later in the medieval period, place names in the Western Isles suggest an immigration by speakers of Old Norse broadly comparable to that which affected the Northern Isles. Yet until the 1990s the Western Isles were the poor relation of Orkney and Shetland in terms of archaeological evidence for Vikings.

With just a couple of exceptions, the available evidence took the form of antiquarian discoveries of silver hoards and burials. These were found throughout the islands, and even on the isolated St Kilda, a Viking warrior was laid to rest beneath a cairn. Also on St Kilda, there is a tantalizing but unverifiable reference to fishermen digging up 'two antique urns,

(Above and left) Oval brooches from the woman's grave at Cnip.

(Below) The sandy headland at Cnip, site of a Viking cemetery.

containing a quantity of Danish silver coin'. The majority of datable silver hoards were deposited in the tenth century, an unexplained contrast with the Northern Isles where most were eleventh century.

Cemetery in the Sand Hills
The first Viking cemetery to be found in the Western Isles was discovered by chance in 1979, eroding grave by grave from the sand dunes at the Cnip headland on the Bhaltos peninsula of Lewis, in the Outer Hebrides.

The first grave to be found, the burial of a woman aged 35–40, is easily recognizable as Viking, for she was buried with a pair of characteristically Scandinavian gilt-bronze oval brooches. Other personal jewelry included a string of 44 glass beads, mostly of segmented form and coloured yellow, blue, silver or gold, a copper-alloy buckle and strap-end, and a ringed pin. In addition, her grave contained a comb, an iron knife, a small sickle, and a small pendant whetstone. A bone needle-case fashioned from the leg bone of a large bird, such as a goose or gannet, held two iron needles. A single rivet with wood adhering to it may represent a plank bier on which she was carried to her final resting place.

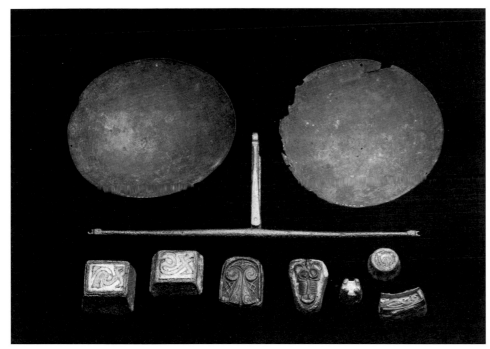

Scale beam, scale pans and weights from a man's grave at Kiloran Bay, Colonsay, Hebrides. The lead weights are decorated with pieces of metalwork cut from fine insular objects.

The next grave to come to light, some 45 m (150 ft) from the woman's grave, was that of a child of about six years old, lying flexed on its side and wearing an amber bead and a simple stone pendant. Then, close to the first grave, three more adult burials were located. Two men and a woman, all aged around 40, had each been buried in a shallow grave within a rectangular kerb of cobbles and large stones. The corpses lay on two different alignments, approximately at right angles to each other; but alignment did not depend upon the deceased's sex. There was also variation in the corpses' positions within the grave – the two males lay on their backs, but the woman lay flexed on her side. Only she had any grave goods with her – a simple bone pin perhaps fastening a shroud, and a small rectangular iron plate of unknown function. Nearby were the tiny graves of an infant aged about six to nine months and of a baby who died at or shortly after birth. Neither grave was marked with a stone kerb, but the infant had been buried with at least three beads and, probably, a bone pin that was found on the surface nearby.

Radiocarbon dating of the oldest child and the three adults suggests that they date from the late ninth or early tenth century; this range could encompass all the excavated burials. The assumption is that these are the graves of Viking settlers and their families, but the reasons why one burial had lots of grave goods and others had none or very few remain conjectural. Are they to do with social status? Or do the differences represent attitudes changing with successive generations? Might they reflect the ethnic origins of the various individuals as natives or newcomers? Cnip, a site favoured for settlement since the Bronze Age, clearly has much more to reveal, in terms both of Viking graves and, presumably, of Viking occupation sites.

Viking burials have also been found on the island of Arran. One of these, the grave of an important woman at King's Cross Point, is helpfully unusual because it contains coins which suggest a date around 850–75. Coins of a similar date were found when the grave of a warrior was dug up on Colonsay in the late nineteenth century. He had been buried with his horse, weapons, portable scales and a set of weights, and various other objects. His body lay within a rectangular setting of edge-set stone slabs, and boat rivets indicated that there had been a boat above or below the body. These two burials, the earliest dated Viking graves in Scotland, probably represent some of the first Scandinavian settlers to colonize the Hebrides.

A woman's burial on the island of Oronsay is noteworthy because she was buried wearing dress jewelry – but not the traditional Scandinavian oval

The destruction and recycling of objects looted by Vikings can also be recognized in the grave of a woman buried at Càrn a'Bharraich, Oronsay, Hebrides. She wore brooches made by adapting decorated cast gilt strips that had been prized off a container for holy relics of, perhaps, ninth-century date.

King's Cross Point, Arran, Hebrides, the site of a ninth-century woman's burial.

need to defend their new settlement. Whatever threat had encouraged the erection of the 'fort', the danger must have passed rapidly, for it was soon abandoned and the site reverted to domestic uses. The houses then erected were distinctly different from those that came before, built largely of turf and in rectangular rather than curvilinear form. Other than this, however, there is little difference in the archaeological 'signatures' of the immediately pre- and post-fort inhabitants of the Udal. Nevertheless, this new method of construction and the discovery of a handful of objects reflecting Viking tastes and origins suggest that it was indeed Vikings who prompted these innovations.

At the time of the Udal excavations, there had been no other investigation of a Viking settlement on North Uist, and only one on South Uist, at Drimore. There, in 1956, a single house dating to the ninth or tenth century was excavated on the machair, the thick layer of shell sand that forms a strip of arable land averaging about 1 km (3,300 ft) wide along the west side of the island. Although the scope of the investigation was severely restricted, finds of soapstone spindle-whorls and bowls, an antler comb and whalebone implements including an unusual 'cleaver', as well as a small conical gaming piece made of bone or ivory, emphasize the Scandinavian affiliations of the occupants.

Archaeological work undertaken in the last 15 years on South Uist has greatly advanced our understanding of the nature and extent of Viking or Scandinavian-influenced settlement in the Outer Hebrides. Detailed survey of the coastal machair identified a series of settlement sites spaced at intervals of about 1 km (3,300 ft). As at the Udal, there appeared to have been some continuity between pre-Viking and Viking Age settlements. To investigate this in more detail, two of the sites were selected for excavation.

At Cille Pheadair, towards the southwest corner of the island, it turned out there was no sign of any settlement underlying the Scandinavian-style occupation which began in about AD 1000. The earliest timber structure, itself a radical departure from local custom, was replaced by a house with cobble foundations, which itself was succeeded by a larger turf-built building. A 5-m (16-ft-6-in) long hearth occupied the central axis of the main room. The fairly basic range of artifacts and other evidence recovered suggest that this was the house of an

brooches. Instead, two thin rectangular gilt-bronze panels from an insular shrine, decorated with interlace designs and amber inlays, had been made into a pair of highly distinctive brooches, reminding us of how Vikings impacted upon local communities and religious centres.

Settling in the Uists

While these burials appear to flaunt the power of the newcomers, one site in the Western Isles is unique for suggesting that Vikings might feel some insecurity in their new surroundings. That site is the Udal, on a sandy promontory projecting from the north coast of North Uist, and excavated in the 1960s–1990s. Continuous local occupation from around 2000 BC, generating mounds of debris and building remains, was interrupted in the ninth century with the building of a small polygonal stone 'fort'. Only 7 m (23 ft) across, the fort's novel structure, as well as its direct superimposition on earlier buildings, has been interpreted as representing a wiping out of the 'natives' by invading Vikings who then felt the

'average' small farmer, not one of the local elite. In contrast, at Bornais, midway up South Uist's west coast, a series of mounds of occupation debris had been building up since the third to fifth centuries AD. Settlement moved to Mound 2 in the seventh and eighth centuries and it was there, eventually, that an important Viking farmstead was sited. As at Cille Pheadair, the earliest Viking-style building was a substantial timber hall. This was replaced by a bow-sided turf building, measuring 19.3 x 5.8 m (63 x 19 ft), which was in use in the eleventh century. Lines of stone slabs formed the inner walls, and prevented the surrounding sand from collapsing on to the floors, which were as much as 1.3 m (4 ft 3 in) below the level of the external ground surface. A large hearth, extending over 9.1 x 1.5 m (30 x 5 ft) occupied the building's central axis.

This form of construction is significant, for it employs elements of pre-Viking, Hebridean Iron Age tradition. Scandinavian tastes in art were represented by an animal design of Ringerike style, incised on a bone cylinder found in the eleventh-century building. The variety of other finds suggests that Bornais was a centre of craft specialization, and that the wealth with which to acquire raw materials was based on the export of herrings. But altogether, the large house at Bornais may represent the estate centre of a locally important Viking settler and his descendants, who over time adopted customs, fashions, manners and tastes that were increasingly distant from those of their original homeland.

The detailed results from Bornais and Cille Pheadair are still being evaluated, but it already seems clear that there was a fairly intensive settlement of the South Uist machair during the Viking Age. This was a superficial 'vikingization' of the native culture, in which farmers simply adapted to the customs and 'world view' of the new Viking overlords. A much more fundamental break with the past came when these long-lived mounds on the coastal machair were abandoned in the high medieval period.

The Aird a'Bhorrain peninsula at the north-west tip of North Uist, Hebrides, looking inland (southwestwards). The Viking and later Norse settlement known in English as the Udal was superimposed upon earlier remains in the area between the two promontories midway along the western (right-hand) side of the peninsula.

COMING TO THE NUB: THE ISLE OF MAN

Viking sites on the Isle of Man.

The Manx parliament meets on the tiered mound of Tynwald Hill, St Johns, traditionally the site of Viking Age assemblies.

The Isle of Man, a fertile hub in the centre of the Irish Sea 54 km (33 miles) long by 22 km (13 miles) wide, was inhabited by British and Irish Christians at the start of the Viking Age, but documentary evidence for the history of the island before the eleventh century is sparse. The Viking presence is, however, confirmed by several strands of evidence. Runic inscriptions suggest that both Norwegians and Danes settled on Man, and place name forms suggest that some of them had already spent time in Ireland, Scotland or England. The island still boasts its own parliament which meets at a stepped earthen mound called Tynwald – another instance of the perpetuation of the Old Norse name *thingvöllr*, meaning 'assembly fields'.

Crucial insights into the interrelationships of the Manxmen and the Vikings have been provided by archaeological excavations, notably those carried out by the eminent German archaeologist, Dr Gerhard Bersu, a refugee from Nazi Germany who was interned on the island as an enemy alien during World War II. It was Bersu who suggested that a site excavated at the Braaid in 1935–37 was not a prehistoric stone circle with accompanying ceremonial alignments, as its excavator believed, but a round house of pre-Viking form besides which Viking settlers had erected two buildings. One of these was interpreted by Bersu as a house with long bowed walls measuring 21 x 9 m (69 ft x 29 ft 6 in) internally; the adjacent rectangular building, measuring 16 x 5.5 m (52 ft 6 in x 18 ft) internally, may have been a byre. If Bersu was right, the structures at the Braaid may represent contact and continuity between natives and newcomers.

The wildly different interpretations of the Braaid were possible in part because it, like other early medieval occupation sites in Man, yielded remarkably few datable objects. This is true also of various small coastal promontory forts which Bersu and others have excavated; nevertheless, the single rectangular buildings that these forts often contain have often been ascribed, on the basis of their shape and layout, to a Viking Age reoccupation of an earlier defended site.

Ships and Slaves

More certainty is possible in the interpretation of some of the Viking burials on Man. The island has a remarkably high number of them – over 20 sites have been recorded – and several have been excavated to rigorous standards. Sadly, this does not apply to the earliest of the excavations, in 1927, at Knoc-y-Doonee, towards the north end of the island. A round mound 15.5 m (51 ft) in diameter and up to 2.4 m (8 ft) high was recognized, belatedly, to have contained a boat. Only the iron clench bolts that had held the ship's timbers together still remained, defining a vessel about 9 m (30 ft) long.

Lying in the centre of the boat was a poorly preserved male skeleton, and badly decayed bones and fragments of harness near the boat demonstrated that a horse had accompanied him. A dog (as the

excavator surmised) or perhaps a joint of meat was also placed nearby. Like so much else about this burial, the records tantalize. Nevertheless, the range of artifacts, including weapons, buckles, a pin and an unusual iron bowl, suggest that this was clearly a man of substance, a prosperous settler.

Higher standards of excavation and recording characterized Bersu's excavations. At Balladoole, on a prominent position just within the ramparts of an earlier Iron Age hillfort, he uncovered a boat burial that had been inserted into a pre-existing Christian cemetery, disturbing cists (small chambers made with slabs of stone) that contained recent burials and treating the semi-decayed bodies with contempt, spreading them out below the boat. This was, perhaps, a symbol of the Vikings' new dominance, further emphasized by the raising of a cairn of stone blocks over the boat, and the erection of a large post atop, close to where the Viking was laid.

The cairn was capped with a layer of cremated animal bones – horse, ox, pig, sheep/goat, dog and cat – somehow symbolic of the dead man's status. Playing the same role within the grave was a selection of horse-riding gear (some perhaps of continental origin), as well as three knives, a shield, an iron cauldron, a hone stone, a ringed pin, and a silver-gilt buckle and strap-end of Carolingian workmanship. Weapons are notably absent. Remains of a woman's skeleton were also found in the boat, but no objects belonging to her, suggesting she may have been a slave sacrificed at his obsequies.

If there is room for debate about the status and fate of the woman in the Balladoole boat, another Manx Viking grave excavated by Bersu, at Ballateare, Jurby, presents a picture of startling clarity. A turf mound there had been thrown up directly

The one round and two rectangular structures at the Braaid, Isle of Man.

Balladoole Iron Age hillfort; the boat-shaped stone setting marks the position of the Viking grave.

The slashed female skull and sword, still in its scabbard, from the burial at Ballateare. Length 95.5 cm (37½ in).

over a burial shaft containing a wooden coffin. In it were faint traces of a human skeleton, clothed in a woollen cloak fastened by a ringed pin. Around the body were placed a ritually broken sword in its scabbard, together with a baldrick, and also a shield that had been ritually slashed, a wooden-handled knife in its leather sheath, and a spear; two more spears lay on top of the coffin. Near the mound's apex the body of a 20- to 30-year-old woman was laid horizontally, frozen in rigor mortis with her upper arms at right angles to her body. A slashing blow from an edged weapon had left a large hole in the back of her skull. There is hardly a clearer cut case of sacrificial slaughter in the Viking world. To emphasize her role as an offering, her

corpse had been incorporated into and covered with a thin layer of cremated animal bones, reminiscent of those found at Balladoole. Similarly, too, there had been an upright timber marker, 70 cm (2 ft 4 in) in diameter, set into the top of the mound.

The Balladoole and Ballateare graves, together with another at Cronk Moar, Jurby, which shares the less dramatic characteristics of its neighbour at Ballateare, can only be dated by typological analysis of the buried objects. A date anywhere in the period 850–950 is theoretically possible, but the current scholarly consensus focuses on the decades either side of AD 900. The dead men were probably first-generation Viking settlers, wealthy landowners, holding to Scandinavian funerary traditions.

The 'Pagan Lady of Peel'

The most recent and spectacular Viking grave from Man represents another aspect of the settlers' story, from a generation or so later. 'The Pagan Lady of Peel', as she has been called, was found in 1984 during excavations on St Patrick's Isle. Close to the only good natural harbour on the island, this site has been chosen for significant functions at several different periods during the last two millennia; on it stand a medieval castle, a cathedral and a parish church.

Excavations north of the cathedral revealed a cemetery that had been in use over hundreds of years. One burial contained the remains of a middle aged woman, about 1.67 m (5 ft 6 in) tall. Among a remarkable collection of artifacts that were buried with her, around her neck was a magnificent string of 71 assorted beads. At her waist two larger amber beads and a fossil ammonite probably adorned an ornamental belt. Beside her was an iron rod (a highly unusual find) originally interpreted as a cooking spit, but possibly a ritual staff. It had been wrapped in cloth amongst which was part of a goose

The Pagan Lady of Peel's necklace, reconstructed from beads that were found clustered near her skull.

PILLARS OF SOCIETY

By the time that the 'Pagan Lady' was buried, the pre-Viking Manx tradition of erecting imposing stone slab memorials bearing Christian cross motifs had been adapted so that they incorporated Scandinavian art styles. A group of these stones that seem to be among the earliest can be dated to the period around 930–950 thanks to the Borre-style ring-chain decoration that is common on them. Most unusually, we also know who made some of them, for two were signed in runes by or on behalf of the sculptor. On the cross at Andreas we are told 'Gautr made me, son of Björn of Kollr', while at Kirk Michael we have 'Gautr made this and all in Man'.

Altogether there are about 70 such memorials, mostly carved on Manx slate in a crisp two-dimensional fashion. Several

are decorated with scenes from Norse mythology. Some of them carry decoration in later Viking styles, showing that the carving of such stones continued into the early eleventh century.

Judged by where the stones have been found, in cemeteries that were important enough eventually to become the sites of parish churches, they probably marked the graves of high-status landowners of Viking descent or affiliation. Within just a few generations, churchyard burial with a Christian stone monument had taken the place of mound burials marked with wooden posts, like those identified at Balladoole and Ballateare.

The cross from Kirk Michael proclaims its Viking links in the use of Borre-style ring-chain ornament, and in the runic inscription recording that it was carved by Gautr.

wing and a bunch of herbs. What she does not have is perhaps equally significant – no oval brooches or their equivalent. Her tomb, a native-style cist grave within an established cemetery at a key prestigious site, is also suggestive. And, although she herself was not buried with precisely datable objects, other more or less contemporary graves in the cemetery contain English coins of the mid-tenth century. All in all, it seems that 'the Pagan Lady' may represent a generation of Viking settlers who were already strongly influenced by the Christian traditions they saw amongst both the natives and their own Viking counterparts in countries around the Irish Sea.

Wealthy Man

The wealth that accumulated on Man is seen in the approximately 20 silver hoards discovered on the island. All but two contain coins, and these show that, with just one exception hidden about AD 900,

there was a peak of hoard deposition in the 960s–990s and another in the 1030s–1070s. Wealth was probably gained from trade and piracy, both linked to the important commercial routes connecting Dublin, Chester, the Western Isles, the Orkney earldom and beyond.

The overall emphasis on coinage rather than bullion in the Manx hoards reflects contacts with the English and Irish economies, and there are indeed brief documentary references which confirm Manx political links with both countries. In 1014, a contingent of Vikings from Man and the Isles accompanied Earl Sigurd the Stout of Orkney on the ill-fated expedition to fight with the Viking/Irish coalition at the Battle of Clontarf, near Dublin. Ironically, it may have been Sigurd's death there that allowed the Dublin Vikings to take control of Man; this would explain why silver pennies struck on Man from the 1020s were variants of the Dublin coinage.

St Patrick's Isle, Peel, looking east, is defended by a later medieval castle within which are a round tower and chapel, a cathedral and bishop's palace; the Viking Age cemetery was excavated to the north of the cathedral, at the far end of the islet.

NORMANDY

In 911, hoping to curtail raiding by enlisting the support of one Viking warband against the rest, the Carolingian ruler Charles the Simple did a deal with the Viking leader on the River Seine. This man was Hrólfr, known to the French as Rollo the Dane; he was a son of the Norwegian Earl of Møre, and nephew of Sigurd 'the mighty', first Earl of Orkney. Under the terms of the agreement, the so-called Treaty of Saint-Clair-Sur-Epte, Rollo promised to end hostilities against Charles, to provide military aid, and to accept Christian baptism. The reward for all of this was a grant of territory in which he and his men could settle – the eastern part of the region known today as Normandy. In 924, with Carolingian power in decline, Rollo was granted the central part of modern Normandy. Finally, in 933 his successor, William Longsword, took control of the Avrenchin and Cotentin, bringing Normandy's western border up to the historic core of what was still the independent kingdom of Brittany. Despite rival Viking incursions, the new counts of Normandy succeeded in holding on to their territory through six generations to William the Conqueror, and beyond.

Scandinavian presence in Normandy is demonstrated by place names with Old Norse and other elements. The Pays de Caux, the coastal strip north of Rouen, is characterized by names with Old English elements, suggestive of Viking settlers who had spent some time in England; in contrast, the north of the Cotentin peninsula, around Cherbourg, has names which suggest Hiberno-Viking immigration from Ireland. As the grant to Rollo coincided with a time when King Alfred's children were beginning their successful reconquest of the Viking settlements in eastern England, and when Irish Vikings like Ingimund (see p. 110) were on the look out for new places to colonize, neither is very surprising. Nowhere, however, do Scandinavian place names outnumber pre-existing Frankish names, and the problem of how many Vikings settled with Rollo remains unanswerable.

In archaeological terms the evidence for Scandinavians in Normandy is limited to ill-documented objects. A pair of oval brooches found in 1865 at Pîtres, on the Andelle in the Vexin area, suggest a Viking woman's grave, the only one known from continental western Europe. It may have been in a Christian cemetery, but there is no other information about the discovery.

Equally tantalizing was the brief exposure of stone settings on the beach at Réville, on the northeast side of the Cotentin peninsula, following a major storm in 1962. Most were recognizable as Frankish graves, but two boat-shaped settings and a cremation deposit may represent Viking graves. After hasty investigation the remains were covered again by the sands. The boat-shaped settings are broadly comparable to those seen, for example, in the Western Isles of Scotland, or at Lindholm Høje in Jutland, but it remains true that Normandy has not yielded a single well-defined and thoroughly investigated Viking burial.

The new counts of Normandy realized the value of trade and Rouen, already an important cathedral city with surviving Roman walls, became the commercial and political centre of their new state. Ironically, it may have been the liquidation of looted church treasures and the influx of Arab silver that started an economic upturn. In the time of William Longsword (c. 928–42) the Rouen mint was revived; as in England, Ireland and Man, the new rulers began to issue their own coinage in imitation of their neighbours. The city had a slave market until the late tenth century, where slaves from Ireland and Flanders, among other places, were sold. Dudo of St Quentin, writing c. 1015, mentions Greek, Indian, Frisian, Breton, Danish, English, Scots and Irish visitors to Rouen, and Rouen's traders are known to have had privileged commercial access to London in the years around 1000. Normandy deniers are found in coin hoards in Ireland and Scotland, as well as in Denmark and further east in Poland and Russia, and it is clear that Normandy's links with the Viking world were maintained up to the early eleventh century. There was a Norman contingent in Ireland at the Battle of Clontarf in 1014; and about ten years later a poet from the Norwegian royal court was in Rouen. Already, however, the Vikings of Normandy were getting increasingly integrated into the French political scene, and Norman interests were reoriented towards the Mediterranean, with successful incursions into Italy and Sicily; and there was also the continuing interest in affairs in England....

Oval brooches representing a Viking woman's grave found at Pîtres (ironically, the site associated with of the edict of 864 forbidding the transfer of weapons to Vikings).

V · NEW FOUND LANDS

'Then the fair wind failed, and northerly winds and fog set in,
and for many days they had no idea what their course was.
After that they saw the sun again and were able to get their bearings;
they hoisted sail and after a day's sailing they sighted land.
They discussed among themselves what country this might be.'
Saga of the Greenlanders

The Greek traveller Pytheas of Marseilles, who wrote a treatise on geography
in about 325 BC, made the earliest surviving reference to Thule, a mysterious
island in the north. Later classical authors repeated and embellished his
account; and thus the notion of Thule was carried into the early Middle Ages
through the copies of their works in the libraries of European monasteries.
Thule was believed to lie in the distant ocean, six days sail from Britain,
guarding the approach to the 'Frozen Sea', which was one day's sail further
to the north. Whether Thule was a real location such as Iceland, or pure
invention, something was thought to be out there. Rumours about Thule
may eventually have reached the ears of Scandinavian seamen.

From their first recorded attack, Vikings had been renowned as much
for their ships and seamanship as for their fighting skills. During the Viking
Age, increasing sophistication in ship-building techniques, combined with
a continually widening sphere of operations, allowed Vikings to explore the
horizons of their world and inexorably to extend its boundaries.

Whether by happenstance or design, the intuitive navigators of the
Viking world were lured westwards to the Faeroe Islands, Iceland, Greenland
and North America.

A detail from Leif Eiriksson Discovers America by Christian Krohg (1852–1925),
a huge picture measuring 3.3 x 4.7 m (9 ft x 18 ft), painted for the Chicago World's Fair
of 1893 and now displayed in the National Gallery, Oslo, Norway. An approximately
half-sized copy was made by Krohg's son, Per, and given to the United States of America's
Senate in 1936 by the Norwegian Friends of the USA; it hangs in the Senate Wing of the
Capitol Building, Washington DC.

THE FAEROE ISLANDS

Map of the Faeroe Islands.

The Irish monk Dicuil wrote a book of geography in c. 825 for the Carolingian court entitled *On the Measurement of the Earth*. In it he devoted a paragraph to a group of small islands, most of them separated only by narrow stretches of water, where Irish hermits had spent time during the previous century: 'But, just as they were always deserted from the beginning of the world, so now because of Vikings they are emptied of hermits, and filled with innumerable sheep and very many different kinds of seabirds.'

Dicuil's description best fits the Faeroe Islands, an archipelago of 18 small islands that lie 320 km (200 miles) northwest of the Shetland Isles and 600 km (375 miles) from Norway's nearest point. The Faeroes jut out of the Atlantic with imposing sheer cliffs of banded volcanic basalt, relics of seismic activity aeons ago. Although the islands are at latitude 62 degrees North, their position in the Gulf Stream gives them a moderate temperature – and a changeable climate. If, indeed, Irish hermits had introduced sheep, that would account for the name Faeroes, which in Old Norse means 'sheep islands'. As yet, the only archaeological evidence that anyone lived there or visited before Dicuil's Scandinavian settlers reached the islands in the generation before 825 comes in the form of radiocarbon-dated pollen cores that indicate the introduction of cereals at some time between 410 and 710.

At present, there is no conclusive archaeological evidence for when the settlement phase began.

Assuming that the equation of Dicuil's '*group of small islands*' with the Faeroes is correct, this tells us that Vikings had reached the islands, either as transient pillagers or permanent settlers, by c. 825. Whether it was their ancestors, or Irish monks, or someone else entirely who was there before, remains unknown, although the recognition on the island of Skuvoy of a group of stone slabs with incised cross designs like those found in pre-Viking contexts in the southwest of Ireland offers support to the scenario of Vikings driving out Irish monks.

The Faeroes were attractive to Viking settlers because, isolated though the islands were, they included places where crops could be grown, and the mountains provided ample grazing. The cliffs teemed with a profusion of seabirds that could provide eggs and meat, and the seas were abundant with fish, whales and seals. The natural vegetation consisted of juniper, heather, willow and sedges – but it almost disappeared once settlers arrived. They brought not only the material necessities of life but also, unknowingly, an array of insects, beetles and other creatures which thrive through their association with humans. Thus the ecosystems on the Faeroes were changed forever.

The so-called *Saga of the Faeroe Islanders*, written in Iceland c. 1200, doesn't survive intact but as fragments incorporated into other sagas. A good yarn but little more regarding the facts surrounding the settlement, it names the founding father as Grímr

Viking Age house remains excavated from 1941–57 at the farmstead of 'Niðri á Toft', Kvívík, on the west coast of Streymoy in the Faeroe Islands, where a stream enters the sea. The nearer ends have been truncated by coastal erosion; the walls as displayed incorporate several different phases of building.

Kamban. His first name is Norse, but the second is Irish, suggesting a Viking who had spent time in the British Isles. Whatever the true historical merits of this claim, it is an oblique indication of where settlers were believed to have originated. On the other hand, one of the handful of runic inscriptions on the islands, a rune stone at Sandavágur on the island of Vágar (now in the church there), dated c. 1200, asserts that 'Torkil Onundarson from Rogaland [Norway] was the first to settle this place'.

These Viking Age settlers on the Faeroes are represented archaeologically by a miscellany of evidence, most of it found only in small quantities. Archaeological excavation in the Faeroes began in 1943, with the discovery of a farmstead at a mound on Streymoy, but chance finds made before then also contribute to knowledge. One of the earliest recorded discoveries occurred in 1863, when gravediggers on the island of Sandoy found a hoard of silver that had been buried in c. 1100. The hoard consisted of a silver armlet and 98 coins from England, Ireland, Germany, Denmark, Norway and Hungary. The islands may appear remote, but they were clearly plugged into the networks of the Viking world.

Only a couple of Viking Age cemeteries have yet been investigated. One at Tjørnuvík on Streymoy came to light in 1956, when about a dozen graves were found. They revealed a range of burial customs like those identified elsewhere in the Viking world, with some corpses buried on their back and others flexed on their side. Objects placed with the dead to accompany them into the afterlife were small-scale personal possessions, the accoutrements of everyday life, such as a knife, a buckle or a ringed pin. In the other excavated cemetery, at Sandur on Sandoy, eleven burials were identified; seven were excavated, and in five of them stone settings defined the graves, a custom also well-known elsewhere in the Viking world. These excavations can hardly claim to provide a statistical sample of the thousands of Viking Age burials that must have taken place on the islands. Nonetheless, among the burials with grave goods there is no sign of even moderately rich burials, and no eye-catching grave mounds like those, for example, on the Isle of Man. Viking Age social relationships on the Faeroes apparently did not need to be reinforced by lavish funeral ceremonies.

Faeroese Settlements

The fullest picture of life on a Faeroese Viking Age farmstead comes from excavations in the 1980s at Toftanes, an ancient settlement site at the village of Leirvík on the east coast of the island of Eysturoy. The farm, dated to the ninth and tenth centuries, lay just above the modern shoreline, beside a

Excavations in and around the church at Sandur, Sandoy, have revealed that the first wooden church was built in the eleventh century, and succeeded by four successive later ones until the present church was erected in 1839. Viking Age graves were found in excavations to the south of the church.

Rune stone from Sandavágur, Vágar, Faeroe Islands, commemorating settlement there by a man from Rogaland in southwest Norway.

The meadowlands just above Lake Eiðisvatn at Argisbrekka, Eysturoy, Faeroe Islands, site of Viking Age shielings.

TAKING TO THE HILLS

Eighteen Faeroese place names incorporate the word *aergi*, which derives from Gaelic and means a shieling – a temporary summer dwelling in the uplands, occupied by people tending their animals on high-level pastures not accessible during winter. This aspect of stock rearing is known from a wide area in Scandinavia, the British Isles and the western Atlantic islands, and is not, of course, exclusively a Viking Age phenomenon. There is another word for this in Old Norse – *saeter* – but it is not clear why some sites were given one name and some the other. Excavation at Argisbrekka, 'the shieling of the slope', which lies 140 m (460 ft) above sea level in northern Eysturoy, has revealed a series of structures. They were all built of turf, without the stone cladding that is typical of Faeroese Viking Age houses. The buildings lay in little clusters, typically with a larger dwelling measuring about 7–8 m (23–26 ft) long and 3–5 m (10–16 ft 6 in) wide, its walls 1 m (3 ft 3 in) or more thick, associated with a few smaller outhouses that were probably used for storage and as workshops. The dating evidence, in the form of a modest selection of artifacts, suggests that this group of shielings was in use during the ninth to eleventh centuries.

(Opposite above) Funningur, in northwest Eysturoy, Faeroe Islands, traditionally the site chosen by Grímr Kamban, the islands' 'founding father', shows the nature of the islands' landscape.

stream which channels water from a natural reservoir formed by a small corrie. The main building was a house that measured approximately 20 x 5 m (65.5 x 16.5 ft) internally. Its walls, 1 m (3.3 ft) thick, were made from inner and outer faces of stones, with turf stacked between to provide insulation. A large rectangular hearth in the western half of the building shows that this was where the family congregated – the eastern, downslope part of the building may have been used as a cattle-byre. Around this longhouse were three smaller buildings of varying dimensions but uncertain functions.

Although the soil conditions did not preserve bone or iron well, several thousand objects, representing the debris of everyday life, were found in and around these buildings. In terms of diet, the animal bones from Toftanes showed that there were some cattle but that sheep (fittingly, in view of the islands' name) were the commonest farm animals. Very few items were of local origin. Soapstone, a soft, easily carved rock imported from Norway or Shetland (see page 127), was used to make a variety of simple items including cooking vessels, weights for fishing lines or nets, and spindle-whorls for making thread. Norway was also the source of schist sharpening stones and querns. Minor luxury items were also imported – a jet arm-ring probably came from England, a bronze disc brooch with Borre-style animal ornament and beads of glass or amber from Scandinavia, a ringed pin perhaps of Irish origin. There was also a surprisingly large collection of wooden items, including building materials, domestic utensils ranging from spoons to barrels, and gaming pieces and part of a gaming board. From the earliest levels came a 40-cm (16-in) tall wooden cross – a remarkable demonstration of Christian belief among the

settlers. Much of the wood would have been deliberately imported, but some may have been driftwood, a natural resource that must not be overlooked. A home-grown resource, at least until it was wiped out through over-use, was the juniper tree. Its strong and flexible roots and branches could be fashioned into ropes, cords and thongs with a multiplicity of uses, from house construction to barrel bindings.

(Right) The remains of a Viking Age farm at Toftanes, seen here looking south. The main house, upper centre, has curving walls which are 1 m (3 ft) thick, each defined by an inner and outer row of stones; there is a long hearth in the western (right-hand) room. A passageway leads from the centre of its north wall to a small irregularly shaped building; south of the main building are two other, smaller structures.

THE SETTLEMENT OF ICELAND

Map of Iceland.

Iceland 'hangs' from the Arctic Circle 500 km (300 miles) northwest of the Faeroe Islands, with its east coast seven days sailing from the nearest point of Norway (Stad). At the time of the Viking settlement it was the world's largest uninhabited island.

Dicuil, the Irish monk who in c. 825 described an archipelago thought be the Faeroes, also recorded that in c. 795 some fellow monks had spent a summer on *Thule*. They reported that for several days in mid-summer the sun hardly set: 'a man could do whatever he wished as though the sun was there, even remove the lice from his shirt'. They also told Dicuil that one day's sail to the north of the island they had found sea-ice. On the basis of these phenomena it is tempting to equate *Thule* with Iceland. *Íslendingabók*, the *Book of Icelanders* written by Ari Thorgilsson, the 'father of Icelandic history', in c. 1120–1130, reports that the arrival of Norwegian settlers caused Irish monks to flee, leaving behind bells, books and crozier; but no archaeological traces of any pre-Viking presence, Irish or otherwise, have yet been found in Iceland.

Medieval Icelanders credited several different individuals with discovering their island. Two storm-tossed mariners who reputedly reached it by chance were Gardar Svavarsson, a Swede heading for the Hebrides, who modestly called it *Gardarsholm*, and Naddod the Viking, a Norwegian sailing for the Faeroes, who named it *Snowland*. Floki Vilgerdason, a Norwegian who sailed to the Shetlands, the Faeroes and then on to what he christened Iceland, allegedly went there on purpose to

attempt a settlement, but gave up. None of these men, however, are mentioned in *Íslendingabók*. Instead, the national honour of being the first permanent settlers has fallen to the Norwegian Ingolfr Arnarson and his brother Leif.

Large areas of Iceland were naturally very inhospitable. Glaciers would have been familiar to anyone coming from north Norway, but a volcanic landscape of lava fields, geysers and sulphur pools would have been a complete novelty, and eruptions were still an intermittent threat. There was some good pasture land, particularly around the fringes of the island, and *Íslendingabók* states that Iceland was originally forested 'from mountain to seashore'. Pollen analysis shows that birch and willow trees, which had flourished in the sub-Arctic climate, retreated in the face of the influx of people; and with deforestation came soil erosion. The unintentional introduction of insects and plants also altered the island's natural ecosystems.

The 'Age of Settlements'

Íslendingabók dates Ingolfr's settlement to 870, and states that the 'Age of Settlements' lasted 60 years. Archaeological evidence is not yet sufficiently precise or plentiful to confirm or deny this short-span chronology (although see box). Few settlement sites have yet provided radiocarbon dates. A series of dates from a site at Herjólfsdalur on the Westmann Islands, which suggested that settlement had begun there in the seventh century, has been much discussed. Rewriting *Íslendingabók*'s chronology can be countenanced; but the lack of any associated seventh- to eighth- century artifacts apparently confounds the case for such early settlement. The debate continues.

Landnámabók, the 'Book of the Settlement' written in the twelfth century, lists about 400 heads of families who were regarded as the pioneers of the Icelandic commonwealth. *Landnámabók* also names the district or area – the fjord, promontory or valley – where each of them eventually set up his homestead. It reports that the entire coastal perimeter and the network of feeder valleys were settled, so that later immigrants had to find new niches in more remote locations. Evidence is accumulating which supports the idea that the favoured locations

Remains of the farm excavated at Herjólfsdalur, Westmann Islands, Iceland; there were at least two main phases of construction before the farm was deserted in c. 1050.

were soon taken up by entrepreneurs who claimed large blocks of land and then sought to fill them with subordinate settlers. The nearest thing to an accurate census of the early Icelandic population is a count made in 1095 to establish the number of free land-owning farmers who had a right to go to the *Althing*, the Icelanders' national assembly. The total, approximately two centuries after settlement began, was 4,560; estimates of the entire population extrapolated from this figure are in the range 40,000–100,000.

Where did the founding fathers come from, and what encouraged them to uproot? Literary sources state that it was the growing power of King Harald Finehair that inspired emigration from Norway. Some settlers allegedly reached Iceland after a sojourn in the British Isles; this would, for example, account for their Celtic names. Recent studies tend to agree that the Viking settlers came principally from Norway or the British Isles, but discount Harald Finehair as a catalyst because his famous triumph over a coalition of rivals at the Battle of Hafrsfjord, probably in c. 885–90, is too late to have instigated this emigration.

An alternative proposal, that a growing population in Scandinavia faced a shortage of cultivatable land, has also been refuted with the suggestion that, on the contrary, farmland was still available in the homelands, where there *was* a further expansion of settlement in the later medieval period.

However, perhaps the key point in that argument is not the amount of potential farmland, but the customs governing its ownership and availability. And while Harald Finehair may not himself have driven out the emigrants, a concentration of power into fewer hands in the late eighth and ninth centuries may have encouraged the dispossessed to re-invent their prestige and authority on a new stage.

An Egalitarian Society

A new land provided the conditions in which society could discard unnecessary conventions and constraints and adapt to novel circumstances. Judging by the range of objects that accompanied the dead into the afterlife, the Icelanders coalesced into a rather more egalitarian society than the ones they had left behind in Scandinavia or the British Isles. The grave goods do not include spectacularly rich assemblages, and the graves themselves did not stand out as monuments in the landscape.

The farmhouses are mostly of similar dimensions, although there are a few appreciably larger houses, showing that some settlers achieved some form of pre-eminence. The largest is the structure at Hofstaðir near Mývatn, which measures 36 x 8 m (120 x 26 ft) internally, and is thus about twice the average size; presumably it was the home of some very important family, and it seems likely that it also served as a cult centre.

Overall, however, the collections of objects recovered from excavated Viking houses share the same, generally rather nondescript, appearance. All of this evidence certainly suggests a community without a great range of social divisions. The concentration on simple tools and equipment that could be produced from local material is well demonstrated by the prevalence of lava, which was used to make lamps, querns and other basic everyday items.

Blades fashioned from obsidian (volcanic glass), which seem often to have taken the place of iron knives or saws, indicate that iron was much more of a prized possession here than in many other parts of the Viking world. It was possible for the Icelanders to extract iron from bog ore by smelting; but judging by the scarcity of iron objects among household debris, they were intent upon recycling as many of them as possible. The commonest

Simulation of a Viking Age longhall farm from a setting in the Thjórsárdalur valley, Iceland, erected in 1974.

King Harald Finehair of Norway's victory at the Battle of Hafrsfjord, which traditionally inspired migration to Iceland, is commemorated by a monument in the form of three Viking swords, 9.2 m (30 ft) tall, at Møllebukta near Stavanger, in southwest Norway. It was erected in 1972, a date then thought to be one thousand years after the battle, and one which fitted the traditional date for the occupation of Iceland; but the battle is now believed to have been later.

imported material was the very mundane soapstone, brought from Norway or the Shetlands, and fashioned into kitchenware.

Thingvellir

According to Íslendingabók, it was in about 930 that the settlers of Iceland established the Althing, an annual gathering open to every free man on the island. The location they chose was in the southwest, the most densely populated area, but was accessible to people coming from all over Iceland. Here, at the spot now known as Thingvellir, is a dramatic ravine formed by the parting of two continental plates. For two weeks in June each year the plain below this ravine must have seethed with a great throng of individuals who 'camped out' in tents or temporary 'booths'. The Althing has been described as the oldest parliament in the world, but this is

DATING FROM FIRE AND ICE

Since the 1930s some Icelandic archaeologists have put much faith in a dating system called tephrachronology. This initially involved linking particular and supposedly distinctive lava flows or layers of volcanic ash found at archaeological sites to specific, historically documented eruptions. Other archaeologists, however, have been highly sceptical about the accuracy of this basic form of tephrachronology; they question both the validity of equating a given lava with a particular historical eruption, and the reliability of correlating lava flows from geographically distant sites.

Nonetheless, one tephra layer, which seems just to predate many of the sites where archaeologists have identified Viking Age settlements, has become known as the landnám ('settlement') tephra. Then, in 1995, scientists reported that they had identified the chemical signature of the 'settlement' tephra within the layers of ice that make up the Greenland icecap. The icecap has grown by a process of annual accretion like the growth rings on a tree, and it is possible to date each year's accretion by counting back from the present; the 'settlement' tephra was in an icecap layer dated to within two years either side of 871.

This seems to provide confirmation that the late ninth century was indeed the heyday of Viking settlement in Iceland; an optimal time when the temperature was slightly milder than today.

The Krafla volcanic system, near Lake Mývatn in northeast Iceland.

(Above) A meeting of the Althing assembly as imagined by the scholarly painter W.G. Collingwood in his work of c. 1897 Thingbrekka at Thingvellir. The tent-like booths in the foreground provide some idea of how participants lived at this annual gathering.

(Left) Thingvellir ('assembly fields'), site of Iceland's Viking Age annual assembly, the Althing. Almannagjá, the volcanic fissure that now forms the main route through the site, can be seen running from bottom left; Collingwood's view of Thingbrekka ('assembly slope') looks back from where the modern path disappears from view (centre left).

probably to aggrandize its origins. The impulse which led to its inauguration is more plausibly explained as a sensible desire to establish a single set of rights and customs in a land of dispersed settlements, where local idiosyncrasies could potentially spring up and become an unwitting cause of friction.

To maintain unanimity, every year an official called the 'Lawspeaker' recited the 'laws', the agreed norms of behaviour, from his position on the 'lawrock'. Ultimately, however, these consensual rules for conduct were enforced by social pressures, and the *Althing* provided the ultimate social forum. It was also the highlight in Viking Age Iceland's social calendar, a time and place for fun and games, for barter and trade, like a great annual fair.

Among the significant events acted out at the *Althing*, the best known is probably the debate in the year 1000 when pagan traditionalists were confronted by the Christian zeal of the powerful Norwegian King Olaf Tryggvason. Unable to determine whether the Christian belief in the Last Judgement was preferable to Ragnorök, the end of the world as portrayed in Norse mythology, the assembly gave the Lawspeaker the task of making a binding decision. A pagan himself, he chose Christianity, sweetening the pill through the retention of the traditional customs of eating horseflesh and exposing unwanted babies to their fate.

Life on the Farmstead in Iceland

Archaeologists have so far explored, to varying degrees, only about twenty Icelandic farms founded before AD 1000. Most are in the southwest and west of Iceland, and they include several sites within the modern capital, Reykjavik, which tradition says was where Ingolfr, the first settler, lived. However, it is the excavations on the northern coast at Granastathir which present one of the best pictures of life on a tenth-century farm in Iceland. Life was focussed on stock rearing, supplemented by fishing and by hunting gamebirds. This economy reflects the difficulties of cereal production at this high latitude, and mirrors the agricultural regime of northern Norway. Indeed, colonists from that area would have had the experience necessary to forge a living in these demanding conditions.

The focus of the biggest building was a main room or 'hall' measuring 16.8 x 7.9 m (55 x 26 ft) externally, enclosing an earth-floored living space of just under 80 sq. m (860 sq. ft). The long walls bowed out gently so that the centre point of the building was wider than the ends. Turf, readily available, was the principal building material, although comfort and appearance may have been improved by the insertion of wooden panelling along the inner faces of the walls. The roof had been supported by two rows of vertical posts standing

Reconstructed interior of a Viking Age house based on that at Stong; salutary for showing how the living space could have been sub-divided for privacy and comfort.

within the building, and this created an aisled effect. The dominating feature in the hall was a 1.2-m (4-ft) long rectangular hearth, approximately in the centre of the building and the symbolic and practical focus of daily life. A second, smaller, hearth was positioned just to the other side of this door, together with a vat and a cistern; this area was presumably partitioned off from the main room, and had its own doorway to the outside, but its function isn't clear. At the other end of the hall another wooden partition defined an area that may have been used for storage. From there a doorway led down into a small room identified as a kitchen because it contained two successive hearths, a concentration of animal bones, and burnt stones identified as pot-boilers.

Just around the building's southeast corner was an annex, built against the hall but entered only from the outside. Inside there was a hearth against the inner wall, and remains of raised earth benches at the far end. The lack of food remains and scarcity of artifacts suggests that this may have been a smoke-house where meat products were prepared for long-term storage, although the presence of benches perhaps argues against this interpretation. Closely clustered around this principal complex was a series of other smaller structures, built in the same way with turf, and perhaps serving as a stall or pig-sty, a barn or cow-house, and a store-room. Slightly further (100 m or 330 ft) away, but still within an encircling turf embankment that defined the farmyard, was a smithy. Altogether the farm was a self-supporting unit, its occupants able to sustain themselves in reasonable comfort. There were, however, social occasions both regional and island-wide, that offered an opportunity for at least some members of the family to broaden their horizons.

SAGAS – FACT OR FICTION?

Until quite recently the Icelandic sagas and other more learned works written in the twelfth and thirteenth centuries were regarded as almost infallible pointers to the sites where named individuals built their farmsteads or famous events took place in the Viking Age, 300 and more years before the stories were written down. It was not surprising, therefore, that Iceland's first archaeologists used them as a guide. And when those archaeologists uncovered buried remains on these sites, they more or less automatically related them to the period in which the sagas were set, even when there was no independent archaeological confirmation of the proposed link.

Today, these literary masterpieces are treated more carefully by archaeologists. Much of the incidental detail in the sagas, such as descriptions of clothing, is now recognized as clearly reflecting the fashions of the medieval period rather than the Viking Age. Less tangibly, the vision of the Viking Age which sagas lay before us is the one current several centuries after the events in question, although oral traditions handed down over many generations may underpin the stirring accounts of heroic characters and epic struggles.

At the time the sagas were composed, references in them to specific places may have been inspired, and/or given an added air of authenticity, by the survival in these places of ruins; these were woven into the narrative, implying, intentionally or not, that they dated back to the period in which the saga was set. Subconsciously, or with art and craft, the saga writers were reinforcing the views of their contemporaries.

A page containing part of King Harald Finehair's saga from Codex Frisianus, an early fourteenth-century Icelandic manuscript of Snorre Sturluson's Heimsksringla. The page measures 31 x 24 cm (12¼ x 9½ in).

GREENLAND

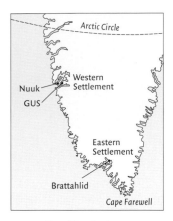

Map of Greenland.

(Opposite) This is the landscape occupied by Eirik the Red at Brattahlid. The church at Qassiarsuk stood just beyond the modern red-coloured church, and Eirik's house was presumably somewhere in the vicinity (although the obvious ruins are later).

Two papal documents dated 1053 and 1055 contain the earliest contemporary references to Greenland, but for a circumstantial account of the settlement we have the Icelandic sagas. The *Saga of the Greenlanders* recounts how, at some time supposedly in the early tenth century, Gunnbjorn Ulf-Krakuson was blown off course while sailing to Iceland from Norway, and sighted land out to the west of Iceland. In 982 Eirik the Red, banished for three years from Iceland for manslaughter, decided to follow this up and to explore what lay beyond the western horizon.

At some point that must have been more than 500 km (300 miles) from Iceland he encountered a starkly inhospitable icebound coastline, but after sailing southwards he rounded a cape and found a west coast indented by a series of long narrow fjords with good pasturage. Eirik returned home from banishment eulogizing the newly christened *Greenland* and determined to settle there. Soon he led 25 ships carrying would-be settlers towards their new home; *Íslendingabók*, written 1122–33, briefly records that this was 14 or 15 years before Christianity was adopted in Iceland – i.e. in 985/6.

If Eirik steered directly towards Cape Farewell, the southernmost tip of Greenland, he would have been sailing with the current of the North Atlantic Drift, but embarking upon a journey of over 1200 km (750 miles); only 14 of his 25 vessels reached Greenland. *Íslendingabók* says that the Viking settlers found human dwellings, fragments of skin boats and stone artifacts like those belonging to the *skraelings* of Vinland. Archaeologists refer to the natives who left these traces as the Dorset people, naming them after the place on Baffin Island where their remains were first recognized. They had been living in the Arctic for hundreds of years, along with other Palaeo-Indian and Palaeo-Eskimo groups. By the time the Vikings arrived, the onset of warmer conditions was encouraging the Dorset Palaeo-Indian people to vacate Greenland, and it may be that the early Viking Greenlanders and the Dorset people rarely, if ever, came face to face in and around the settled areas.

Eirik settled in Eiriksfjord, at the heart of what is known as the Eastern Settlement. The name is geographically confusing, for 'Southern' would

be a more helpful description. This settlement area eventually extended along a coastline of about 200 km (125 miles), towards the southern tip of Greenland's western side. Northwards, beyond a 500-km (300-mile) strip of shoreline uninhabitable because of the small amount of available grazing land, the so-called 'Western Settlement' was established in the area where the capital Nuuk (Gothåb) stands today. In both, the favoured locations for farmsteads were in the inner fjords, well back from the coast. Altogether, the sites of about 400 Norse farms have been located in the Eastern Settlement and about 80 in the Western, although it's not certain that all were occupied simultaneously. It was never to be a densely populated landscape – estimates of population are notoriously difficult to substantiate, but it has been suggested that there were only about 2,500 settlers at the zenith of the Greenland colony.

Brattahlid

The archaeological site on Eiriksfjord associated with the saga story of Eirik the Red is Brattahlid. Groups of stone-built ruins are plainly visible there, and since the nineteenth century there have been several different campaigns of excavation, all initiated in the hope of finding traces of Eirik's settlement. The obvious ruins still visible today belong to later medieval buildings, considerably later in date than Eirik's time. Yet in one place, at the straggling modern village of Qassiarsuk, just a few hundred metres from Brattahlid, archaeologists have come face to face with early Viking settlers.

In 1961, when a school hostel was being erected, the workmen unearthed several human skulls. Archaeological excavations at the spot in 1962–5 revealed a cemetery of about 150 individuals, who had been buried around a tiny turf-built church which measured only 2 x 3.5 m (6.5 x 11.5 ft) internally. Radiocarbon dating of nine skeletons indicated dates in the period 1000–1100/1200, the uncertainty over the end date being due to inherent methodological factors. There were no later dates, and also virtually no intercutting of earlier graves by later ones, a common phenomenon in cemeteries that remain in use over a long period.

Together, these facts suggest a relatively short-lived cemetery serving quite a small community living hereabouts at about the time of the original Viking settlement.

It is tempting, given the proximity to Brattahlid, to link this church and cemetery with the story told in Eirik the Red's Saga, of how Eirik's son, Leif the Lucky, introduced Christianity to Greenland in ...... Eirik was not impressed by the new religion but his wife, Thjodhild, embraced the faith and built a church, which she sited some way away from the farmstead so as not to aggravate Eirik. Only later was it necessary or desirable to construct the church that was the predecessor of a larger, stone-built church that now stands within its walled rectangular graveyard some 200 m (220 yd) away, close to the remains of other buildings. Whether this story records historical reality, or was concocted to explain the presence of seemingly isolated church ruins that were still standing when the saga was written, is an open question.

The cemetery provides an insight into living conditions here in the first generations of the settlement. Very few people lived beyond the age of 45; for those who had safely negotiated the dangers of birth and infancy and reached the age of 20,

(Below) Simulation at Brattahlid of the little church excavated at Qassiarsuk, Greenland; it is constructed entirely of turf and sods, apart from the timber western gable.

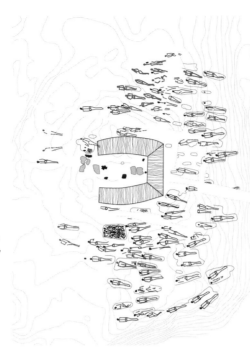

Plan of the church and cemetery, dating to c. 1000 – 1100/1200, excavated at Qassiarsuk near Brattahlid, Greenland. Men (shown in black) were mostly buried south of the church, women (shown in red) to the north. All had their heads to the west, in the normal Christian fashion.

But more coveted still were the tusks, for walrus ivory was a luxury commodity which commanded a high price abroad, and so could be used to pay for the basic necessities of life that the Greenlanders had to import. The main hunting grounds for the walrus were 600 km (375 miles) and more to the north of the Western Settlement, in and beyond Disko Bay, but such was the lure of the walrus that the Greenlanders must have devoted great efforts to their summer hunting trips. The fruits of these trips are represented in the ecclesiastical treasuries of northwestern Europe, for at a time when elephant ivory was virtually unobtainable it was walrus ivory, durable but delicate, that was chosen for the carving of devotional crosses, bishops' crozier and other religious items.

The Farm Beneath the Sand

The remains of farmsteads occupied by the Greenland Norse are usually easy to identify, for the outlines of their walls are normally still visible, and their shape is unlike that of any native Inuit buildings. Nearly 50 of these 'ruin groups' have been investigated since the nineteenth century, although in many cases the investigations were on a very limited scale. The nineteenth-century investigations used simple methods to achieve simple results, and they contribute little to our understanding of the settlement. It is now recognized that most of the excavated sites can be dated to the thirteenth and fourteenth centuries, but this isn't at all surprising since their excavators dug within and around the ruined buildings but did not remove the walls to see what lay below. Yet it is only by adopting this procedure that a more accurate and complete understanding of earlier phases of occupation can be gained.

The insights that can be won through a carefully recorded dismantling of ruins to reveal underlying structures have recently been demonstrated on a site in the Western Settlement. In 1990 two caribou hunters came across timbers sticking out of a river bank about 80 km (50 miles) east of Nuuk. The site is now known as GUS, from the initials of its Danish name *Gården Under Sandet*, 'the farm beneath the sand'. This sand, which had been deposited by stream channels fed by the expansion of a nearby glacier, covered the farm to an average depth of 1.5 m (5 ft). The new climatic conditions of the Little Ice Age, which started in about 1350,

the average life expectancy was about a further 15 years. And it wasn't only natural causes that depleted the population. Among the disarticulated remains of 13 individuals found in a mass grave were three individuals with head injuries caused by a sharp weapon such as a sword or an axe. All, perhaps, were victims of combat or feuding. A knife blade discovered stuck between the ribs of another male skeleton also suggests that all was not sweetness and light in this community.

The immigrant Greenlanders had to adjust their accustomed farming practices in order to ensure their own survival. The environmental differences between the Eastern and Western Settlements also dictated some variation in the emphases placed upon different food sources. Cattle and sheep were the principal farm animals in both areas, but it seems that goats were commoner in the Western Settlement, where their omnivorous habits were better suited to the ground cover. It is clear that fishing and hunting were vital, with both seal and caribou becoming important sources of food to both communities. Walrus bones are also found widely distributed, but although the meat would doubtless have been a useful food resource, other parts of the walrus were even more significant. From the hides the Greenlanders could fashion the ropes that were so important for their ships.

Excavations from 1991–96 at the GUS site, east of Nuuk uniquely revealed the entire history of a Viking settlement in Greenland from its Viking Age origin to its abandonment in the medieval period.

had evidently polluted the river, a vital water supply, as well as devastating the production of fodder for cattle. The farmers had been left with no alternative – they had to abandon their home. Likewise, archaeologists had no qualms about attempting a total excavation of the farm, for the river which had revealed the remarkably well-preserved timbers was steadily destroying the site through erosion. For a month or so each summer in the years 1991–96 the site was excavated and, for the first time in Greenland, the walls of buildings were carefully dismantled after excavation and recording, in order to reveal the remains of even earlier structures below.

The earliest building on the site, provisionally dated c. 1000–50, is a three-aisled house that measures about 12 x 5 m (39 ft 6 in x 16 ft 6 in) internally. The walls were up to 1.9 m (6.3 ft) thick, and were built entirely from blocks of turf. Courses of turves laid horizontally separated others angled at 45 degrees, giving a herringbone effect. The side walls may have been about 1 m (3 ft 3 in) tall; the taller gable ends were probably faced internally with wooden panelling. The roof was made of wattles and long thin strips of turf, resting on horizontal wooden beams and large rafters. It was supported by two rows of wooden posts, thus creating the aisled appearance. In the central space, which was 15–20 cm (6–8 in) below the original ground surface, was a long hearth, while the two side aisles were made into raised wooden benches, about 1.5 m (5 ft) wide, for sitting and sleeping on. At the northern end, immediately beyond an

entrance door in one of the side walls, was a 2-m (6-ft-6-in) long kitchen area which contained a cooking pit and a barrel stand.

This is the first building of this type found in Greenland, and one of very few which have been interpreted as belonging to the early stages of the settlement. Among the objects found in this earliest phase of the farm is an important series of textile fragments, including items of wool, goats' hair and linen. Geological identification of the stone objects shows that most, including sharpening stones and a strike-a-light for making fire, were collected relatively close to the settlement. At least one, however, a chalcedony strike-a-light, probably comes from the Disko Bay area, about 600 km (375 miles) north of the farmstead. Perhaps it shows contacts with the Palaeo-Eskimo Dorset people.

Plan of the original turf-built farmhouse at the GUS site in Greenland. Later it was used as an animal shed; at that time it was abutted by a new pantry with evidence for the positions of storage barrels, with traces of a new house beyond.

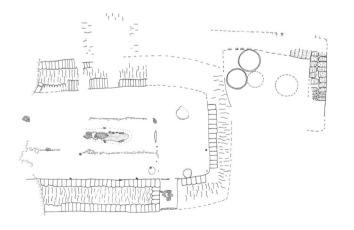

FURTHER WEST: VINLAND

The earliest writer to refer to lands west of Greenland was the monk Adam of Bremen, who wrote in c. 1070, recording information given to him by King Svein Estrithsson of Denmark (1047–74). Svein knew of 'another island discovered by many in that ocean. It is called Wineland because wild grapes grow there, producing the best wine. Unsown crops also grow there as we have learned not from fabulous conjecture but from reliable report of the Danes'.

Travellers' Tales?

Most famously, the thirteenth- and fourteenth-century authors of the *Saga of the Greenlanders* and *Eirik the Red's Saga* refer to these western lands, albeit in somewhat contradictory terms. Their discovery is attributed to an Icelander, Bjarni Herjolfsson, who in 986 set sail for Greenland but missed his landfall. Blown on westwards, Bjarni sighted a coastline with varied terrain but didn't land, and managed to sail safely back to Greenland. There, his story reached the ears of Greenland's founding father, Eirik the Red; and it was his son, Leif Eiriksson, who bought Bjarni's ship, enlisted some of his

crew, and set out to retrace Bjarni's route. He gave names to the different areas he encountered: *Helluland* ('flatstone land'), was probably part of Baffin Island, and *Markland* ('woodland') was probably an expanse of the Labrador coastline.

Eventually he located a more congenial place to establish a base camp which became known as *Leifsbuðir*, and spent the winter there. One of his crew, a German, is credited with recognizing the wild grapevines that prompted Leif to name the area *Vínland* ('wineland'). Next year Leif returned home; *en route* he rescued a shipwrecked crew, including the captain and his wife Gudrid, from a reef off Greenland. This added further lustre to his adventure and provided him with a nickname, Leif the Lucky.

Leif's brother Thorvald undertook the next expedition and again based himself at *Leifsbuðir*. The sojourn reportedly lasted over three winters before Thorvald went exploring further north and was killed by natives whom the explorers called *skraelings*. A third brother, Thorstein, who had married the now-widowed Gudrid, died before he could complete his attempt to maintain the

Épaves Bay ('Wreck Bay'), near the village of L'Anse aux Meadows, Newfoundland, where traces of Viking Age buildings have been excavated. Their outlines are displayed on the near side of the recreated building visible at centre right.

Eiriksson tradition. It was a wealthy Icelandic merchant called Thorfinn Karlsefni who became the next leader of a successful expedition to *Vínland*. He had sailed to Greenland, spent the winter at Brattahlid and married Thorstein's widow Gudrid. Together with a crew of 65, they followed Leif's sailing directions and arrived at *Leifsbuðir*. After two winters, the birth of a son called Snorre (the first white man to be born in North America), and two battles with *skraelings*, Thorfinn Karlsefni sailed back to Greenland; he went on eventually to settle in Iceland with Gudrid. The *Vínland* adventure ended, at least so far as the sagas were concerned, with a final voyage by Leif Eiriksson's sister, Freydis. Depicted as a woman beside whom Lady Macbeth would look cuddlesome, she too made use of *Leifsbuðir* before sailing back to Greenland with a much depleted crew.

L'Anse aux Meadows

The testimony of the sagas, coupled with a sixteenth-century Icelandic map of the north Atlantic upon which were marked *Helleland*, *Markland*, *Skraelinge Land* and *Promontorium Winlandiae* ('the *Vínland* promontory'), inspired the Norwegian Helge Ingstad to believe that traces of a Viking presence might be found in northern Newfoundland. Local residents eventually brought him to a site at L'Anse aux Meadows, on Épaves Bay, where the outlines of ancient buildings could be recognized. Épaves Bay faces westwards, with the coast of Labrador plainly visible just 50 km (31 miles) away, and despite the shallowness of the bay, this was a place favoured for occupation by native North Americans on several different occasions both before and after the year 1000.

Excavations by Anne Stine Ingstad during 1961–68 revealed evidence for this native occupation, but also identified eight buildings, together with about 125 artifacts, that were clearly not in the native tradition. The vast majority of these objects were iron nails, and the discovery of traces of an iron smithing furnace confirmed the presence of foreigners. The crucial item, however, was a copper-alloy dress pin of the type known as a ringed pin; this form of cloak fastener is widely distributed throughout the western sector of Viking activities, and is virtually a trademark of Viking presence. A glass bead, a soapstone spindle-whorl, a fragmentary bone needle and whetstones for sharpening fine objects like needles, all of which are characteristic of Scandinavian occupation sites elsewhere, confirm that the occupation is to be dated to the Viking Age.

Excavations undertaken by the Canadian Parks Service in 1973–76 investigated other parts of the site. Boggy areas had preserved organic objects, among them carpenters' wooden debris, lengths of rope made from spruce roots, and a birch-bark container. All of these, too, are acceptable in a North Atlantic Viking Age context; in particular, the wooden debris and the concentrated distribution of the nails suggest that ship repairing was one of the activities carried out here. Finally, a series of radiocarbon dates indicates that the site was occupied in the period 980–1020. All of this is compatible with the saga references to voyages around and just after the year 1000, and it does seem credible that L'Anse aux Meadows is the site of *Leifsbuðir*.

The buildings are of two main forms. Large multi-roomed structures, of the type known as halls, are interpreted as houses, albeit incorporating a workshop. Constructed of turf sods laid against a timber framework, and possibly panelled with wood on their inner faces, they had a central hearth, and low wooden platforms along the side walls which were used as beds and for sitting upon. The roofs were also made of turf sods, resting on an underlay of branches supported by the roof timbers. The function of smaller 'pit buildings', which were dug into the ground, is less easy to diagnose.

Small birch-bark container, sewn with spruce roots, found in the boggy area at L'Anse aux Meadows. Height 9 cm (3½ in).

Ringed pin of copper alloy (length 10 cm (4 in)) from the L'Anse aux Meadows site; the single object most telling of a Viking presence there. Similar objects have been found over much of the north-looking world.

OLAF IN MAINE

A late eleventh-century Norwegian coin found at Naskeag Point, near Brooklin, Maine; the only impeccable archaeological evidence for Viking contacts with the area of the modern USA.

The only Viking object from the United States of America which is both genuine and found in an ancient archaeological context is the so-called Maine penny. This is a silver coin with a cross motif on one side and an animal design on the other. Experts say that it was minted for the Norwegian King Olaf Kyrre (1067–93). It was found in 1957 during the excavation of a native American site at Naskeag Point near Brooklin in Maine, 1,250 km (775 miles) as the crow flies from L'Anse aux Meadows. The excavations established that a large settlement had been occupied there during the summer months over many centuries, c. 900–1500. One of its functions was as a trading place for goods collected from a widespread native trading network, extending from Labrador to Pennsylvania. As this native trade was carried on without using coins, the Maine penny's value was as a rarity, an unusual small piece of decorated metalwork, and the fact that it had been pierced by a small hole near its edge suggests that it had been worn as a pendant. It seems likely that the coin represents some form of contact between Scandinavians and natives, not necessarily in Maine, and that it had been brought to Naskeag Point and lost there by someone attending the annual jamboree. Its loss may have occurred in the late eleventh or twelfth century, thus demonstrating that contacts between the extremities of the Old World of Western Europe and the New World were not extinguished with the abandonment of *Leifsbuðir*.

Simulation of one of the halls excavated at L'Anse aux Meadows; compare with the interior of the Stong house shown on p.154.

One suggestion is that they served as living quarters for individuals of low status, such as slaves; another is that they were the very first buildings, quick and simple to erect when the explorers first arrived. Taking the three halls together, there could have been 70 to 90 people living there – more than enough to crew three ships. A few artifacts used in typically female activities, such as spinning, suggest that some women were present.

One hall incorporated a smithy, one a carpentry shop and one a shed for boat repair. Absent, however, were traces of the barns, byres or enclosures associated with farming livestock. Yet the recovery of three butternuts (white walnuts), which have never grown north of the St Lawrence valley, show that foodstuffs were being gathered from 800 km (500 miles) south of L'Anse aux Meadows.

It may have been there, too, that grapes were found – vines do not grow in north Newfoundland. The butternuts and wine suggest that *Vínland* included the south part of the Gulf of St Lawrence, including New Brunswick, Nova Scotia and, perhaps, Maine. Indeed, their presence may be the clearest indication of the site's function, as an explorers' and exploiters' base, a way-station from which to range out in search of valuable natural resources that could be brought back for storage at the depot before being shipped back the 3,200 km (2,000 miles) eastwards to Greenland, a voyage that could have taken anything from two weeks to two months.

Whether L'Anse aux Meadows is the site of *Leifsbuðir* or the base for other, unrecorded near-contemporary voyages to North America, all the signs are that Viking occupation there didn't last very long. Despite its attractions, the investment of manpower necessary to sustain a viable settled community, particularly in the face of hostile natives, was too much for the small population of Greenland.

Visits to North America by Greenlanders continued for several centuries, however, as is shown by the scatter of late Norse objects found at a variety of native sites, and by contemporary documentary references. But despite this, *Vínland* proved to be beyond the permanent reach of the Vikings.

A butternut found at L'Anse aux Meadows. Butternuts would not have grown north of the Gulf of St Lawrence; it thus demonstrates Viking contacts further south.

Reconstruction of a group of buildings excavated at L'Anse aux Meadows, Newfoundland.

VI • EXPRESSIONS OF IDENTITY: RELIGION AND ART

Religion and art were means by which the Vikings expressed and affirmed their identity; an identity with a pedigree that extended back well into the preceding centuries. 'Viking' religion was not an invention of the Viking Age, but a development of the common inheritance of Germanic northwest Europe. Key elements can be traced as far back as the Early Iron Age; the Roman writer Tacitus recorded some of its essence in the first century AD. It celebrated aspects of the natural world and of the human condition – elemental forces such as fertility, natural phenomena such as thunder, human wisdom, prowess in battle – matters that were of common concern across large tracts of the ancient world. Similarly, artists and craftsmen of the Viking Age drew on a common Germanic artistic legacy, adopting and adapting elements that were centuries old. Well-known motifs were expressed in a succession of new styles that maintained the identity of tradition while imbuing it with new resonances.

A mystical link between Viking Age religion and artistic craftsmanship is that of the shape-changer. In the supernatural realm the powerful god Odin was able to assume the form of others; and this attribute may sometimes have been reflected in the rites and rituals of worship. Meanwhile, in the real world, it was craftsmen who were the shape-changers. Carvers, for example, gave form and meaning to shapeless blocks of raw material. Metalworkers were doubly potent in this regard, transmuting ores into metals before fashioning them into shapes and, where appropriate, finishing them with elaborate decoration. Indeed, such were the skills and powers associated with the arts and crafts of smithing that they were celebrated in mythological stories such as that of Völund the smith. Völund, also known as Weland or Wayland, married a Valkyrie, but then lost his bride and was captured and hamstrung by a cruel king. He gained his revenge by killing the king's sons and making drinking vessels from their skulls, by ravishing the king's wife, and then escaping through the air, on wings that he had fashioned himself.

Embroidery of wool on a linen background from Skog church, Hälsingland, Sweden. The three figures are believed to have dual meanings. They simultaneously represent (from left to right) the saintly kings Olaf Haraldsson (1015–30), Knut IV of Denmark (1080–86) and Erik IX of Sweden (1150–60), and the pagan gods Odin (next to the tree on which he was hung), Thor (holding a hammer-like cross) and Frey (holding an ear of corn representing fertility).

A PAGAN WORLD

When the first Viking raiders struck, Scandinavia was outside the Christian network, beyond the boundaries of bishoprics. For their Christian victims, paganism was one of the Vikings' defining characteristics, something that differentiated them from almost all other near neighbours; English and Irish chroniclers referred to their enemies as *pagani*. Although Christian missionaries operated in all the Scandinavian countries from the ninth century onwards, and Viking traders and settlers became increasingly familiar with Christian customs and beliefs, heathens they remained until the Danes officially accepted Christianity in the mid-tenth century, and the Norwegians and Swedes followed suit in the years around 1000.

The Vikings did not worship a single all-powerful deity, but honoured a plethora of gods and goddesses among whom some were pre-eminent. The gods' supernatural counterparts and adversaries were the giants, together with an assortment of monsters and dwarfs. Gods, humans, giants, dwarves and all other forms of Norse mythic life inhabited a complex cosmic world that was divided into many parts. The centre of the entire universe was *Yggdrasil*, the great sacred ash tree that spanned the cosmos. Miðgard, literally 'the enclosure in the middle' where humans lived, was created around the tree, and it, in turn, was surrounded by ocean, in which lived Jörmungand, the world-encircling serpent. The gods lived in Ásgard, close to but distinct from Miðgard; some giants dwelt in Jötunheim ('giant home'), separated from Miðgard by various rivers, and others lived with trolls and other

SOURCES FOR THE SUPERNATURAL

There are no detailed contemporary descriptions of Viking Age religious beliefs or practices in Scandinavia. The most coherent account of Old Norse paganism was written in about 1220–30 by the Icelandic nobleman Snorre Sturluson. In a prose work he called *Edda* ('Poetics') he presented the pantheon of Viking gods and a cosmology of their universe, introducing it from his Christian perspective as a rational but misguided attempt to explain the world's natural forces. Glimpses into this supernatural world are also provided by the so-called *Poetic Edda*, a collection of 29 poems on gods and heroes written down in Iceland between 1250 and 1300. When and where these 'Eddic' poems were originally composed is highly debatable, and some seem to date from the Christian rather than the pagan era. They may therefore have been influenced by stories from the Christian Bible or by other aspects of

contemporary Christian thinking. Skaldic verses – carefully contrived, highly allusive riddle-like poetry composed by Viking Age skalds (court poets) – are yet another source of mythological and religious nuggets, and some offer the earliest indigenous written references to Scandinavian pagan beliefs and practices.

An Icelandic manuscript of c. 1680 (Árni Magnússon Institute AM 738 4to) contains an illustrated version of Snorre's Edda. Left: Valhalla, guarded by the gods' watchman, Heimdall, and with the mythical goat Heidrún on the roof. Right: the world serpent Jörmundgand is hooked by Thor's fishing line baited with an ox head (compare with the illustration on p.113).

unspeakably horrible creatures in Útgard on the outer fringes of the cosmos.

This sacred world was not static and frozen, but incorporated a dimension of time. The world had been created from a great void called *Ginnungagap*, and the present order would end in apocalyptic destruction at *Ragnarök*, after which a new world would arise. Renewal of a sort was also available to individual Viking warriors who died after showing great valour in battle. They would be chosen by the Valkyries, female assistants of the powerful god Odin, and join the feasting in Odin's great hall, Valhalla. For others, death took them to an under world called Hel.

Adam of Bremen, writing in *c*. 1070 on the basis of information provided by King Svein Estrithsson of Denmark, recounts that a pagan temple at Uppsala in Sweden contained images of three great gods, Odin, Thor and Frey; and other written sources combine to indicate the characteristics attributed to these gods. The most important god was Odin (known to the Anglo-Saxons as Woden, the god after whom Wednesday is named). He had forfeited one eye in return for a drink from the well of wit and wisdom; and he had been willing to be hanged in order to acquire and understand the esoteric magical powers of runes. In keeping with this thirst for knowledge, he had two ravens, Hugin and Munin, who brought him news from all corners of the world. Odin was the god of battle, able to change his shape, a cunning deceiver, the god of poetry and of numerous other aspects of life.

Thor, the thunderer, the killer of giants with his magic hammer, was the second great figure of the Viking pantheon (Thursday is his day). Straightforward and reliable, neither as clever nor as deceitful as Odin, he was a game for anything. In a drinking contest with the giants he was given a drinking horn with its tip in the sea, yet still managed to swallow so much that the tide ebbed. On a fishing trip with a giant he hooked the fearsome World Serpent and would have hauled it from the deep if the frightened giant hadn't cut his line. An Eddic poem claims 'Odin gets the noblemen who fall in slaughter, but Thor gets the kin of slaves', thus suggesting that Thor was the popular god of Everyman. Miniature Thor's hammers, usually made of silver and suspended around the neck, were certainly the most popular amulets of the

Panel from the cross shaft at St Martin's church, Kirklevington, North Yorkshire, England. Odin with his ravens perched on his shoulder, or Christian iconography?

Viking Age, worn by warriors such as the one buried at Repton, Derbyshire in 873 or 874 (see p. 38). Even today, Thor is common as an element in Scandinavian men's Christian names.

The third principal Viking god was Frey, chief of the fertility gods, and brother of Freyja, goddess of love and sex. Frey was the god of favourable weather needed to ensure good harvests and abundant produce, and by extension he was associated with wealth and general prosperity. A famous phallic figurine from Rällinge, Södermanland, Sweden, is thought to represent Frey.

Cult Sites

Despite the broad commonality of religious belief across Scandinavia that is detectable in the documentary and other sources, there is no suggestion that there was any uniformity of cult, rites or ritual imposed by a centralized priesthood. The very concept of a separate priesthood seems to have been alien; instead, there are references in later Icelandic sources to a class called

Copper alloy bearded and helmeted figurine from Rällinge, Södermanland, Sweden, its prominent phallus suggestive of fertility and thus of the god Frey. Height 6.9 cm (2³/₄ in).

(Opposite) Copper-alloy mount (c. 3 x 6 cm (c. 1¼ x 2⅓ in)) from a man's cremation grave of c. 700 at Solberga, Östergötland, Sweden, showing a man paddling/steering a boat and fishing; his line is grasped by a creature with hair knotted in a female style. This may represent Thor fishing for the world serpent (compare with the illustrations on pp. 166 and 113).

goðar who exercised both secular and religious responsibilities. Chieftains and kings convened and led large-scale sacral functions on a local, regional or national level, while family devotions of whatever sort were probably at the behest of the head of the household. Some religious festivals and ceremonies took place in the open air, for example in sacred groves of trees, commemorated in the place name lund; but because political and religious leadership was the joint function of local chieftains, their homes or estate centres doubled

as focal points for religious ceremonies. Indeed, a skaldic verse written in c. 980 describes mythological pictures decorating the hall of an Icelandic chieftain in the generation before the official conversion to Christianity.

In terms of tangible archaeological evidence, buildings and objects excavated at Storagård ('the big farm enclosure'), Tissø, in western Sjaelland, Denmark, are plausibly interpreted as the remains of one such cult centre. Both the name Tissø, which means 'Tyr's [a war god's] lake', and finds

PICTURING THE GODS

On the island of Gotland, off the eastern coast of Sweden, is a collection of about 450 decorated stones that are unique in the Viking world.

There is virtually no independent dating evidence for the stones, but a fragment of one of the earliest type was found discarded in a grave that also contained fifth-century brooches, while at the other end of the sequence some have designs incorporating Christian-influenced cross motifs. A few include inscriptions dated by expert runologists to the tenth or

eleventh centuries, but an assessment of when most of these stones were erected depends solely upon artistic criteria of style and content. Virtually all have been moved from their original location, but the earlier ones, which belong to the pre-Viking period, may have served as grave markers. The later stones were erected, sometimes in pairs or groups, as memorials or markers in the landscape.

The slabs are mostly limestone, and up to 3 m (10 ft) tall. Their shapes vary; the earliest are nearly rectangular

with a slightly convex top and slightly concave sides, like a slightly flared axe-head; the majority, which date perhaps to the eighth to eleventh centuries, are often described as phallic- or mushroom-shaped. Their distinctive shape also resembles that of the doors of the famous Norwegian stave churches, and so it has been suggested that the stones represent 'doors' to another world. Their decoration took the form of horizontal bands of motifs, incised and originally highlighted with coloured pigments.

Few original examples of colour have survived, but there are some traces of black and red, and the monuments must have been of very striking appearance. The motifs on the Viking Age stones include ships with remarkable details such as rigging, warriors fighting, and other human figures in a wide array of clothing.

Supernatural or mythical scenes can also be identified, for some of the figures have recognizable attributes – Odin's eight-legged horse Sleipnir, Valkyries, and winged figures who may be either Odin or Völund, the flying smith. These stones are thus an important pictorial source for how the Viking Age portrayed its myths.

Picture stone from Tjängvide 1, Alskog, Gotland, Sweden. A female, presumably a Valkyrie (left), offers a drinking horn to the rider of an eight-legged horse, which must be Sleipnir, the mount of Odin. This may represent the welcoming of the dead to Valhalla.

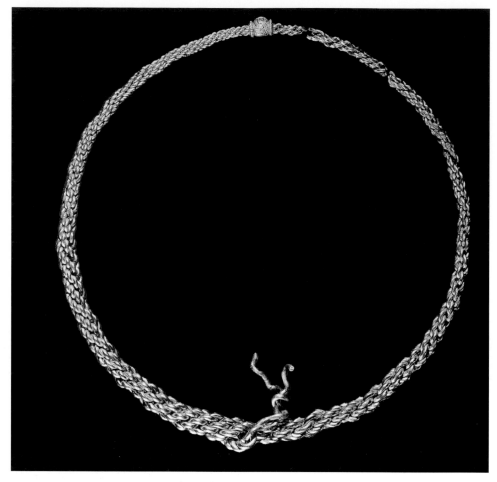

Gold neck-ring made of four double-twisted rods; one half of one of these rods was removed in antiquity (from bottom to top right). Maximum diameter 32 cm (12¹/₂ in). Found by chance in 1977 at Tissø, Sjaelland, Denmark.

Lucky charms in the shape of a Thor's hammer were popular forms of jewelry (see also p. 107). This is one of the more elaborate examples, made of silver and ornamented carefully with ring-and-dot ornament.

of weapons which may have been ritual deposits in that lake, suggest that there was a religious focus in the vicinity. Large-scale excavations at Tissø have revealed that the site, the estate centre of a local or regional dynasty, fulfilled a range of functions from the 600s to the 1100s. There is copious evidence for large-scale craft activities, notably smithing; there are highly prestigious objects such as a gold neck-ring weighing over 1.8 kg (4 lb); and evidence for trade and foreign contacts includes a Byzantine lead seal of a type found at the international trading sites of Ribe and Hedeby (see p. 23 and p. 60).

Each successive rebuilding of the site's focus included an impressive hall building. In its earliest form, in the seventh to eighth centuries (the immediately pre-Viking era), this hall measured 36 by 11.2 m (118 x 36 ft 9 in); its main timbers were set in massive post-holes 3 m (10 ft) deep that suggest some very special and imposing form of construction. Off one end of the hall was an enclosure containing another building, and it is thought that this part of the complex was the focus of cult activities. A similar layout of hall and adjacent enclosure was maintained into the ninth and tenth centuries; 25 Thor's hammer amulets, and cult figurines of Odin, Thor and Tyr, were found in this area. In a final phase of rebuilding in the tenth to eleventh century these two focal buildings were each given new constructional and architectural forms, and a multi-chambered building on the supposed cult site may be its replacement as a church.

Elsewhere, at structurally impressive sites that may also have served as chieftains' farms, other types of archaeological discoveries have been interpreted as aspects of pagan ritual. For example, concentrations of animal bones may represent the remains of sacrifices and/or ritual feasting. Tiny rectangular sheets of gold, decorated with human and fantastic figures, have been found in the postholes of buildings dating to the beginning of the Viking Age; they may have been deliberately placed there as votive deposits to emphasize and reinforce the ritual aspects of the buildings' use (see p. 11).

THE SIGURD SAGA

The Viking myths deal not only with deities but also with heroes, men of superhuman qualities who were favoured by the gods. Among the best-known heroes is Sigurd the Volsung, slayer of the dragon Fafnir, winner of a great treasure hoard, and tragic lover of the Valkyrie Brynhild. The narrative story of Sigurd's deeds is known from Eddic poems and from Volsunga Saga, and scenes from it are found carved as accompaniments to several Christian runic inscriptions in Scandinavia. But Sigurd was a popular figure whose epic travelled early and travelled well across the Viking world. Tenth-century carvings from the Isle of Man clearly depict episodes from the Sigurd saga, notably Sigurd roasting of the dragon's heart, and sucking his thumb after burning it on the roasting spit. These scenes were critical to the story because, through contact with the dragon's blood, Sigurd gained the power to understand the twittering of the birds in the trees around him. Their song alerted him to a treacherous attack by his foster-father; forewarned, he was able to foil it. The thumb-sucking also occurs on a fragment of a contemporary carving from Ripon cathedral, Yorkshire; as a hero defeating evil, an analogy of Christ, Sigurd was welcome in a Christian milieu.

(Right) Detail from the cross-slab at Andreas, Isle of Man, showing the hero Sigurd roasting doughnut-shaped slices of the dragon Fafnir's heart on a spit over a triple-tongued flame.

(Below) Scenes from the story of Sigurd incised into the rock at Ramsund in Sweden. Sigurd, at bottom right, slices his sword into the dragon Fafnir. The runic inscription records the building of a bridge to assist Christian salvation in the next world. The panel is 4.7 m (15 ft 5 in) wide.

Consigned to the Other World

Ritual is most tangibly presented in the graves and cemeteries that have been discovered throughout Scandinavia. The sites that have been investigated must represent only a small proportion of the burial grounds in use at some time during the Viking Age, just as the number of individual graves that has been excavated scientifically can be only a tiny fraction of the Viking Age population. Yet there is an enormous variety of burial rites. Some corpses were cremated, others were buried in inhumation graves. Ashes could be placed in a container, heaped in a pile, or scattered across the burial site; bodies could be laid in a range of postures, within or without any coffin or bier, oriented in any direction, placed singly or in groups, and accompanied by any or none of a wide range of grave goods, some of which might be deliberately 'killed' by being bent and made unusable. Graves might be advertised with a memorial of stone or timber, contained within a kerb of stones that might be one of several possible shapes, and/or covered by a cairn or mound; they might be disposed singly, within a family group or be part of a large cemetery.

Regional custom, social class and current politics were among the factors that determined the nature of an individual's burial rites. Social class is sometimes reflected in the magnificence of the rites – the amount of wealth disposed of in the grave goods, the amount of effort put into creating the grave and its marker. It is this conspicuous consumption that encourages the categorization of graves as 'royal', 'aristocratic', 'chieftain's', and so on. Women's graves – identifiable on the basis of osteology and by the range of grave goods – include some in the richest stratum.

The importance of regional custom can be seen when comparing the burial rites recorded from across Scandinavia. On the island of Öland, close to the eastern coast of Sweden, cremation and inhumation seem to have been utilized contemporaneously, while on the island of Bornholm, further south, only inhumation, often within elaborately patterned stone settings, was practised.

Islands, of course, lend themselves to the development of distinctive practices; compare the 'island' north of the Limfjord in Jutland, where cremation was the norm, with the emphasis on inhumation in the remainder of that peninsula. And yet the adjacent large Danish islands of Fyn and Sjaelland shared broadly similar inhumation rituals to 'mainland' Jutland, and so too did the southwest corner of Scånia, now part of Sweden but often under Danish control in the Viking Age. The reasons for these variations are not yet well understood.

A Witch and a Warlock

In a cemetery of about 30 graves found just outside the late tenth-century circular fortified enclosure at Fyrkat, in Jutland (see p. 187), one female burial stood out. Laid in a wagon-body (a well-known if very occasional form of coffin or bier), she had none of the standard types of Viking Age female jewelry with her, but instead there was a wide range of other objects. Some of them, including two silver toe-rings, which are wholly exceptional, and a bronze box-brooch of Gotlandic form, suggest that she may have come from the eastern Baltic.

Below her waist, and probably hung originally from a belt, was a series of small items. Many appear to be amulets or charms, including a

Box brooch made from gilt bronze and silver, from Gotland, found with other unusual items with the female burial in Grave 4 at Fyrkat, Jutland, Denmark. Diameter 5.8 cm (2¼ in).

miniature silver chair of a type found in other unusual female graves in Scandinavia. By her side were an iron roasting spit and a wooden staff, and two drinking horns. At her feet an elaborate wooden box contained textiles, above which were a pig's jaw and a clump of owl pellets. Here, too, were tiny fragments of what may have been a ritual metal staff – a composite bundle of rods with knobs at intervals along it. Such items are extremely rare but occur, like the miniature chairs, in unusual female graves.

One final remarkable discovery was several hundred seeds of the plant henbane (*Hyoscamus* sp.), perhaps originally contained in a sheepskin pouch. Henbane is a potent potion. Applied as an ointment, it can give the effect of flying; vaporized, it induces drowsiness. The presence of so many exceptional objects among this collection,

particularly the amulets, pig's jaw, owl pellets and henbane, suggest that they represent the apparatus of a priestess, a seer, someone in touch with the other world.

Even centuries after Christianity had been officially accepted, the power of pagan or heathen belief can still be detected. At Hvidegården by Lyngby, near Copenhagen, in a man's grave dated to c. 1200, was a purse containing a goshawk's claw, a grass snake's tail, a Mediterranean conch shell, a fragment of mussel shell, a small wooden cube, an amber bead fragment, pebbles wrapped in a pigeon's gut, and the lower jaw of a young squirrel. These items have no practical value, but may have been some form of key to the supernatural, perhaps related to divining the future.

The cemetery at Lindholm Høje, Jutland, Denmark has graves marked with stones in a variety of forms, including ship-shaped settings.

ART AND CRAFT MYSTERIES

The myths and cults of the Viking world certainly required and encouraged the talents of a range of craftsmen. Their skills were deployed, for example, in the creation of cult figures, memorials and amulets. At some cult sites, such as Borg in Östergötland, Sweden, craftsmen seem to have worked near the focus of worship, in this instance making amulets. Yet these craftsmen, like the rituals themselves, must have been controlled by local chieftains who had an underlying political motive. Their objective was to bolster the hierarchy of social stratification that underpinned the cult practices and their own pre-eminent position; and they recognized that this hierarchy could be reinforced and society manipulated through the craftsmen's products. The chieftains accrued prestige both by patronizing skilled craftspeople capable of contriving lavish and elaborate items, and also through having access to the raw materials that the craftsmen worked. So while the

inclusion of smiths' tools such as tongs and hammers in some high-status Viking graves may reflect personal prowess in these arts, a more important signal from their presence may have been that the dead person (and his kin) controlled key resources. Aristocratic patronage underpinned the artistry and craftsmanship of the Viking world; status and authority were asserted through the products of the craftsmen.

Animal Instincts

The single dominant motif common to the three centuries of Viking art is an animal; hence the art is described as zoomorphic. The beast went through a great variety of transformations during these centuries, and in many examples it is impossible to determine what family of the animal kingdom is represented, let alone what species, for this is an abstract and allusive art. There are occasional instances of naturalistic representation in Viking

Sixth-century gold bracteate from Åsum, Skåne, Sweden, its suspension loop broken from its top in antiquity. The figure riding a horse at the centre is almost overwhelmed by the mass of concentric circles around it.

Age art, but the norm was an interlaced mesh of convoluted and stylized elements. Viking artistic taste was fashioned by the same influences that permeated much of Europe; the raiders and the raided shared many common artistic conventions, themes, motifs and treatments.

The ancestry of this zoomorphic art can be traced back to quadrupeds that appear as part of the decorative scheme on some of the thin, circular medallion-like objects known as bracteates, decorated on one side only, which were made in Scandinavia from about 450 to 550 (see p. 17). These gold objects were clearly based upon late Roman gold coins and medallions, for some of them have copied the human busts of their models. Other provincial Roman objects that had reached Scandinavia were also decorated with animal designs, and together they provided the underlying inspiration for what was to be an enduring fashion, not only in Scandinavia but all over the Germanic areas of Europe, including Anglo-Saxon England, as well as Celtic areas such as Ireland and Scotland.

Styles I and II

The first main transmogrification of this Roman-influenced Germanic art in Scandinavia is contemporary with the bracteates. Known to archaeologists as Style I, the principal component is a single animal, often so contorted in order to make it fit the available space that its zoomorphic essence is almost lost. Additionally, the Scandinavian craftsmen had adopted a late Roman decorative technique called chip-carving, in which V- or wedge-shaped incisions and notches are used to define and ornament the design. This can be imitated in cast metalworking as well as in the woodcarving from which it originated; it gave metalwork a glittering and faceted appearance, but also contributes to the difficulty in recognizing that the design is animal-based, for it characteristically dismembered the beasts into angular blocks.

By the late sixth century the more rhythmical and symmetrical Style II had been introduced to Scandinavia, as it was all over the Germanic world. Its geometric interlaced designs are much more comprehensible and, once the viewer has come to understand the stylistic conventions, the animal elements stand out. Over the next century and a

half, master craftsmen across Scandinavia developed a wide range of further variations on the animal ornament theme. These, in turn, led on to the repertoire that was current at the start of the Viking Age, between c. 750 and 850.

Viking Age Art Styles

Viking Age art styles have traditionally been defined by key objects of high artistry which embody the particular characteristics and conventions of their group. The six successive styles now differentiated have been named after the places of ritual – burials, memorials, a church – where these key objects were found. Three of the styles were defined by archetypal objects made from metals, and one by a series of carved stone monuments. This ratio of three to one hardly mirrors the relative rarity of stone carving until the later stages of the Viking Age, and it is metalworking that has provided most of the evidence for Viking art. Remarkably, the contemporary styles at either end of the Viking Age were defined partly or wholly in relation to woodcarvings.

However, this importance of woodcarving in terms of labelling styles hides the fact that the artistic skills of the woodcarver, together with those of craftsmen and women working in other organic materials, notably leather and textile, are grossly under-represented in the archaeological record. The only organic materials to be adequately represented are animal bone, deer antler and morse ivory; the former two were so commonly available as to be utilized for mundane items, whereas walrus ivory was a luxury good, retained for high-status objects.

Two discoveries have come to represent artistic taste in the period 750–850. They are a group of gilt bronze metal mounts from Broa, on the Swedish island of Gotland, and the assemblage of objects found in the magnificent ship burial at Oseberg, on the west side of Oslo Fjord in Norway. The precise dating of the Broa mounts is a matter of art-historical judgment; in contrast, recent advances in tree-ring dating have proved that the Oseberg ship, with its important carved decoration along the prow- and stern-posts, was built in about 820, and that the burial itself took place in 834. Together with S-shaped animals that have ribbon-like bodies, semi-naturalistic animals and birds, and simple stylized human face masks, a

(Top) Style I animal interlace on the hilt of a sixth-century ring sword found in Grave V at Snartemo, Vest Agder, Norway.

(Centre) Gilt bronze animal mask on a strap end from Vendel, Sweden. Two garnets form the eyes of a large animal head; they each also mark the hips of Style II animals whose heads are at the base of the design.

(Above) Gilt silver brooch from Rinkaby, Skåne, Sweden, with a mask-like animal face typical of Borre-style art at its four corners.

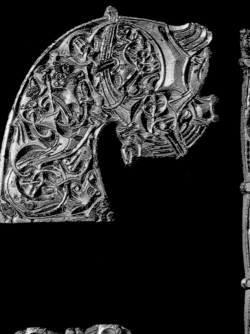

totally new element now takes its place in the artists' repertoire. This was the so-called 'gripping beast', named because it characteristically grasps either itself, an adjacent animal, or the frame within which it is portrayed.

The form of the beast varies enormously – it includes the wraith-like humanesque figures on the Oseberg ship's prow, and the three-dimensional beasts of the 'Carolingian' head-post, also from Oseberg. They presumably emanate from several different craftsmen or workshops, and demonstrate that items of very different appearance could be equally fashionable.

Around the mid-ninth century, at the time when Scandinavians were establishing their Irish *longphoirt*, settling in Scotland and intensifying their attacks on England, Scandinavian tastes were turning to new stylistic developments defined as the Borre style. The name comes from another ship burial in the Oslo Fjord area, where a series of gilt-bronze mounts was found. Gripping beasts remain part of the repertoire; so too are ribbon-bodied animals, often with their heads turned backwards and lightly entwined with narrow bands called lappets that spring from their bodies. Taut, symmetrical knotwork, exemplified by the so-called 'ring chain', is a trademark of this style, as are small animal masks seen full face.

The later ninth to mid-tenth centuries, the era that encompassed the Viking settlements in England and Ireland, brought out the beast in Scandinavian art in what is known as the Jellinge style. The archetypal object comes from the royal burial at Jelling, Jutland, Denmark, where the

(Opposite) Copper-alloy bridle mounts from Broa, Gotland, Sweden. Animal ornament, identifiable from the face masks of the various beasts, is contained within precisely defined geometric shapes. A particularly obvious 'gripping beast' motif, a paw grasping the frame, is seen at bottom centre.

(Left) The prow of the ship from Oseberg, Vestfold, Norway, carved in c. 820 with animal interlace. There are also human figures, but they are out of sight, on the tingl that connected the port and starboard sides.

(Bottom left) The Jellinge style of art, characterized by ribbon-like animals, was popular in the period c.875–950, and takes its name from the silver cup deposited in 958/9 in the burial at Jelling, Jutland, Denmark. Height: 4.2 cm (1⅝ in).

burial chamber has a tree-ring date of 958–59. It is a small silver cup, with undulating, ribbon-bodied animals entwined around its bowl. Each creature has a pigtail lappet springing from the back of its head, which is seen in profile, and another lappet curls from its upper lip. The animal's body is outlined by double contour lines, with the central strip infilled with pelleting. All we know about the date of the cup's manufacture is that it was before 958–59, but a definitely earlier manifestation of the style is found in yet another of the Oslo Fjord ship burials, this time the one at Gokstad. There a bed-post or tent-post, decorated with a typical Jellinge-style animal head, is dated by dendrochronology to 895–96.

The single animal motif continued to dominate in the period 950–1000. It was the design inlaid with silver into an iron axehead found in an aristocratic grave at Mammen in north-central Jutland, Denmark, which gave the Mammen style its name; the wooden chamber containing the burial there was made of timber cut down in the winter of 970–71. The double-contoured animal became fuller bodied, prominent spirals joined legs to body and, diagnostically, plant-like tendrils entered the repertoire. Symmetry was of no concern. The fact that the creature on the Mammen axe is usually described as a bird serves as a reminder that a naturalist would struggle to identify many of these creatures. The design on the other face of this axe has no recognizable animal characteristics, being composed solely of vegetable tendrils. It may represent the mythological world tree, *Yggdrasil*, or the Christian tree of life; the bird, too, could be interpreted as either Christian or pagan in meaning. Once again the link between art and belief is present, as it is with the more majestic and more recognizable beast of Mammen form that is entwined with a snake or serpent on one face of the great stone monument further south in the Jutland peninsula, at Jelling (see pp. 182–184).

Developing seamlessly out of the Mammen animal was the great beast of Ringerike style, named

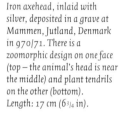

Iron axehead, inlaid with silver, deposited in a grave at Mammen, Jutland, Denmark in 970/71. There is a zoomorphic design on one face (top – the animal's head is near the middle) and plant tendrils on the other (bottom). Length: 17 cm (6¾ in).

Gilt bronze ship's prow vane from Heggen, Modum, Buskerud, Norway, decorated with two splendid Ringerike-style beasts replete with tendrils. Width 27.8 cm (11 in).

Openwork silver brooch in the Urnes style, c. 1100, from Tröllaskógur, Rangarvallasysla, Iceland. Height 4 cm (1½ in).

after a series of carvings on sandstone slabs from the Ringerike area, near Oslo, Norway. This was the art style fashionable during the first half of the eleventh century, and it is associated particularly with the reign of King Cnut, who introduced it to England. Tendrils continued to be important design elements, although they were sometimes clustered in groups or clumps; spirals retained their prominence, the animal body was still double-contoured, and sometimes the entwined snake was also present.

As the eleventh century wore on a more graceful interlace came into favour, represented on a grand scale by carved wooden panels from an earlier building that were incorporated into the twelfth-century church at Urnes (see p. 185), in the Sogne-fjord area of western Norway. A sinuous quad-ruped, delicate yet energetic like a greyhound, with fine spiral hips and pointed-almond eye, is enmeshed with and bites on a somewhat slimmer version of itself. This second beast has a similar head to the quadruped but only one front leg, and just a foot where its rear limb might be. The third creature in the Urnes menagerie is a snake-like tendril that weaves and loops between the other two. The style occurs also on a series of Swedish rune stones, and formed the basis for elegant openwork brooches that were popular across Scandinavia and in Britain well into the twelfth century, beyond the end of the Viking Age.

Five generations of a single royal dynasty span the peak of Danish Viking Age power in the decades to either side of the year 1000, and lay the foundations of the medieval kingdom of Denmark. This was an era when kingly power was made even more visible than it had been previously – in military might, in administrative control, in economic regeneration and in religious change. All of these developments have left major monuments, and the investigations which archaeologists have undertaken, particularly over the last few decades, have yielded important results that have redefined our understanding of the aspirations and achievements of Viking Age kings. It was also a time when Viking attacks on England recommenced; these evolved into major invasions and, ultimately, met with unprecedented success. King Cnut (now more familiar in England as Canute) became the ruler of a large slice of Scandinavia as well as of England.

His English successes had measurable impacts in Denmark; in 1018 his disbanded army brought 82,500 pounds of silver home with it, together with a heightened appreciation of Anglo-Saxon town life, coinage and other socio-political and economic traits. This transfusion of silver and ideas led, for example, to the introduction of Anglo-Saxon mint masters to create a new coinage for Cnut in Denmark, and the appearance of relatively mundane English goods and fashions at Danish sites such as Viborg – tangible evidence for the reality of a 'Viking world' around the North Sea in the early eleventh century.

Bound figure of Christ on the large rune stone from Jelling, Jutland, Denmark, ordered by King Harald Bluetooth and carved in the period c. 960–8.

THE CULT OF KINGS AT JELLING

To judge by the impressive monuments raised by him and for him, the foundations of the later Viking Age Danish state were laid by King Gorm. It was he who commissioned a rune stone at Jelling, in central Jutland, that includes the earliest recorded use of the name Denmark: 'King Gorm made this monument in memory of Thyre his wife, Denmark's adornment'.

Gorm and Thyre were later commemorated by their son, King Harald Bluetooth, who raised a larger and spectacularly ornamented runic monument at Jelling. The inscription proclaims Harald's triumphs: 'King Harald commanded this monument to be made in memory of Gorm his father and in memory of Thyre his mother – that Harald who won the whole of Denmark for himself and Norway and made the Danes Christian'.

These rune stones are the main clues to the significance of a remarkable complex of monuments among which they stand. Harald's stone is positioned exactly midway between the two largest mounds in Denmark. The southern mound, now 77 m (250 ft) in diameter and 11 m (36 ft) tall, is marginally the bigger. Excavations in 1861 and 1942 found no trace of any grave within or below it, although a large post had been implanted into its summit. It seems most likely, therefore, that it was designed as a memorial.

The northern mound was first examined in the 1820s, and was investigated again in 1861 and 1942. At its core is a small earlier mound that marks the northern end of an enormous ship-shaped stone setting. The setting was obliterated when this earlier mound was massively enlarged and encased in turf in the Viking Age. Inside it a timber-lined chamber grave was constructed with a wooden roof, walls and floor. Dendrochronological dating of samples from the chamber has proved that the timbers were felled in 958–59, and this is assumed to be the date both of the chamber's construction and of its former occupant's death. The southern mound, which also lies over part of the ship setting, is thought to be approximately contemporary.

The chamber grave had been broken into and emptied in antiquity. However, the little that was left behind reveals that the chamber had contained sumptuous furnishings. The most famous

Two faces of the three-sided stone at Jelling, Jutland, Denmark, carved by order of King Harald Bluetooth in the period c. 960–85. The animal design is in the Mammen style, a progression from the ribbon animal of the Jelling cup (see p.177) towards the full-bodied Ringerike beast (see p.179). The inscription on the second face records that Harald raised the monument in memory of his parents, and that he made Denmark Christian.

surviving object is a small silver goblet with an animal design engraved around its bowl (see p. 177). The Jellinge art style takes its name from this piece. More unusual still are fragments of carved wood, painted in yellow and red. They include pieces of openwork interlace design and another representing a human figure, but their function isn't clear. Other small items of horse-riding equipment indicate that this was the grave of a man who had been buried in a traditional, pre-Christian fashion. The

obvious suggestion, given the date, is that this was the original resting place of King Gorm.

The other component of the Jelling monument complex is the stone-built church which stands just to the north of Harald's rune stone. Although this church was built around AD 1100, excavations in 1976–79 revealed that there are traces of three successive timber churches below it. The earliest of these, which may go back to the time of Harald Bluetooth, was the largest. Indeed, it is much

The great stone at Jelling, Jutland, and the smaller rune stone raised by King Gorm in memory of his wife. There are three lines of runes on the hidden face of Gorm's stone; the visible line, read from bottom to top, contains in its middle, between two sets of double dots, the earliest use of the name Denmark. Height of Gorm's stone: 1.40 m (4 ft 7 in).

larger than other early timber churches in Scandinavia, and on a scale appropriate for a royal church. Remarkably, below its eastern end was a chamber grave, like that in the northern mound; within the chamber was the skeleton of a strongly built man who had been about 1.70 m (5 ft 7 in) tall. Associated traces of gold wire, representing garments of the highest quality, and small silver ornaments made and decorated in the style of the goblet found in the northern mound, all re-emphasize the importance of this individual. Yet his bones were found in jumbled disorder. The explanation may be that these are the remains of King Gorm, exhumed from his pagan burial place in the northern mound and re-interred in accord with the new religion promulgated by his Christian son King Harald. If this is so, however, why weren't Queen Thyre's remains treated in the same manner? Her place of burial remains stubbornly problematic.

The ceremonial complex at Jelling, Jutland, Denmark. From bottom left: the south mound, from which six stones of the earlier setting protrude; the church, with the two rune stones outside its south porch; the north mound, site of an emptied chamber grave.

CHRISTIAN VIKINGS

Although Harald Bluetooth boasted that he made the Danes Christian, this was not the earliest infiltration of Christianity into Scandinavia. The German monk Ansgar, eventually archbishop of Hamburg and Bremen, undertook some missions himself to Denmark and Sweden between 826 and 865, and also promoted other missionary work there.

Widukind of Corvey, a contemporary of Harald Bluetooth, wrote that the Danes had long been Christian but that they still worshipped old gods; a state of belief similar to that of some of the earlier Scandinavian settlers in the British Isles, who assimilated elements of Christianity with their pagan beliefs. Indeed, the familiarity with Christianity that resulted from raiding, trading and settling overseas assisted the accommodation of the new religion back in Scandinavia; all of the early missionaries to Scandinavia came from either Francia or England, two areas that had been heavily exposed to the Vikings.

Among the reasons why Christianity appealed to Scandinavian kings was that it allowed them to take control of local and regional religion away from the petty chiefs and aristocrats who lead the worship in pagan religion. Simultaneously it bolstered their own authority through being seen as God's anointed one. Kings could use the bishops whom they sanctioned to unify belief and minimize regional fragmentation; and becoming Christian took away one of the reasons that powerful neighbours could use to justify any aggression. So there were political dividends associated with the new for kings.

At the individual level, some people seem to have embraced the new religion, as the pious wording on some eleventh-century rune stones suggests. The more general move away from sending a corpse to the next world accompanied by grave-goods is also associated with the change in beliefs, and deprives archaeologists of one of their most fruitful sources of artifactual evidence.

The timber church erected at Jelling by Harald has been identified in excavations, but there are relatively few traces of the other timber churches built during the first century of official Christianity in Scandinavia, although some highly decorated fragments, such as those from Urnes in Norway, do survive.

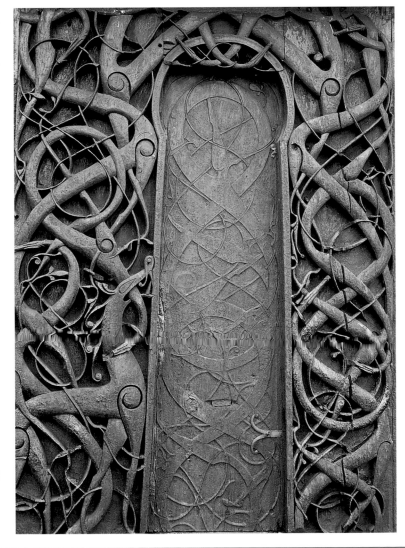

Door panel from an earlier church, erected perhaps in the mid-eleventh century, incorporated into the stave church at Urnes, Sognefjord, Norway.

KING HARALD'S POWER BASES

Reconstructed building based on remains excavated within the camp at Fyrkat, Jutland.

Harald Bluetooth succeeded his father, King Gorm, on the Danish throne in 958–59. He was probably aged about twenty-five, and he ruled until his death in 985–87. Fairly early in his reign, in 968, he strengthened the great Danevirke earth rampart, which defended Jutland against German aggression (see p. 23). Documentary sources indicate that he was a militarily active king, fighting the Germans in 974 and again, with greater success, in 983; archaeology has demonstrated how he wielded power in Denmark and welded the country together under his control.

One strategy was to construct a series of circular strongholds at key points throughout the kingdom. Four of these sites, built with geometrical precision, have now been firmly identified. The first to be investigated, at Trelleborg, on a promontory defended naturally by two converging rivers, is strategically located just 3 km (2 miles) from the western coast of Sjaelland. Its circular earthwork, then of unknown date, was still recognisable in 1933 when a motorcycle club bought the land in order to turn it into a speedway track. A programme of survey and excavations which began in 1934 went on until 1942; it had to be extended in 1936 when an air photograph revealed a previously unknown outer rampart that strengthened the defences across the neck of the promontory, on the obvious line of attack.

Inside a 4-m (13-ft) deep V-shaped ditch, the circular rampart, 17.6 m (58 ft) wide, defines an area 134 m (440 ft) in internal diameter. Originally the rampart stood to a height of about 7 m (23 ft), held in place at front and back by vertical timbers;

RAVNING

Across a wide and marshy river valley at Ravning Enge, about 10 km (6 miles) south of Jelling, is a bridge or causeway made from timbers felled in 979–80. Doubtless it was built to speed movement to and from Jelling; despite its apparent mundane functionality, it is another remarkable indication of Harald Bluetooth's power to mobilize resources.

The scale of these works is anything but mundane. The bridge, which is about 750 m (2,460 ft) long and 5.5 m (18 ft) wide, is supported on over 300 sets of four massive wooden piles. Each of these 1,200 piles had to felled, shaped, transported, pile-driven and trimmed off before the decking was put into place about 1.5 m (5 ft) above the surrounding

ground level. The bridge could carry loads of 5 tons.

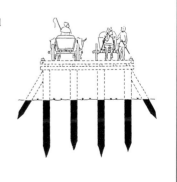

The remains of posts driven into the ground at Ravning Enge allow the form of a timber causeway or bridge across boggy ground to be reconstructed.

presumably there was a palisade at the top to protect the defenders. Four gateways, at north, south, east and west, each only 3 m (9 ft 10 in) wide, pierced the rampart, which was supported at these entrances by a stone lining behind a timber facing, to prevent it from collapsing.

Between opposite gateways ran timber-paved streets, which were underpinned by timber piles. The streets divided the interior into four equal portions, and within each quadrant four large, bow-sided buildings were laid out in a square so as to enclose a courtyard. These buildings were about 29.5 m (96 ft) long and 8 m (26 ft) in greatest width. Each was divided into a large, 18-m (59-ft) long, central hall with a stone hearth in the middle, with smaller rooms at each end. Another 15 buildings of similar shape, although slightly smaller in size, stood within the outer rampart. There, too, was a cemetery containing 157 individuals, most of them males.

Tree-ring dating has shown that the Trelleborg fortress and another like it at Fyrkat, in Jutland, were constructed in 980–81, in the reign of Harald Bluetooth. Two more sites, at Aggersborg on the Limfjord in north Jutland and at Nonnebakken on Fyn, are so similar that they too are attributed to the same bout of construction; and there may be yet another camp of broadly similar appearance and date to Trelleborg in Skåne, southern Sweden. It seems most likely that they served as regional centres of control, as places where taxes could be collected, as symbols of Harald's power. Any king who could harness the resources needed in their construction was clearly a force to be reckoned with.

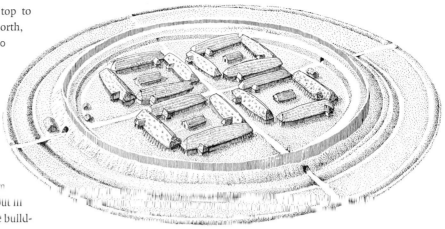

(Above) A visualization of how the camp at Fyrkat may have looked in the late tenth century.

(Below) Harald Bluetooth's fortress at Trelleborg. The circular inner defence is split into four quadrants by roads leading from the gateways, and within each quadrant four bow-sided buildings create an enclosed courtyard. Similar buildings stand inside an outer rampart defending the headland.

SVEIN FORKBEARD'S INVASIONS OF ENGLAND

Svein Forkbeard succeeded his father Harald Bluetooth on the throne of Denmark sometime in the years 985–87. After a generation or so of peace, Viking raids on England had resumed in 980 when seven ships attacked Southampton. A decade of sporadic raids aimed principally at the southwest of England and Wales heralded more sustained aggression from 991 onwards. In that year a force targeted first Kent and then East Anglia. Among its leaders may have been both King Svein Forkbeard and Olaf Tryggvason, grandson of King Harald Finehair of Norway.

Their operations looked destined to come to a sticky end when they were bottled up on the tidal island of Northey in the estuary of the River Blackwater, just outside Maldon in Essex, by the forces of the local Anglo-Saxon ealdorman. But rash chivalry or bravado on the part of the English permitted the Vikings to regroup on the landward side of the causeway, where battle was joined. Ealdorman Byrhtnoth was killed early in the action but his warriors fought on in heroic fashion to the last man. Their valour and loyalty were celebrated in an Old English epic poem, *The Battle of Maldon*, an unusual by-product of Viking aggression:

All determined that their choice should be
To die on that field, or avenge their loved one.

The Vikings, in contrast, celebrated the receipt of £10,000 in return for a respite from further attack. This was the first payment of what became known as Danegeld.

Svein and Olaf next cooperated in 994, when they attacked London unsuccessfully. Thwarted, they sailed off on a destructive course around the southern English coast until, in the happy possession of another £16,000 of Danegeld, they came to overwinter at Southampton. With a guarantee of safe conduct Olaf Tryggvason was then conveyed 'with great ceremony' to Andover in Hampshire where he was baptised under the sponsorship of the English king Aethelred, who 'bestowed gifts

(Above) *Silver coin minted for King Svein Forkbeard of Denmark (985–1014). Its design imitates contemporary English pennies, but the portrait side has the Latin legend ZAEN REX AD DENER (Svein King of Denmark).*

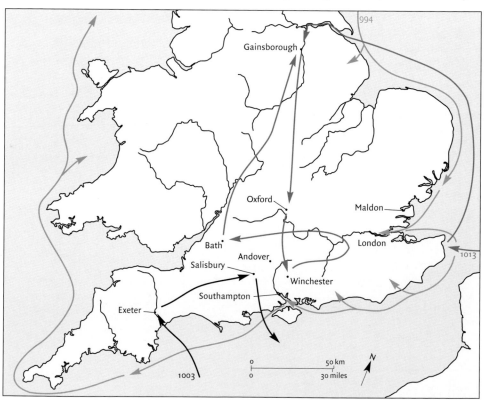

Map showing Svein Forkbeard's main invasions of England.

on him royally'. Thus bribed and feted, Olaf promised that he would leave England and never attack it again – a promise which he kept.

After Olaf Tryggvason's departure in late 994, Viking attacks on southern England continued virtually every year without respite. Incapable of inflicting a decisive defeat on the invaders, the English under King Aethelred II unraed (literally 'noble counsel no-counsel,' but known as 'the unready') plotted to kill Danes settled in England who were thought to have collaborated with the Vikings. This resulted in the so-called St Brice's Day massacre of 13 November 1002. Aethelred's view of these Danes is revealed in a document written shortly afterwards, in which they are described as 'sprouting like weeds among the wheat', and the deed itself is characterized as 'a most just extermination'.

In Oxford the Danes barricaded themselves in a church; undeterred, their English pursuers burned it down. These details from Oxford are the only indication of what really happened on St Brice's Day, but whatever the intention and the extent of the massacre, it certainly did not deter the Vikings from attacking England, for Svein Forkbeard reappeared the next year.

As the years passed England also became the target of other Viking leaders. A Dane called

VIKING CHRISTIAN SOLDIER

Olaf Tryggvason's English booty underwrote his successful attempt to seize power in Norway in 995. He promoted Christianity in his realm, often at the point of a sword, and also initiated a Norwegian currency by issuing coins that imitated those of his Anglo-Saxon godfather, King Aethelred.

His success was short-lived, for he had many enemies, both internal and external. Foremost among them was his erstwhile ally King Svein Forkbeard of Denmark, who wanted to restore the Danish supremacy in Norway of which his father, King Harald Bluetooth, had boasted on his Jelling rune stone. In 1000 Olaf was defeated in a sea-battle at Svold, a location that has not been firmly identified. With no other means of escape, he reportedly leapt off his great ship, the Long Serpent, and was never seen again. Danish power in Norway was reasserted, with the Vik area of Oslo Fjord under direct rule and other regions parcelled out to various allies.

A drowning warrior, possibly representing Olaf Tryggvason of Norway at the Battle of Svold, from a thirteenth-century manuscript.

Thorkell 'the tall' led an army that landed in 1009. By then King Aethelred was prepared to try just about anything in his fight against the Vikings. One psychological ploy that he contemplated but then abruptly abandoned was a remarkable re-minting of the silver penny coinage on which, in a total break with tradition, there was no portrait of the king himself. Instead, Christian religious motifs were to be emblazoned on both sides of the coins. Such designs were common on the late Anglo-Saxon coinage; for example, the Hand of God had appeared earlier in Aethelred's reign. Now, however, a Dove, presumably the Holy Spirit, on one side, was coupled with the Lamb of God on the other. Perhaps this coin was initially intended to accompany a three-day period of national prayer and fasting that was called in 1009 shortly after the arrival of Thorkell's army. And it may be that its rapid withdrawal, before large-scale minting got underway, was because the king's advisers realized that a coin without Aethelred's portrait might send out precisely the wrong message, that he himself was about to vanish from the scene.

Thorkell's army ravaged successfully until, in 1012, they were bought off with Danegeld; the

The tidal causeway over the Blackwater Estuary at Maldon, Essex, associated with events of 991 recounted in the Old English poem The Battle of Maldon.

'going' rate was now £48,000. King Aethelred also purchased the allegiance of Thorkell together with 45 of his ships, a policy that was paid for by the imposition of a new tax, *heregeld* ('army tax').

Bizarrely, recruiting Thorkell may have deepened Aethelred's troubles, for Svein Forkbeard may have seen a Thorkell/Aethelred alliance as posing a long-term threat to his own position in Denmark. Svein invaded England in 1013, sailing into the Humber Estuary and up the River Trent to Gainsborough in Lincolnshire. A southward march met no resistance until he reached London but, when other parts of the south submitted, London followed suit. King Aethelred fled to his brother-in-law in Normandy.

Svein enjoyed his victory for barely a month, for the *Anglo-Saxon Chronicle* recorded 'the happy event' of his death on 3 February 1014. Aethelred returned to England and forced Svein's son, Cnut, to sail back to Denmark; but the respite was brief, for Cnut led his army back to England in 1015. The denouement of this long-drawn-out series of campaigns started with the death of King Aethelred in April 1016 and climaxed with that of his son and successor Edmund Ironside in November 1016. The war-weary Anglo-Saxons, bereft of any obvious natural contender for the throne, accepted that this left England in Cnut's hands.

Silver penny minted for King Aethelred II unraed ('the unready') invoking Christianity as a weapon against Vikings. One side shows the Lamb of God (Agnus Dei) and there is a dove, representing the Holy Spirit, on the other.

Weaponry found in the River Thames at London Bridge may represent losses during Viking attacks.

CNUT'S ANGLO-SCANDINAVIAN EMPIRE

Silver penny minted for King Cnut in England, during the period 1024–30. He is shown wearing a helmet and holding a sceptre, in the manner of his English predecessors; the Latin legend, reading from top, proclaims +CNUT REX ANGLOR (Cnut king of the English).

Cnut's strategy for holding on to the kingdom of England during his longish reign (1016–35) was to maintain the institutions of the Anglo-Saxon church and state, albeit with new personnel whenever and wherever necessary. There was essential continuity in coinage and taxation, governance and the law – even in the person of the queen, for Cnut married Emma of Normandy (also known as Aelfgifu), Aethelred's widow.

Cnut also endowed many churches and monasteries with lavish gifts. One instance of such an act is captured on a manuscript written for the New Minster at Winchester in about 1031, which contains a representation of Cnut and Emma presenting a huge cross made of silver and gold on the altar there (illustrated on p.194). Cnut may also have commissioned a stone frieze, fragments of which were found in the archaeological excavation of a part of the Old Minster at Winchester that was built in about 980 and demolished in 1093–94. On the left is a mail-clad warrior; to the right, more diagnostically, an animal licks the face of a person lying bound on the ground. This is interpreted as the representation of an episode from the *Volsunga saga*, commissioned by Cnut in another bid to stress common elements in Anglo-Scandinavian traditions. It has even been suggested that the famous Old English epic poem *Beowulf*, which celebrates the deeds of its Danish hero/king, was another product of Cnut's propaganda campaign of reassurance to his new Anglo-Saxon subjects.

Overall, however, the new Scandinavian king and his court had a relatively limited impact on the arts in England. Among the handful of objects with a pure Scandinavian pedigree is a stone panel, probably a head- or foot-stone grave marker, found in 1852 on the south side of the churchyard at St Paul's Cathedral, London. A runic inscription on one edge records 'Ginna and Toki had this stone laid'. Both these names are Scandinavian, and the burial was presumably that of a follower of Cnut. The stone's decorated face bears an animal design in so mainstream a version of the Ringerike style (see pp. 178–179) that it was probably carved by a Scandinavian

(Right) Fragment of a stone frieze from the Old Minster, Winchester, Hampshire, England, showing a wolf licking a bound figure, and a warrior wearing protective mail and a sword. This may represent a scene from the Volsunga Saga.

(Below) Map of Cnut's empire.

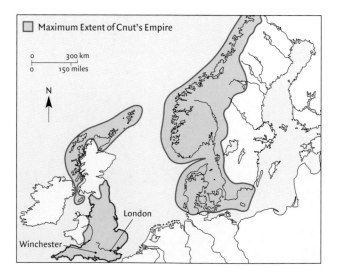

Maximum Extent of Cnut's Empire

0   300 km
0 150 miles

N

London

Winchester

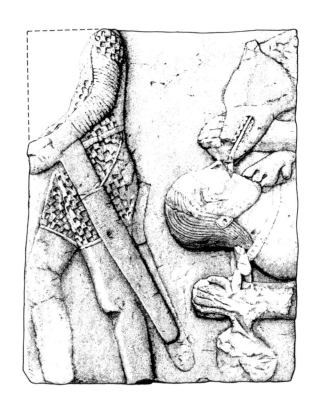

REAPING THE REWARDS – A SILVER HARVEST

Over 60,000 Anglo-Saxon coins minted between about 975 and 1050 have been found in Scandinavia and countries on the south shore of the Baltic Sea, a remarkable increase in the numbers from the preceding century and a half of Viking interest in England.

These 60,000 are likely to represent just a fraction of the number that were transported across the North Sea, for the majority would have been melted down into bullion or, eventually, re-minted into native coin. Although it may be that some of the coins represent the profits from commercial ventures between Germany and England which later ended up further north and west, the presumption has been that these coins made up the *heregeld* tax or the tributes of Danegeld that were paid to Viking warriors.

Certainly, the families of Viking participants in these raiding armies were pleased to boast of the financial rewards harvested in England – at Yttergärde in Uppland, Sweden, a rune stone records:

Ulv took three gelds in England.
The first was that which Tostig paid.
Then Thorkell paid
Then Cnut paid.

Rune stone at Yttergärde, Uppland, Sweden, recording multiple success in Viking raids against England in the early eleventh century.

Stone grave marker from St Paul's Churchyard, London, decorated in the Ringerike style of the early eleventh century that was popular in the court of Cnut (1016–35).

craftsman. Extensive traces of red, blue and white paint allow the vivid original appearance to be reconstructed with confidence.

Cnut connections

Meanwhile, Cnut was overtly embraced within the interlocking network of Christian Europe's royal families. Whereas his grandfather, King Harald Bluetooth, had been at war with the German emperor Otto I, Cnut was a guest at the coronation of the German emperor Conrad II in Rome in 1027. Later he saw his daughter Gunnhild betrothed to Conrad's son, the future Emperor Henry III. With Cnut's success, the dynasty of Gorm graduated from being Viking irritants to full-blown participants in international power politics. And in this they set an example that other Scandinavian leaders would want to emulate.

This illustration from the Liber Vitae (Book of Life) from New Minster, Winchester, Hampshire, England which commemorates the monastery's benefactors, shows King Cnut and his wife, Emma, dedicating a new golden cross on the church's altar. Drawn in c. 1031, this is the only contemporary representation of Cnut.

ST OLAF OF NORWAY

Secure in the backing of the English laity and ecclesiasts, Cnut was able to spend time exerting his power in Scandinavia. After the death of his brother, who had ruled Denmark after their father Svein, Cnut moved successfully in 1019 to add this to his dominions. In Norway, after the defeat of Olaf Tryggvason, Danish sovereignty had been exercised on behalf of Svein Forkbeard through the family of the Earls of Lade (Trondheim). But in 1015 the Norwegian Olaf Haraldsson entered the stage. He had been with Thorkell 'the tall' in England in 1009–12, and then a Christian convert in the service of Duke Richard II of Normandy; now he defeated the pro-Danish contingent in a battle in the Oslo Fjord area.

By 1025 an alliance of Olaf and King Anund Jacob of Sweden felt able to threaten Denmark, where Cnut had already weathered the possibility of rebellion. Cnut, however, was able to defeat them, and in 1028 he expelled Olaf altogether. He thus reasserted his dynasty's control of Norway and of parts of Sweden. Olaf was killed two years later in the Battle of Stiklestad (near Trondheim) while attempting a comeback to power. His appeal to nationalist sentiments meant that within a short time he was regarded as a saint; and his cult spread rapidly and widely around the Viking world. In York, for example, Earl Siward, the English king's representative in the city, was buried in 1055 in the church he had dedicated to St Olaf. Having been appointed earl by Cnut, but from 1042 owing allegiance to the reinstated Anglo-Saxon dynasty, perhaps the dedication was a means of reinforcing his Scandinavian credentials to York's Anglo-Scandinavian population, while simultaneously sending a message that his heavenly intercessor was an opponent of Cnut and his deposed lineage.

A painted wooden panel of fourteenth-century date from the Trøndelag area of Norway, now in Trondheim Cathedral, depicting the events of St Olaf's death in battle and enshrinement The large figure of Olaf carries a royal orb and an axe, the symbol associated with him.

TOWN LIFE IN SCANDINAVIA

Silver coin struck for King Olaf Eriksson 'Skötkonung' of Sweden (c. 995–1022) and a fragmentary lead strip (top) used for testing the coin die for a similar coin, found at Sigtuna, Uppland, Sweden in 1990.

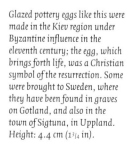

Glazed pottery eggs like this were made in the Kiev region under Byzantine influence in the eleventh century; the egg, which brings forth life, was a Christian symbol of the resurrection. Some were brought to Sweden, where they have been found in graves on Gotland, and also in the town of Sigtuna, in Uppland. Height: 4.4 cm (1³/₄ in).

It was in the later tenth and early eleventh century that urban centres began to proliferate in Scandinavia. Before this time only a very few sites had relatively large, closely packed, permanent or semi-permanent populations who made their living not solely through agriculture but also through the practice of diverse crafts and trade. These places were the small group of international trading centres, located on key long-distance routes that linked Scandinavia to the surrounding territories (see p. 56).

Now, a second tier of places started to emerge in the hierarchy of settlement, functioning as regional centres and local market places. Among them are Viborg and Roskilde in Denmark, Trondheim in Norway, Lund in southwest Sweden and Visby on Gotland. Elusive in the historical and archaeological record, they are nonetheless detectable, sometimes mentioned as the seats of established or would-be bishoprics, sometimes as the locations of royal mints. Most were in lands under Danish control, in modern Denmark and southwestern Sweden.

Excavated remains of these places are few and far between, but Århus in Jutland indicates some of the characteristics that can be expected. Incredibly small by modern standards, Århus was defined and defended by an earth rampart and outer ditch; the enclosure was about 250 m (820 ft) in diameter, with an area of only 4–5 ha (10–12 acres). A wood-paved road ran around the inner face of the rampart, and there were timber buildings with floors in cellar-like cuttings below the surrounding ground level. They served as both houses and workshops for craftsmen.

Excavations at Søndersø in Viborg, central Jutland, have uncovered a metalworker's workshop erected c. 1018; other evidence from nearby suggests a spate of building activity at about this time. Perhaps a royal residence was constructed here when Cnut returned from England – coins were minted for him at Viborg in c. 1018. However, after seasonal use for a few years, perhaps corresponding to the annual presence of a royal entourage, the workshop was finally abandoned c. 1030; Viborg's urban development started in earnest in the mid-eleventh century, perhaps in conjunction with the bishopric that is first mentioned c. 1065.

Sigtuna stands on the shore of Lake Mälaren in east-central Sweden. The town consisted of about 100 property plots, each 8 m (26 ft) wide and laid out to one side or the other of a road that ran parallel to the lake shore. A royal residence stood close to the centre of the town; excavations opposite there in 1990 revealed the foundations of a building within which was found part of a silver coin of King Olaf Eriksson 'Skötkonung' ('tributary king'), who ruled c. 995–1022. More significantly, there were two pieces of lead sheet with impressions from the coin dies used to make these coins. Additionally, there were traces of craft or industrial activities including gold-smithing, bronze casting, bead making and working in walrus ivory. It is possible that this site was where Olaf's Anglo-Saxon moneyers created his first silver coins, before Swedish craftsmen mastered the skills of die manufacture and coin production. Rune stones at Sigtuna which mention members of a Frisian guild testify to commercial contacts with western Europe, and objects such as a painted ceramic 'Resurrection egg' from Kiev, and Byzantine pottery, indicate a continuation of eastern trade, albeit one no longer focused on the Muslim world.

(Above and right) Two views of a model of Århus, Jutland, laid out on a grid plan. There was a settlement on the north side of the River Århus from the late eighth century. Defensive ramparts were first erected in the early to mid-tenth century, perhaps by King Gorm (see p. 182); his son, King Harald Bluetooth, had the defences enlarged and strengthened.

VIII • THE END AND AFTER

The consolidation of centralized monarchies in Denmark, Norway and Sweden in the eleventh and twelfth centuries, and the incorporation of these nations into the European networks of religion, trade and politics, created a straitjacket that curbed the individualistic enterprises which had characterized the Viking Age. Out in the Atlantic, however, it was the new lands—the Faroe Islands, Iceland and Greenland that preserved traces of their Viking Age origins for rather longer.

Within the British Isles modern political geography is much simpler than was the case in the eleventh to thirteenth centuries, when there were still opportunities for former Viking power blocks to maintain and even enhance their identity. Power in Ireland was contested between leading regional dynasties and, latterly, with Anglo-Norman invaders.

By 1100 England had more or less its present extent except for uncertainties about the line of its northern border. Scottish kings now directly controlled the Lowlands and the lands north to the River Dee, for the Picts and the Strathclyde Britons no longer had an independent political existence, and the Northumbrians had given up their claims to the Lowlands. The country had a new name – Alba – but large parts of it were still not controlled by the Scottish kings.

In the southwest, there were independent lordships in Argyll and Galloway (a land not of the Galls/foreigners/Vikings, but of the Gaels/gaelic speakers). The Western Isles were firmly in Scandinavian hands and remained so until 1266. Further north, beyond the River Dee and modern Aberdeen, lay the kingdom of Moray, homeland of Macbeth (king from 1040–57) and a force to be reckoned with until the reign of the Scottish king David I (1124–53). To the north of Moray was territory controlled by the Earls of Orkney. The Earls served two masters – they held Caithness through homage to the king of the Scots, but Orkney and Shetland were ultimately the possessions of the Norwegian kings, and were surrendered by them only in 1469.

Detail from A Viking's Funeral by Sir Frank Dicksee, painted in 1893 and now in Manchester City Art Galleries. This late Victorian romanticized picture shows a Viking chieftain's body in a burning ship being pushed out to sea by men including one wearing a horned helmet. The ultimate inspiration may have been either the Old English poem Beowulf, or Snorre Sturluson's description of the funeral of Baldr in his Edda.

Harald Hardraada ('the Ruthless') was the last of the great Viking warriors, adventurers whose careers spanned large tracts of the Viking world. Of King Harald Finehair's lineage, he was a half-brother of the former Norwegian king, Saint Olaf Haraldsson. In 1030, at the age of about fifteen, he had fought alongside Olaf in his attempt to regain control of Norway at the Battle of Stiklestad. After his brother's defeat and death there, Harald left Scandinavia; he served as a mercenary leader fighting for Russian princes, and then joined the Byzantine emperor's elite Varangian Guard (see p. 200), posted to Bulgaria, Sicily and Syria. Rich, successful and charismatic as a brave commander, he returned in 1045 to Norway and was accepted as joint ruler by his cousin, King Magnus. When Magnus died in 1047 Harald was left with absolute power.

For almost twenty years he fought against the Danish King Svein Estrithsson, but after peace was negotiated in 1064 he turned his attention to England. In 1066 he led a fleet across the North Sea, into the Humber Estuary and up the River Ouse. He was heading towards York, in company with his ally, the English defector Earl Tostig, brother of England's King Harold. Harald's ships moored at Riccall, 16 km (10 miles) downstream from York, and on 20 September his army advanced to Fulford, on the city's outskirts. There they were confronted by an English force, hastily assembled from the region. These defenders, reported the *Anglo-Saxon Chronicle*, 'fought against the invaders and caused them heavy casualties, and many of the English host were killed and drowned and put to flight'; the Norwegians had won a hard-fought battle.

On 25 September Harald and his men, still based at Riccall, marched 20 km (13 miles) eastwards to collect tribute and hostages at Stamford Bridge. There they were surprised by the English king, who had rapidly marched north to defend his realm. In the ensuing battle both Harald and

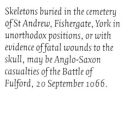

Skeletons buried in the cemetery of St Andrew, Fishergate, York in unorthodox positions, or with evidence of fatal wounds to the skull, may be Anglo-Saxon casualties of the Battle of Fulford, 20 September 1066.

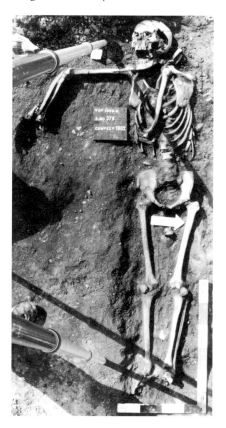

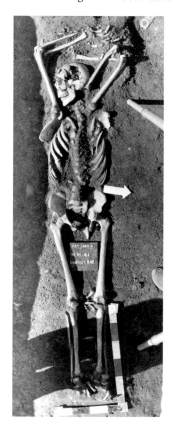

hARO L D REX INTERFEC TVS EST

Tostig were killed, and the fleeing Norwegians were pursued back to their ships at Riccall. Some 300 ships had invaded; only 24 were needed to take the survivors back home.

Relics of the Battles?

Tangible relics from the battles of Fulford and Stamford Bridge are elusive, but two cemeteries may hold the remains of warriors killed in these encounters. On the outskirts of Viking Age York, close to the street Fishergate which led towards Fulford, stood a small wooden church.

In its surrounding cemetery, clustered in a group together, were the burials of young men, several of whom had marks on their bones made by swords, spears, arrows and axes. Might these be the skeletons of defeated defenders from the battle of Fulford, only 3 km (2 miles) up the road? As for the Viking victims of Stamford Bridge and its aftermath, might some of them still lie in the unmarked cemetery found in 1956 by a farmer digging mangelwurzels in a field beside the River Ouse at Riccall?

The Last Danish Invasions

Hardraada's defeat wasn't the end of Scandinavian attacks on England, even though within weeks of his defeat the country had succumbed to William the Conqueror's Normans. In 1069 the Danes mounted an invasion that culminated in the capture of York castle and the seizure of much treasure. This was merely the prelude to an invasion in 1070 by the Danish king that resulted in further looting but no political change; another Danish attack in 1075, when much plunder was taken from York Minster, also had no longer term consequences.

This was the final Danish attack of the eleventh century to meet with even moderate success; a planned invasion in 1085 was aborted, and the threat of a Scandinavian coup disappeared.

King Harold of England's death in battle at Hastings in 1066 was recorded in the Bayeux Tapestry. It brought a sixth generation Norseman – Duke William 'the Bastard' of Normandy – to the throne of England.

LOST KINGDOMS IN THE WEST

*In Lewis Isle with fearful blaze
the house-destroying fire plays;
To hills and rocks the people fly,
fearing all shelter but the sky.
In Uist the king deep crimson made
the lightning of his glancing blade;
The peasant lost his land and life
who dared to bide the Norseman's strife.
The hungry battle-birds were filled
in Skye with blood of foemen killed,
And wolves on Tiree's lonely shore
dyed red their hairy jaws in gore.
The men of Mull were tired of flight;
The Scottish foemen would not fight,
And many an island girl's wail
was heard as through the Isles we sail.
On Sanda's plain our shields they spy;
from Islay smoke rose heaven-high,
Whirling up from the flashing blaze
the king's men o'er the island raise.
South of Kintyre the people fled,
scared by our swords in blood dyed red,
And our brave champion onwards goes
to meet in Man the Norsemen's foes.*

(Below left) Silver ingots,
coins and a plaited armring
from the Glenfaba, Isle of Man,
hoard, buried in the early
eleventh century.
(Below right) Silver coin minted
for King Magnus Barelegs of
Norway (1093–1103).

On and off the west coast of Scotland, politics in the eleventh to thirteenth centuries were complicated and fluid. Scandinavian settlement in the Western Isles or Hebrides had resulted in it being called *Innse Gall*, the 'Isles of the foreigners'. Maccus or Magnus Haraldsson, 'king of many islands', had attended King Edgar of England at Chester in 973; his brother Guthroth, the first recorded 'king of Innse Gall', died in 989.

Thereafter the earls of Orkney extended their sphere of control to embrace the Western Isles, and a Hebridean contingent fought with Earl Sigurd the Stout of Orkney at the Battle of Clontarf in 1014, hoping to maintain unfettered access across the Irish Sea to the wealth of the Hiberno-Viking trading centre of Dublin.

Conversely, rival Irish kings competing for the overlordship of Dublin sought domination of the Irish Sea through control of the Isle of Man. Indeed, one tangible testimony to the close links between Dublin and Man in the early eleventh century was the brief appearance of a Manx penny coinage, based on the style of contemporary Dublin issues.

The wealth of Man in the eleventh century is demonstrated by a hoard of silver in a lead container, discovered at Glenfaba in 2003. Buried in the 1020s, it comprised 464 silver coins, 25 ingots

and a plaited silver armring, weighing in total 1.3 kg (2lb 14 oz) and making it the largest complete Manx hoard in existence. The Glenfaba and other broadly contemporary Manx hoards clearly indicate that the island was a rich place, in which both bullion and/or coinage were used in transactions. The coins in the Glenfaba hoard had been minted in Dublin, in a wide variety of Anglo-Saxon mints, on Man itself, and at other mints in the Irish Sea region – testimony to the island's nodal position in this 'Viking lake'.

Later, in about 1079, Godred Crovan, a member of the Dublin dynasty, engineered a decisive moment when, in the words of the *Chronicles of the Kings of Man and the Isles*, he 'gathered a massive force and came by night to the harbour which is called Ramsey'. This invasion of Man established a dynasty of Manx kings that was to endure, with interruptions, until 1265, and which also ruled in the Hebrides. The extent of his dominion is echoed in the name of the Bishopric of Sodor and Man – Sodor, which embraces the Hebrides, is derived from the Old Norse *suðreyar*, 'the Southern Islands', so named with reference to the Northern Isles of Orkney and Shetland.

This entire area of the Northern and Western Isles came under formal Norwegian overlordship in 1098, when King Magnus Barelegs of Norway seized the Earldom of Orkney and then demonstrated his power by sailing into the Irish Sea and ravaging his way through the Hebrides. Bjorn Cripplehand, the king's poet, celebrated the voyage in a passage of skaldic verse preserved in Snorre Sturluson's *Heimskringla* (see margin).

King Magnus landed on Man, fought and defeated Anglo-Norman earls on Anglesey ('Earl Hugh killed in Anglesey by sea rovers' reported the *Anglo-Saxon Chronicle*) and then turned back for home, progressing north again through the islands. King Edgar of Scotland, whose writ held no weight in this area, was quite content to

THE LEWIS CHESSMEN

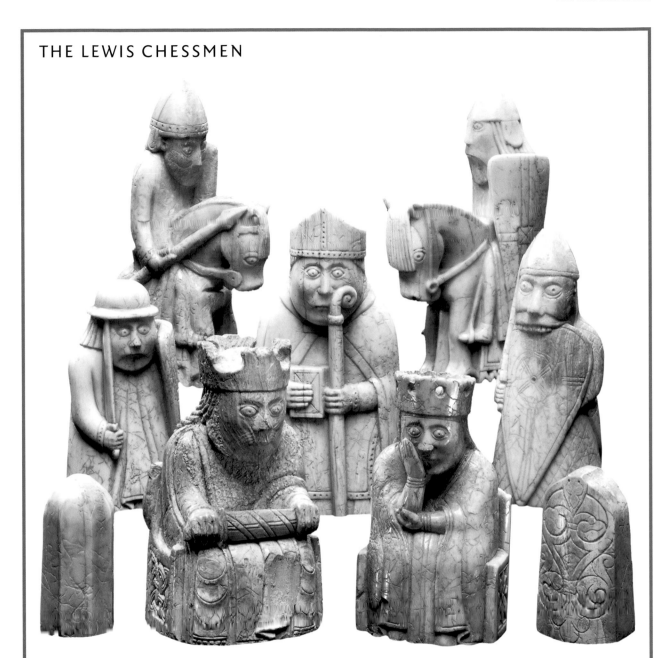

In or about 1831, in the sandhills at Uig on the western coast of the Isle of Lewis, in the Outer Hebrides, a remarkable group of 93 pieces of carved walrus ivory was discovered. Most were chessmen, making up the majority of four sets; perhaps they were the stock of an itinerant trader who was forced to conceal and was then unable to retrieve them. Boldly carved, and decorated with Romanesque motifs, they can be dated on stylistic grounds to the period 1150–1200. Their closest parallels come from Norway, and in particular from Trondheim, where the archbishopric of Norway was created in 1152/3. They are a physical manifestation of the links between the Western Isles and Norway, which retained sovereignty over this part of Scotland until 1266.

A selection of chess pieces, carved in Norway in the later twelfth century, and found on the Isle of Lewis, Western Isles of Scotland. The king figure, front left, is c. 10 cm (4 in) tall.

maintain his own territorial integrity by ceding control of the Hebrides to Magnus, and thus Norway joined England and Scotland as principal power brokers in the British Isles. To cement a strategic alliance, Magnus married his nine-year-old son to the five-year-old daughter of the King of Munster, in southwest Ireland – but when Magnus was killed in Ulster (northeastern Ireland) on another expedition in 1103, presumably aimed at curbing Ulster's abilities to threaten shipping in the Irish Sea, this match was cancelled. Norwegian overlordship remained, however: 'In the Northern Ocean beyond Ulster and Galloway are a number of islands.... Almost all of them are held by and are subject to the Norwegians... who keep their eyes ever on the ocean [and] lead, above any other people, a piratical life...' wrote Gerald of Wales in c. 1185 in his *Topography of Ireland*.

Rise and Fall of a Summer Warrior

Into this arena, at some time in the 1120s or 1130s, emerged the figure of Somerled. Little is known for certain about the origins and ancestry of this warlord who was to become king of the *Innse Gall*. His Norse name means 'summer warrior' or 'Viking', and he may have been a chieftain of mixed Scotto-Norse extraction whose power base was in Argyll. He rose from this historical obscurity to become powerful and successful enough to marry the daughter of the Manx king; on his father-in-law's death, and egged on by the king of Ulster, he made an attempt to seize the throne of

Man. After winning a bloody sea battle on 5–6 January 1156, the kingdom of Man and the Isles was divided; Somerled took control of the southern Hebrides and the Manx king retained Man, Skye, Lewis and Harris. Two years later Somerled returned to Man, defeated his rival for a second time, and seized the whole kingdom for himself. The Manx king fled to seek assistance in Norway, but Somerled's extended realm remained intact until he died in 1164 leading a force from the Hebrides, Argyll, Kintyre and Dublin in a strike against Scottish power on the Clyde.

Endgame in the Irish Sea

In the century after Somerled's death his descendants, collectively known as the MacSorleys, contended among themselves and with the equally fractured Manx dynasty of Godred Crovan for supremacy in the Irish Sea. Initially their struggle didn't attract the attention of the kings of Scotland and Norway, both of whom had other, more pressing, concerns; but this changed in the 1220s when the kings of Scotland became intent upon imprinting their hold on these western areas through which they were vulnerable to invasion. When the Manx king asked for help from King Håkon IV of Norway in 1230, he sent an expedition that killed various MacSorleys and captured Rothesay Castle on the island of Bute. This did not deter the long-term ambitions of the Scots' king, and the Manxmen in turn continued to ally themselves firmly with Håkon.

Runic inscription in St Molaise's Cave, Arran, VIGLEIKR S*ALLAR?RÆISS(T) – Vigleikr stallari reist – 'Vigleikr the marshall carved'. This relates to a historical event in 1263 during King Håkon IV's expedition from Norway to the Western Isles of Scotland.

Harald of Man married Håkon's daughter in Bergen in 1248, but the returning couple were drowned in the treacherous waters off the southern tip of Shetland. The decisive action came in 1263 when Håkon led his fleet via Orkney and Skye to Man. Turning northwards, he captured Rothesay Castle again; Vigleikr, his marshall, the son of a priest, found time to visit St Molaise's Cave on Arran and carved a runic inscription there. There followed a series of skirmishes in the Clyde Estuary, later dignified as the 'battle of Largs', which preceded Håkon's death on Orkney. With his

Norwegian patron dead, the Manx king Magnus then did homage to the king of Scots who, on Magnus' death without an heir in 1265, took control of Man. In 1266, by the terms of the Treaty of Perth, Norwegian overlordship of the Hebrides was sold back to the Scots for a lump sum of 4,000 marks and a promise of annual payments of 100 marks; Norwegian relations with Scotland entered a new and friendlier phase. One branch of the MacSorleys, the MacDonalds, was eventually recognized by the Scots' kings as Lords of the Isles, and maintained that position from the 1330s until 1493.

Rothesay Castle, Bute, Scotland; the circular stone enclosure represents the castle attacked by Norwegian expeditions in 1230 and 1263; the projecting towers are later additions.

ENDING THE EARLDOM IN THE NORTHERN ISLES

(Opposite) The Brough of Birsay, a tidal island off Birsay Bay in Mainland, Orkney, has remains of Viking Age buildings. Orkneyinga Saga records that Earl Thorfinn Skullsplitter built a church at Birsay in the mid-eleventh century; but the church on the Brough (centre) is later than his time, and Thorfinn's church may have been at Birsay village, on the Mainland.

While the Western Isles were the battleground of rival invading dynasties, the Earldom of Orkney remained until 1231 in the hands of the family descended from Thorfinn Skullsplitter, Sigurd the Stout and other heroic figures from the Viking past. Under their rule, some Orkney men continued in the good old Viking ways – as late as the twelfth century, Svein Asleifarson of Gairsay undertook raiding expeditions every summer, attacking the Hebrides and even the Scilly Islands, off the southwest tip of England, and using his share of the plunder to maintain his farm and lands.

Orkneyinga Saga, a History of the Earls of Orkney that was written in Iceland around AD 1200, records how a century earlier the power struggle between different branches of the earl's family pitched Magnus against his cousin Håkon. A meeting of reconciliation in 1117 on the island of Egilsay ended with Magnus being captured and then killed by a blow to the head administered by Håkon's cook. He was buried at Christ Church, by the earl's palace at Birsay. His tomb attracted worshippers, miracles were claimed, this veneration developed into a cult, and popular acclaim declared Magnus to be a saint. The canny Earl Rognvald realized that this was a cause that would bring him support and,

(Right) St Magnus' church, Egilsay, Orkney Islands, was built in c. 1140 to commemorate his death there in 1117.

THE BONES OF SAINT MAGNUS

In 1919 during renovation of St Magnus's cathedral in Kirkwall, loose stones in the rectangular pillar in the south arcade of the choir were removed. Carefully concealed behind them, perhaps at the Reformation in 1560, was a wooden box that contained most of a male skeleton. The skull had signs of an injury consistent with Orkneyinga Saga's account of Magnus's death, and this, together with the obvious care with which the coffin had been hidden, suggests that these are indeed the remains of St Magnus. They are now

re-interred within this cathedral, which is itself a remarkable testimony to the status assumed and enjoyed by the Earls of Orkney.

The human remains retrieved in 1919 from concealment within a wooden box inside a pillar at St Magnus' Cathedral, Kirkwall, Mainland, Orkney.

with his backing, work began in 1136 on building a new cathedral at Kirkwall to house St Magnus's remains. Within a few years the remains of St Magnus were transferred there; the last mention of his relics was in 1263 when the Norwegian king Håkon IV unsuccessfully sought to stave off his approaching death by a visit to St Magnus's shrine.

Last Days of the Orkney Earl

The temptation for successive generations of the feuding Orkney earls to further their own fortunes through involvement in Norway's civil wars led, in 1195, to their disastrous defeat at Florevåg, just north of Bergen. The repercussions included the detachment of Shetland from the earldom and its direct rule by the Norwegian king. The last earl descended from Thorfinn Skullsplitter was killed in 1231 in a cellar in Thurso, Caithness, in the very north of mainland Scotland, where he had unsuccessfully tried to hide from drunken Norwegians. His death foreshadowed the extinction of the entire family line when their ship, with all their leading men aboard, was lost in the following year during its return from Norway. The Orkney earldom then passed to other families who, in a replay

MESSAGES IN THE MOUND

Just after New Year 1153, according to *Orkneyinga Saga*, a raiding group of earl's men took shelter from a snowstorm in the stone-lined entrance passage and chambers of *Orkahaugr*, the prehistoric burial mound now known as Maeshowe ('moss mound'), on Mainland, Orkney. At some later date the roof of the chamber collapsed and the mound became impenetrable, and so it wasn't until 1861 that an 'excavation' revealed not only the impressive and massive stone construction but also the largest collection of runic inscriptions known anywhere in the British Isles. Some 33 inscriptions have been identified, employing both

the runic alphabet and also what are known as 'twig' runes. The form of the runes themselves and the language they represent both suggest that all the inscriptions, although the product of several different sets of visitors, can be dated to the decades on either side of 1150. Many are short graffiti such as 'Ottar carved these runes'.

A more ambiguous message, positively genteel when compared to some others within the mound, records 'Ingibjorg, the fair widow. Many a woman has gone stooping in here. A great show-off'. Whatever might have compelled these Orcadian ladies to visit Maeshowe (if this is

no more than wishful thinking on the part of the writers), several other inscriptions suggest that some people entered in the hope of enrichment – 'It was long ago that great treasure was hidden here.' Another inscription tells us that 'Jerusalem men [crusaders] broke into this mound', and this is entirely possible, for in 1151–53 Earl Rognvald made just such a pilgrimage to the Holy Land, accompanied by a group of Norwegians. Perhaps it was their runic expertise that accounts for the competence of the Maeshowe inscriptions.

(Below) These runes from Maeshowe assert that treasure had been removed from the mound.

(Below) A beast carved on the wall of Maeshowe in the mid-twelfth century; it is a descendant of the Ringerike style animals of over a hundred years earlier.

of events in the Western Isles, found themselves squeezed ever tighter between the kings of Norway and Scotland.

These monarchs disputed, among other matters, about the annual payment by the Scots of 100 marks for the Hebrides that had been agreed in the Treaty of Perth of 1266, but which the Scots had chosen to forget. It was the resolution of this by another paper transfer of funds that finally closed the dispute, after the king of Norway betrothed his daughter to the Scottish king with a dowry fixed at 60,000 Rhenish florins. Not having the ready cash, he mortgaged Orkney to the Scottish king for 50,000 florins in 1468 and then, in 1469, after raising only 2,000 of the remainder, he threw in Shetland as well in recompense for the missing 8,000. Additionally, the Scots' outstanding payments on the Treaty of Perth since 1266 were cancelled. Although until as late as 1749 kings of Norway intermittently floated the idea of repaying the 60,000 florins and repossessing the Northern Isles, 1468–69 marked the formal end of Scandinavian power in the British Isles, almost 700 years after the dawn of the Viking Age.

(Above) Kirkwall Cathedral, Mainland, Orkney, built as a shrine to St Magnus from the 1130s onwards; the west front was begun in c. 1200–1225, but the higher parts are later still.

(Left) Earl's Bu, Orphir, Mainland, Orkney; described in Orkneyinga Saga as where twelfth-century earls had a great drinking hall and a fine church. The remains of a round church are visible in the churchyard, perhaps built by Earl Hákon Paulsson who, after killing St Magnus, went on a pilgrimage to Jerusalem, where he would have seen round churches. Excavations have revealed traces of buildings (left foreground) that may be part of the earl's residence.

FROM NORSEMEN TO ANGLO-NORMANS IN IRELAND

A silver penny of Sihtric 'Silkbeard', king of Dublin, the first Viking to strike coins in Ireland in c. 997. The legend (starting bottom left) reads SIHTRC REX DIFL, 'Sihtric king of Dublin'.

After the Battle of Clontarf in 1014 (see p. 142), the Hiberno-Norsemen of Dublin continued to be pawns in the rivalries of Irish provincial kings, who intermittently inserted their own, Irish, nominees on to the throne of Dublin. The Dubliners were subdued by either force, threats, or bribes for their support, which brought with it a call on their militarily significant fleet. Dublin also continued to be an important economic centre, the focus for trade with English ports across the Irish Sea. The important trade in slaves seems to have climaxed in the eleventh century, when Bristol in southwest England was the main trading partner. By 1102, however, the Norman kings of England had prohibited slave trading, and this sealed the fate of Dublin's slave merchants.

These economic links with England can be identified in the new coinage initiated on behalf of Sihtric 'Silkbeard', the Hiberno-Norse king of Dublin, in about 997. The new pennies were modelled on recent coins struck for the reigning English king, Aethelred II, and this copying of English coins was continued in the Dublin mint throughout the eleventh century. Coins imitating the earlier imitations were also produced, their designs becoming increasingly degenerate. None of these coins has been found in England, where a policy of demonetizing imported foreign coins by melting them down into bullion was strictly enforced, but they do occur in Scandinavia, attesting to continuing Irish contacts across the North Sea.

In 1169 Irish dynastic rivalries resulted in the introduction of Anglo-Norman military reinforcements into Ireland. Their first target was Wexford, another of the Hiberno-Norse coastal towns. In 1170, first Waterford and then Dublin fell prey as more Anglo-Normans sought their fortune in Ireland; but when the English King Henry II exerted his ultimate authority over the ambitions of these opportunist adventurers and made the invasion a royal enterprise, he made sure that these vital ports were surrendered into his own control. Indeed, in 1171 he celebrated Christmas at Dublin. An Anglo-Norman colony was planted in the city; the thread of continuity with a distant Viking past was severed.

THE SHIPPING NEWS

The routes plied by Dublin's fleets have recently been elucidated thanks to the science of dendrochronology – the study of tree-ring patterns as a means of dating and analyzing wooden artifacts. This technique has been applied to the so-called Skuldelev 2 vessel, a 30-m (100-ft) long warship deliberately sunk in Roskilde Fjord, Denmark in the later eleventh century, and excavated in 1962. To everyone's surprise, it has revealed that the vessel was built in southeastern Ireland, probably in Dublin, in 1042. A quarter of a century later it was repaired at a location somewhere around the Irish Sea.

Its arrival in Denmark may be a direct consequence of the Norman conquest of England.

After the defeat and death of King Harold at the battle of Hastings in 1066, his son Godwine fled to Ireland. With military assistance from Irish allies in Dublin he attacked Bristol in 1068 and Exeter in 1069, both without success. At about this time it is recorded that members of his family went to the court of the Danish king; even if the Skuldelev 2 ship did not itself carry them across the North Sea, it is the type of prestigious vessel appropriate for such a mission.

Another remarkable discovery further highlights the continuing importance – and dangers – of the Irish seaways. Some 29 km (18 miles) off the Pembrokeshire coast, protruding from the Irish Sea, are the rocks of Smalls Reef. There, 11 m (36 ft) below the surface, a diver found a brass sword guard decorated in the Irish version of the Urnes style, and made c. 1100–1125. This is all that survives from a ship, probably plying between Viking ports in Ireland and Wales, which was wrecked there in the early twelfth century.

The Smalls Reef sword guard, probably made in Ireland, with Hiberno-Viking Urnes-style decoration.

FROM FEUDS TO FEUDAL ICELAND

Until the mid-twelfth century Iceland maintained its unusual social structure as a commonwealth of free landowners, dispersed in farmsteads around the island. Remarkably, their interrelationships were not dependent on authority enforced by kings or war-leaders. Instead, the rudimentary government system devised during the Age of Settlement operated largely on the basis of consensus, fostered through local leaders and founded ultimately on an elaborate legal system. Yet although it was politically self-contained and owed allegiance to no external power, Iceland was economically dependant on contacts with Norway for a range of necessities and also for luxury goods. In the thirteenth century, however, a small number of leading families rose from local prominence to vie for island-wide supremacy. The period of the 1220s to the 1260s is known as the Age of the Sturlungs, after one of the principal dynasties; the bitter family feuds of this era are preserved in the pages of a series of family histories collectively known as the Sturlunga sagas. Eventually, in 1262–64, these rivalries induced the Icelanders to succumb to the blandishments initiated by King Håkon IV of Norway, who offered them political stability, trading assurances and the continuation of their own legal system if they acknowledged him as their overlord. Although for some time this was an arrangement that fulfilled its promises and improved the lot of the Icelanders, it formally marked the end of a remarkable Viking Age social experiment.

SNORRE STURLUSON – POLITICIAN AND POET

It is a member of the Sturling family, Snorre Sturluson (1178/9–1241), a leading political figure in the last days of the Icelandic commonwealth, to whom we are indebted for some of the Icelandic literature which illuminates important aspects of the Viking Age. Episodes from his eventful life, worthy of its own saga, were recorded in his nephew's composition *The Saga of the Icelanders*, and he can also be traced through a variety of other contemporary sources.

For long periods he was Lawspeaker at the *Althing* assembly (see p. 152), and he profited both from this position and from influential marriages. Involved in the web of political contention and the violence that surrounded it, he sought to increase his power and prestige by courting the patronage of the Norwegian king. In the midst of this busy life he found time to write the *Prose Edda*, the *Saga of St Olaf*, the history of the kings of Norway known as *Heimskringla*, and also, perhaps, the *Saga of Egill Skallgrimsson*, the story of an Icelandic farmer, Viking and skald. Egill was apparently of rather strange appearance, with, according to the saga, 'a broad forehead, heavy brows, a nose not long but very wide, lips broad and full, the chin unusually broad and the whole jawline, a thick neck and shoulders broader than most men have, harsh looking and fierce when he was angry. He was of good size, taller than anyone else, with thick wolf-grey hair, and he soon became bald. While he sat, he dropped one eyebrow down towards his cheek, raising the other up to the roots of his hair. Egil had black eyes and dark brows.'

Ultimately Snorre Sturluson miscalculated in his alliances and was deemed an enemy by the Norwegian king; his son-in-law, who had turned against him, led the attack on his house at Reykholt on 22 September 1241 which ended with his murder in the cellar.

Egill Skallgrimsson, as depicted in a seventeenth-century Icelandic manuscript.

(Below) A page from the Prose Edda.

GREENLAND: EXTINCT/EXTERMINATED/EXITED?

Knowledge of how the Greenland colonists were faring in the centuries after the initial settlement comes through some archaeological discoveries and, principally, from documentary sources. These reflect the concerns of kings and churchmen, who both wanted to exert control over the Greenlanders. *The King's Mirror*, a Norwegian work of c. 1220–30, records that the Greenlanders imported timber and iron, and in return exported hides, skins, walrus ivory and ropes.

Their best hunting grounds, which they called Norðsetur, were in the far north, in and beyond Disko Bay, lands then occupied by what archaeologists call the Thule people, ancestors of the present native Inuit population of Greenland. The name was coined because a variety of basic European goods dated to the thirteenth and fourteenth centuries has been found on sites in the Thule district north of Melville Bay; Thule artifacts found at Norse farms in the Eastern Settlement confirm that there were trading or other contacts between the two peoples.

More precise proof of the Greenlanders' ventures northwards comes from a runic inscription, carved on a 10-cm (4-in) long piece of Greenland phyllite, found in 1823 in a cairn at Kingittorsuaq, north of Upernavik. This is above latitude 73 degrees North, nearly 1,000 km (625 miles) north of the nearest permanent Norse settlement. The inscription records that three Greenlanders built the cairn on the Saturday before Rogation Day (i.e. in late April); unfortunately the year is not recorded, but runologists suggest that the inscription was carved c. 1300. It seems inconceivable that three hunters would have travelled so far to the north so early in the year, and they may have been forced to overwinter in this inhospitable terrain. There is also documentary evidence that the

Greenlanders continued to make at least sporadic forays westwards to North America. In 1347 there is a record in the Icelandic annals of a Greenland ship that was storm-tossed to Iceland after a voyage to *Markland*. Their vessel was described as 'smaller than a small Icelandic trading vessel'; perhaps this size reflected the scarcity of timber. in Greenland. Indeed, the Greenlanders visit to Markland was probably in search of timber to replace damaged, lost or aged ships. Without seaworthy vessels, the Greenlanders would be isolated.

In 1261 King Håkon IV of Norway had formally extended his power to embrace Greenland. The

(Right) The Bishop of Greenland's estate centre at Gardar (Igaliku) incorporated large storage buildings.

(Below) The Kingittorsuaq stone, a runic inscription from the north of Greenland dating to around 1300. Length: 10 cm (4 in).

Greenlanders were forbidden to use their own ships for trade, and thenceforth relied on the Norwegians, and particularly the merchants of Bergen. The ship that acted as this lifeline was known as the *Greenland Carrier*; but when the vessel was lost in 1367 or 1369 the Norwegians didn't replace it. They didn't need to – the luxury exports that Greenland supplied, such as furs and hides, were becoming more readily available from nearer sources such as Russia, while walrus ivory was becoming less fashionable with the opening up of supply routes that brought the larger, African elephant ivory to Europe. For the Greenlanders, however, the loss of this mercantile link spelt disaster. Already, by c. 1350, it seems that the Western Settlement had been abandoned, and when

Denmark became the dominant partner over Norway in 1397 there was probably even less royal interest in Greenland.

The other vested interest in Greenland was the church, and it was the bishops of Bergen who were most directly concerned. Their motives included generating revenue through church taxes, and the imperative question of pastoral leadership, as well as the care of souls. A bishop's residence and farm had been established at Gardar, with by far the largest storehouse on Greenland, capable of holding produce and goods rendered as tax; and a cathedral was eventually built there too. But after the death of Bishop Alfr in 1377 no medieval bishop ever set foot on Greenland again.

The 14-cm (5½-in) high head of a bishop's crozier, carved from walrus ivory, found in a thirteenth-century grave at Gardar (Igaliku), Greenland

Disappearing from History

Visits to Greenland seem to have become increasingly rare after the loss of the *Greenland Carrier* in the 1360s, and the last recorded contact with the Norse Greenlanders was by a group of Icelanders who were driven off course to Greenland in 1406. They remained for four years before returning home, presumably because it took that long to repair their ship. During their stay in Greenland they witnessed the burning of a man for witchcraft, and took part in a wedding service in the church at Hvalsey. The couple apparently left Greenland when the ship sailed back to Iceland in 1410 – a sign of the times? With this ceremony, a testament to apparent normality, the Greenlanders disappeared from recorded history. After that, Greenland and lands to the far west were ignored by Europeans – until, in 1492, Christopher Columbus reached Central America and, in 1497, John Cabot landed on Newfoundland.

Probably the most important single reason for the Greenlanders' predicament, even more important than the loss of the *Greenland Carrier*, was the steadily deteriorating climate, which limited the agricultural opportunities for the Norse farmers. It also increased the amount of ice coming down the coast and this, in turn, may have affected the availability of driftwood. Furthermore, it encouraged the Thule Palaeo-Eskimos to venture further south. On at least one occasion there was conflict; the Icelandic annals record in 1379 that 'the *skraelings* made a hostile attack on the Greenlanders, killed 18 men and captured two boys and made them slaves'. When this took place isn't clear, but a *Description of Greenland* written in 1350–1400 reports 'Now the *skraelings* have the whole of the Western

The church at Hvalsey, scene of the last documented events in the Norse settlement of Greenland in the opening decade of the fifteenth century.

Settlement, there are only horses, goats, cattle and sheep, all wild, but no inhabitants, neither Christian nor heathen'. If true, we see the Norse settlement contracting. Thule people lived a life in tune, in terms of food and clothing, with this harsh environment; the Norse, by contrast, showed a fatal unwillingness to adapt, preferring to maintain customs and habits better suited to life in Scandinavia and the British Isles.

The memory of the Greenland settlement lingered on, however, and in 1605 King Christian IV of Denmark sent the first of three expeditions to rediscover the Norse settlement, with James Hall of Hull in Yorkshire as pilot and navigator. The expedition managed to kidnap some Inuit but found no Norse, and it wasn't until the missionary activity of Hans Egede from 1721 onwards that traces of the lost colony began to be recognized. Over the years the settlement's disappearance has been blamed on attacks by natives, attacks by foreign pirates (English, German, or Basque), and plague. Most probably, however, the settlement ended with a whimper rather than a bang, as climatic deterioration gradually persuaded the remaining Greenlanders that, while they still had enough seaworthy vessels, they should retreat (unrecorded) back to Iceland. For long it has been believed that the styles of clothes used as shrouds in the cemetery at Herjolfsnes, on the southernmost tip of Greenland, indicated that burials continued there until the 1500s. Now, however, radiocarbon dating suggests that the clothes are earlier than previously believed, that their stylistic/fashion affinities are local rather than distant, and that the cemetery fell out of use by c. 1450. Only a generation or so after the Hvalsey nuptials, Greenland may have been left to the Inuit.

(Above and left) Clothes preserved in graves in the churchyard at Herjolfsnes followed late medieval European fashions rather than adapting to suit the worsening climate.

IX · NATIONALISTS, ROMANTICS, MADMEN AND SCHOLARS

The early seventeenth-century Danish search for the long-lost colony in Greenland was a search for physical reality; it was also a manifestation of a new interest in the Viking Age past that had been ignited by nationalism, fuelled by the Enlightenment and then inflamed by Romantic sentiments. At the beginning of the nineteenth century it was precocious Scandinavian scholars who first ordered the remains of antiquity into a chronological scheme; this marked the start of a transition from dilettante antiquarianism towards methodical archaeology, and initiated the process of scientific examination of ancient remains.

Meanwhile in the United Kingdom, parallel processes had given their due share of attention to the Viking Age. British scholars and their aristocratic patrons were therefore open to the arrival of Scandinavian experts who were able to confirm that some aspects of the archaeological record on either side of the North Sea displayed close similarities.

As the nineteenth century progressed, spectacular discoveries, particularly of well-preserved Viking ships, maintained the momentum in academic and public interest. As the Vikings entered popular culture they offered something to everyone – barbaric plunderers and heroic warriors, daring seamen, intrepid adventurers, enterprising traders, allusive poets, master craftsmen. Archetypes harnessed to a spectrum of political causes, they still excite strong passions and are eagerly – sometimes too eagerly – sought to legitimate identities, theories and even commercial brands. A thousand years and more since bursting onto the world scene, Vikings are still a potent force.

The annual Up-Helly-Aa celebrations in Lerwick, Mainland, Shetland, always involve members of the Guizer Jarl's squad dressing as 'Vikings'. Panache is probably more important than historical accuracy; the absence of horned helmets in this particular year – 2006 – was purely fortuitous. More importantly, a modern 'tradition' is maintained, and a good time is had by all in the depths of midwinter.

In England, where sixteenth-century politics and religion inspired an interest in the good old days of an independent Anglo-Saxon state, scholars knew about the contemporary chronicles that had charted the wars of the English and the Vikings, and recorded the names of successive kings and war leaders. The chronicles thus provided a guide to the dating of coins bearing these kings' names, making them the one category of Viking Age artifacts which could be confidently identified.

Otherwise, guesswork was the order of the day. All sorts of earthworks and artifacts, from Stonehenge to the first-century BC musical horns found near the great Irish ritual centre at Navan, County Armagh, were assigned to the Vikings by

seventeenth-, eighteenth- and early nineteenth-century antiquarians who were simply groping in the dark. This was the era when the name 'the Roll-right Stones', long given to a late Neolithic (c. 2000 BC) stone circle in Oxfordshire, was believed by some to relate to 'Rollo the Dane'. Simultaneously, new names such as 'Danes' Graves' and 'Danish Fort' were coined willy-nilly for unexplained ancient monuments across Britain and Ireland.

Just about any newly discovered traces of old boats were also attributed to Vikings. In 1882, for example, just two years after the Gokstad ship was excavated in Norway, the Monmouthshire and Caerleon Antiquarian Association in south Wales reported an 'Ancient Danish Vessel discovered at

Wagner's Ring cycle of operas inspired artistic invention in the quasi-Viking sphere, such as the costume worn by the Norwegian Kirsten Flagstad in singing the role of Brynhild at the Metropolitan Opera House, New York, in the 1930s.

HORNED HELMET SYNDROME

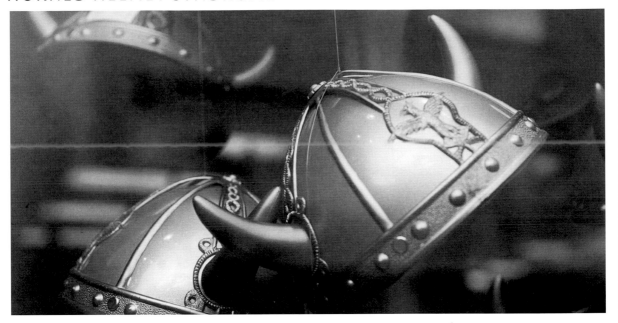

For many people today, a Viking's distinguishing feature is his horned helmet. It's an image reinforced in cartoon strips, a recurring and instantly recognizable caricature. Why this should be is difficult to define precisely. Surviving Viking Age helmets are few and far between, but none of them have horns.

There are indications, however, that horned helmets of some sort may have formed part of the ritual regalia worn in some religious ceremonies. Several two-dimensional copper-alloy representations of bearded male heads with horns springing from them have been found in sixth- and seventh-century contexts in Anglo-Saxon England and in Sweden, and are thought to reflect a cult of the Germanic/Viking god Odin. The 'horns' may represent his two ravens, Hugin and Munin (see p. 167).

Famously, a small bronze 'plaque' with a similar representation was found at Torslunda, on the Swedish island of Öland, in 1870; it may have encouraged the myth of the omnipresent warrior's horned helmet when, for want of any real examples of helmets, it was illustrated in Du Chaillu's popular book *The Viking Age* in 1889. More likely, however, there was simply a long-cherished belief that Viking helmets should have some form of embellishment; even classical representations of the Roman god Mercury's winged helmet seem to have been copied in nineteenth-century pictures of Vikings.

This belief may have been bolstered by horned (probably ceremonial) helmets, now known to date from the Bronze Age and Iron Age, which were found in Scandinavia and Britain during the nineteenth century. And at a time when German military helmets were crowned with a spike like the top of an iron railing, perhaps horns didn't seem so outlandish and risible as they do today.

Ubiquitous equipment for anyone playing at Vikings in the modern world, the plastic horned helmet provides a perfect opportunity for kitsch.

Bronze plaque from Torslunda, Öland, Sweden, showing a horned-helmeted warrior alongside what may be a warrior dressed in a wolf's skin. The scene thus has ritual rather than war-like connotations.

the Mouth of the Usk'. This was pure wishful thinking. So too was the identification of an 'ancient vessel', discovered in the channel of the River Rother in Kent in 1822, which was 'supposed to be one of the fleet abandoned by the Danes after their defeat in the reign of King Alfred'. Associated pottery is now known to indicate a date some 700–800 years later.

The mid-nineteenth century, however, brought new precision to Viking studies. In 1846–47, at the command of King Christian VIII of Denmark, the young Danish archaeologist J.J.A. Worsaae visited Britain and Ireland in order to study Viking Age remains. Struck by the similarities between British and Scandinavian archaeological discoveries, he published in 1852 an influential book entitled *An*

Account of the Danes and Norwegians in England, Scotland and Ireland. There he confirmed the Scandinavian origins of a range of weaponry and jewelry, found principally in graves in Scotland and Ireland.

This was the first of a series of scholarly exchanges across the North Sea that contributed to a growing understanding of Viking Age antiquities. In some cases, it was the opinions of Scandinavian experts that allowed English antiquarians to assert that Viking finds had been made – it was, for example, on the say-so of the Director of the Danish National Museum, Dr Sophus Müller, that objects found in York were recognized in the 1880s for what they were. Otherwise, it was the publication and receipt in Britain of ever more refined and comprehensive surveys of the Scandinavian material in the late nineteenth and twentieth centuries that aided the correct identification of newly excavated material.

Up-Helly-Aa

On the last Tuesday every January in Lerwick, on Mainland, Shetland, a simulated Viking ship is put to the torch by a squad of men extravagantly dressed as Vikings. This is the open-air culmination of Up-Helly-Aa, Britain's most famous and most recognizable winter festival, one which nowadays is inexorably linked with Vikings. Not all participants are dressed as Vikings, however; most sets of 'guizing' costumes are very different and very diverse. For this is not the manifestation of a Viking tradition, unbroken for a millennium; indeed, Lerwick was not founded until the seventeenth century. Rather, it is a new, urban Christmas-time revelry, originating in the early nineteenth century when masked and costumed figures discharged pistols, sought food and drink on people's doorsteps, and tarred their houses if they were refused. By the 1840s flaming barrels of tar were towed around the town as part of this very unruly festivity, and it wasn't until the 1870s that anarchic revelry was tamed and muted into a respectable, increasingly choreographed, pageant-like occasion. New traditions were quickly established, and by the early twentieth century they had come to focus on a romanticized Norse past.

Vikings and Politics

In twentieth-century Europe Viking symbolism was adopted or shunned by a range of political causes. In France the region of Normandy proudly adopted the distinctive profile of a Viking ship's prow as its regional symbol. In Germany, which disputed the border territory of Schleswig-Holstein with Denmark, interest in the heroic past of the early medieval period had been fostered by Wagner's use of Old Norse myths in his Ring cycle of operas completed in 1874.

The climax of the Up-Helly-Aa festival in Lerwick, Mainland, Shetland, comes with a Viking ship being dragged through the streets of the town by the flame-bearing throng, after which the ship is ceremonially burnt.

(Far left) The year 1911 was an opportunity for the City of Rouen (Normandy, France) to celebrate a romantic millenary vision of their Viking heritage.

(Left) A Nazi poster 'For Denmark Against Bolshevism' (c. 1942) harnessed a clean-cut Viking image to the support of a 'Germanic' master race.

(Below) The city of Novgorod, Russia, now identifies the Viking phase of its existence in a lapel badge; this was not politically acceptable in the communist era.

Vikings were adopted in some quarters as honorary Teutons, and their intrepid colonizing was hijacked by the Nazis as propaganda in support of Hitler's bid to rule the world. Further to the east, however, racial purity for post-revolution Russia and its later twentieth-century empire involved stout denial that Vikings had played any significant role in the founding of the Russian kingdom which was, at least officially, a purely Slav creation. Discoveries of Viking artifacts were suppressed and Soviet academics were constrained to toe the Communist Party line. Only with the end of the communist regime in the 1990s was there the start of a new openness to discuss the issue of the Rus and their origins (see pp. 96–101). Soon Novgorod chose to advertise its links with the Vikings, and incorporated a Viking ship into the city's logo.

LATTER-DAY VIKINGS

The foundation in 1892 of the Viking Club, alias The Orkney, Shetland, and Northern Society, was a sign of the contemporary interest in things Viking; in 1912 it became The Viking Society for Northern Research, and still continues to promote Viking studies.

In 1919 the Norwegian Research Fund decided to undertake a major investigation of Viking remains in the British Isles (later extended to Normandy and the coastal lands of northwest Europe). A series of experts was dispatched in 1925–26 to study museum collections, and the fruits of their labours were published in five volumes in 1939–40 under the title Viking Antiquities in Great Britain and Ireland. A sixth volume of synthesis and additional material appeared in 1954. By that time, in the wake of a Second World War during which covert maritime links known as 'the Shetland bus' were maintained between Shetland and occupied Norway, the British Council and the University of Aberdeen combined to arrange in 1950 a gathering of British and Scandinavian scholars in Lerwick, Shetland. Christened 'The Viking Congress', this turned out to be the first of a series of meetings which have been held periodically ever since at venues that alternate between the Scandinavian homelands and 'the Viking colonies'.

REDISCOVERING THE VIKINGS IN THEIR HOMELANDS

Within Scandinavia, interest in the distant past was rekindled in the seventeenth century. The meteoric rise and fall of Swedish empire around the Baltic Sea and a decline in Danish power further fuelled a rivalry between the two kingdoms. Both started to foster an interest in their own pasts, setting out to establish the antiquity, the pedigree and the superiority of their people, and to legitimate their territorial aspirations.

It was by chance rather than design that Viking Age antiquities played a part, for prominent among ancient monuments in the countryside, particularly in parts of what today we know as Sweden, were rune stones. These were an obvious target for antiquarians, who were able to read the runic inscriptions. Indeed, as early as 1591 the Danish governor of Holstein had ordered an engraving to be made of the ancient monuments at Jelling (see pp. 182–184) which included the runic inscriptions and their translation. The Swedish King Gustavus II Adolphus created the Royal Antiquarian Office in 1630, and in 1684 a law was

passed to protect archaeological material found in the ground by paying a reward to the finder.

Interest in the gamut of Nordic antiquities was maintained throughout the eighteenth century. Early prehistoric tombs attracted most attention, but Viking Age remains were sometimes unearthed – in 1751, for example, what must have been a Viking ship burial was found on Rolvsøy, Østfold, Norway, but nothing was preserved. In other cases it was literary texts such as *Heimskringla* – the thirteenth-century history of the Viking world – that were used as a guide as to where and why to excavate, albeit with little success.

In 1752 King Frederick V of Denmark determined to make his country's heritage accessible to a greater European audience and commissioned a history of Denmark. Only two volumes were published, in French, in 1755–56, but together with their English translation *Northern Antiquities* that appeared in 1770, they stimulated great interest. Although there were excavations in the 1680s on Björkö, which was correctly

This early representation of Jelling in Jutland, Denmark, published in 1591, shows most of the principal monuments visible today (compare with p.184). It was, above all, the runic inscription and its references to Viking Age kings that commanded attention.

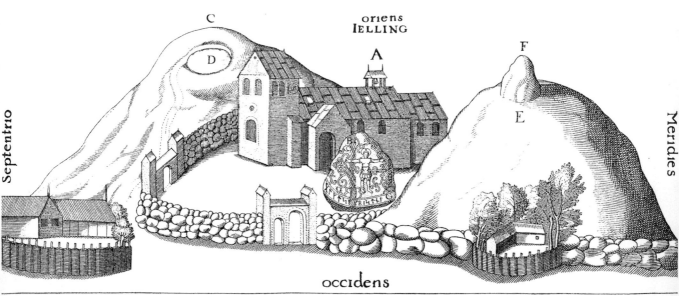

identified as the location of the Viking Age town of Birka (see pp. 64–65), and also at Old Uppsala (see p. 22), where trenches were dug and recorded with a care and attention way ahead of its time, there was still uncertainty about the dating of almost all prehistoric objects.

It wasn't until 1816 that the Dane C. J. Thomsen set out the basic principles which divided the ancient past into Stone, Bronze and Iron Ages, an archaeological classification that remains fundamental to this day. In this scheme the Viking Age was recognized as the very latest prehistoric epoch, at the end of the Iron Age. This scientific approach allowed the artifacts that are characteristic of the Viking Age to be identified clearly, and to be described in a series of critical publications that informed Scandinavians and foreigners alike about what objects could reliably be attributed to the Vikings. Excavations continued to reveal important Viking Age remains – in 1820 work on the northern mound at Jelling revealed the timber tomb chamber of King Gorm (see p. 182), while in 1861 it was the royal initiative of King Frederick VII of Denmark that instigated further investigation of the Jelling mounds.

Antiquities were not exclusively the preserve of the antiquarian, however. The naturalist Hjalmar Stolpe came to Birka in search of ancient insects trapped in amber; the bug he caught, however, was archaeological, and his excavations in 1871–78 brought to light a wealth of objects. His trenching embraced both the large cemeteries at Birka and the area formerly occupied by the Viking Age town referred to in contemporary writings. Normally, however, Viking Age settlement sites could not be located from surface remains. In contrast, graves were often identifiable as mounds, and since there was a strong possibility that they would contain collectable objects, they were the aspect of Viking Age archaeology most frequently investigated.

Meanwhile in Vestfold, Norway, the first of a series of stunning Viking ship burials from the region was dug out of a large mound at Borre in 1852. By all accounts the 17-m (55-ft-6-in) long ship was magnificently furnished – but most of the objects vanished during the digging, and the ship itself does not survive. In 1867 another ship burial was exposed when a large mound at Tune on Rolvsøy, Østfold, on the other side of the Oslo Fjord, was dug into. The grave had been plundered

Royal interest in archaeology among the Scandinavian royal families has a long pedigree; here, King Frederick VII of Denmark visits excavations at Jelling, Jutland in 1861.

Udgravningerne i Jellinge 2den Afdeling Juli 1861   N:8.

MANUSCRIPTS

The spirit of the Viking Age was also preserved through the collection of Icelandic manuscripts that contained the texts of sagas, poems and other works that dealt with Viking Age 'history' or with heroic deeds set in the Viking Age. These manuscripts had been relatively safe in the hands of the Icelandic church throughout the Middle Ages, but with the new version of the faith that came with the Reformation in the mid-sixteenth century, and the introduction of paper, the original vellum manuscripts were no longer accorded the same status as previously.

Danes, and to a lesser extent Swedes, both began to collect these treasures. Some ended up in national libraries, others in the hands of cultured collectors. The most significant collector

was the Icelander Árni Magnússon (1663–1730), a professor at the University of Copenhagen, who made extended tours of his native land in the service of the Danish king. Part of his library was destroyed in a great fire that swept through Copenhagen in 1728, but many of the most significant manuscripts survived.

On the last day of his life Árni Magnússon bequeathed his Danish possessions, including the magnificent manuscript collection, to Copenhagen University. In 1772, by the royal authority of King Frederick V, the Arnamagnaean Foundation came into being, charged with looking after the collection and making its contents widely accessible; in 1956 the University opened the Arnamagnaean Institute

with a permanent staff to carry out these aims.

For Icelanders of the nineteenth and early twentieth centuries who were determined to re-establish an independent Republic, the manuscripts represented the written proof of their country's identity. With the establishment of the Republic of Iceland in 1944, the question of returning these cultural treasures to their native land was debated, and in 1961 the Danes agreed to hand them back to Iceland.

Árni Magnússon, an Icelander working for the Danish court, brought together an important collection of manuscripts in Copenhagen in the early eighteenth century. Since full Icelandic independence in 1944, the collection has been returned to Iceland.

in antiquity, and many of the surviving fragile objects and large segments of the ship itself were destroyed when they were exposed to the air, but an archaeological excavation managed belatedly to salvage some of the remains. In 1880, however, a properly conducted excavation of the better preserved and larger ship burial at Gokstad, in Vestfold, stirred the Norwegian nation. A contemporary account enthused about 'things of which nothing corresponding thereto has ever been found from so remote an age, and which in fact we never had the slightest hope of being able to find... the most valuable archaeological discovery of the period.' The remains of boat and cargo were taken to Oslo and preserved; in a gentle riposte to the Columbus celebrations of the previous year, a replica of the ship, called *Viking*, was sailed across the Atlantic in 1893.

This accumulated experience in scientific examination of ship burials was called upon again in 1903–04 when the most ornately furnished ship of them all was excavated at Oseberg, also in Vestfold. Although the ship was crushed into hundreds of pieces by the weight of the overlying burial mound, its elegantly carved decoration, the elaborate range of wooden items and the remains of textiles were just some of the attributes that singled it out. Painstakingly pieced back together, it was moved in 1926 to a specially built Viking Ship Hall at Bygdøy, Oslo, where the two other surviving ships joined it in 1932 to become something of a shrine to the Viking Age.

(Opposite below) The nineteenth century saw improvements in the techniques of archaeological excavations, at least in the recording of Viking graves excavated at Birka, Uppland, Sweden by Hjalmar Stolpe in the last quarter of the century.

(Left) In 1926, after conservation treatment, the Oseberg ship was transported through the streets of Oslo to a purpose-built display in the suburbs at Bygdøy.

(Below) The early ninth-century ship being excavated from its burial mound at Oseberg, Vestfold, Norway in 1904; it was so well preserved that only a little propping of the prow was necessary at this stage.

MEANWHILE IN AMERICA...

In 1837 the Dane Carl Christian Rafn published his book *Antiquitates Americanae* which, for the first time, made translations of the Vinland sagas available to the nascent American nation and thereby excited interest – particularly among immigrant Scandinavians – in the Viking episode of their past. Rafn was subsequently introduced to an unusual stone structure at Newport, Rhode Island, which he interpreted as the baptistery of a church built by Norse settlers in the twelfth century, despite local belief that it had been erected by Benedict Arnold, governor of the colony, who had emigrated to America in 1635. Indeed, Arnold's will referred to his windmill, and he had probably based this innovative windmill tower on a windmill built in 1632 at Chesterton in Warwickshire, England, that had itself perhaps been designed by the architect Inigo Jones.

Rafn's attribution has been discredited by a variety of modern investigations; at the time it was first propounded, however, it inspired the poet Henry Wadsworth Longfellow. In his poem of 1841 'The Skeleton in Armour', Longfellow wove together the discovery of a native American burial found at nearby Falls River, which he asserted was a Viking, and the Newport Tower, which poetically became the Viking's home. In the popularity of this work, and in its influence in perpetuating and enhancing the Viking past of America, fiction thus became not only stranger, but stronger, more influential, than truth.

Canada too received immigrants proud of a Viking past. In 1875 a group of about 200 Icelandic emigrants were granted land in an area about 50 miles (80 km) to the north of Winnipeg. The main township was christened Gimli, a name taken from Norse mythology and meaning 'the great hall of heaven'; with this expectation of paradise, the settlers soon established the Republic of New Iceland, covering an area of 1,200 sq. km

The tower at Newport, Rhode Island, USA, poetically but wholly erroneously associated with Vikings.

THE VINLAND MAP – GENUINE OR FAKE

The so-called Vinland Map has caused widespread interest and controversy because it purports to be a representation of North America drawn in the early to mid-fifteenth century, 50 years or more before Europeans 'discovered' America. The map is remarkable for its portrayal of a very large island to the west of Greenland; the island is named, in Latin, 'Island of Vinland, discovered by Bjarni and Leif in company'. The implication of this inscription is that the map-maker had got his information from a tradition that went back to the age of the Vikings.

The map first came to attention in 1957 when it was bought in Geneva by an American dealer in rare books. It was subsequently sold to Paul Mellon, an American philanthropist, who presented it to Yale University Library. In 1964 a small group of scholars pronounced the map a genuine work of c. 1440, but in 1974, following scientific examination, Yale announced that the map 'may be a forgery'. This about-turn was based on the fact that the map's ink contained anatase, and on the belief that this would not have been available in the quantities allegedly present on the map before the commercial production of anatase began in 1920.

Further scientific examinations in 1985 suggested that the anatase was present only in tiny quantities compatible with medieval production, and this led to a further re-evaluation of the map, which Yale again pronounced to be genuine in 1995.

Doubts remained, however, and the overwhelming scholarly consensus is that the Vinland Map is a modern forgery, based on sixteenth-century Portuguese maps, and made by a knowledgeable scholar. Indeed, it has been suggested that the forgery was perpetrated in the 1930s by an Austrian Jesuit priest, Father Joseph Fischer, an expert on ancient maps. His purpose, it is alleged, was to lodge a scholarly protest against Nazi attempts to associate the Third Reich with ancient Norse culture. The Vinland Map contains many saints' names, and thus it links the church, rather than secular power, with the discovery of America.

The Vinland Map – still an object of contention, despite scientific analyses.

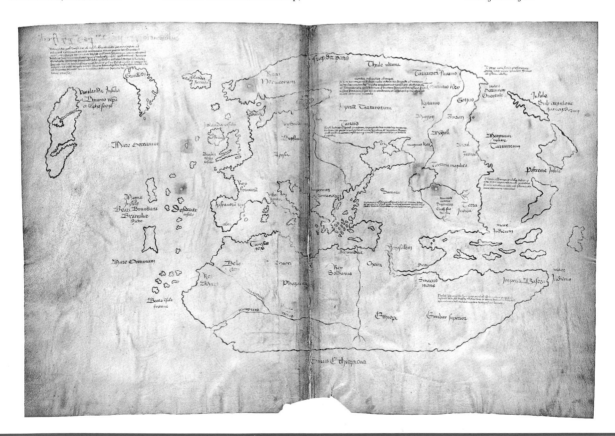

(460 sq. miles). Their numbers boosted by further Icelanders, some seeking respite from the fall-out of volcanic eruptions, the Republic maintained a quasi-independence until it was absorbed into an expanded province of Manitoba in 1887. The Icelandic tradition lives on, and to commemorate their origins the townsfolk in 1967 erected a huge Viking statue, 4.6 m (15 ft) high.

In 1899 a Swedish immigrant farmer at Kensington, Minnesota, brought to attention a stone that he claimed to have found on his farm in the previous year. Its distinguishing characteristic is a long runic inscription that describes a disastrous voyage of exploration undertaken to this area by a group of Goths (Swedes) and Norwegians from Vinland in 1362. The 'Kensington Stone', as it came to be known, was immediately decried by leading Scandinavian experts as 'a crude fraud, perpetrated by a Swede with the aid of a chisel and a meagre knowledge of runic letters and English'. Several more recent commentators have seen it as a witty hoax, an understandable and essentially harmless joke, given the time and place. Indeed, some have claimed that the inscription deliberately incorporates clues designed to alert readers to its true origin.

It was only when a Norwegian-American from Wisconsin, Hjalmar Holand, acquired the stone in 1907 and began a vigorous campaign to proclaim its authenticity, that things changed. The 'Kensington Stone' began to achieve the status of icon for some people and became a bête-noir to others. Not a single modern internationally-acknowledged expert in runes considers that this is a genuine fourteenth-century inscription; meanwhile true believers, unburdened by this depth of comparative knowledge, detect an academic conspiracy (without explaining why there should be one) and continue to uphold the stone's authenticity and historical accuracy and value.

(Above) The stone from Kensington, Minnesota, USA, obviously a late nineteenth-century creation to expert runologists but, for others, a treasured symbol of their pride in Scandinavian roots.

(Right) Huge statue of the archetypal popular Viking erected in 1967 at Gimli, Manitoba, Canada, to commemorate the area's settlement by Icelanders in the late nineteenth century.

THE VIKINGS: PAST, PRESENT AND FUTURE

The last half century has seen enormous advances in our understanding of the Vikings. A number of 'landmark' investigations have attracted and enhanced this interest over the decades, including the remarkable recovery of the Viking ships from the waters of Roskilde Fjord in 1962, the continuing excavations in Novgorod and, latterly, Gorodisce, the investigation of the Danish Viking camp at Fyrkat in the 1950s and early 1960s, the 1976–81 'Viking Dig' in York and the earlier and simultaneous excavations in Dublin.

Public concern has prompted governments to safeguard cultural remains of all periods, including the Viking Age; ironically, this has meant that there has been much more archaeological excavation (analytical destruction) of sites which stand in the way of modernization and re-development.

It is now almost impossible to keep abreast of the amount of new data and their implications. Simultaneously, the exponential growth in scientific means of investigating the past – dating methodologies, physical, chemical and biological analyses, and so on – has opened entirely new horizons of study, such as the environment of the Viking Age. Increasingly subtle historical, linguistic, literary and art historical discourse has prompted new questions and provided new avenues along which to approach the subject.

An enormous amount of excavation and research spread across a wide range of academic disciplines has taken place. Some of this has, in turn, encouraged much wider popular interest in the Vikings, whether as visitors to educational attractions such as the Jorvik Centre in York, or as participants in Viking-themed events.

As I write, some new studies are addressing areas of the Viking world, such as the west coast of Ireland, which have hitherto been overlooked or dismissed as lacking evidence, while others are critically reassessing older material. The picture of the Vikings is now as different from that drawn 50 years ago as was the wide extent of Viking power and influence c. 1000 from the much more circumscribed limits of their ambit two centuries earlier. Viking studies are in a state of healthy ferment, with new themes and topics under academic attack.

Viking balls were fashionable in later nineteenth-century Sweden, and represent an era when antiquarian imagination had hardly been influenced by archaeological discoveries. Serious twenty-first-century Viking re-enactors can base their costumes on a wide range of excavated objects. Whatever the inspiration, the appeal of the Vikings appears undiminished.

GAZETTEER

National, regional and local museums and visitor centres around the Viking world may contain artifacts, exhibitions and displays relating to Vikings. But exhibitions change, so please check the internet for the latest information.

Denmark

As well as The National Museum in Copenhagen and a network of regional museums, there are significant displays at the Ribe Viking Museum (reconstructions, excavated artifacts), at the Lindholm Høje site museum adjacent to the memorable cemetery with its stone-marked graves, and at Moesgård Museum near Århus, where there is a reconstruction of a house from Hedeby, a collection of rune stones, and so on.

The excellent Roskilde Ship Museum displays the conserved remains of the Skuldelev ships, together with full-scale replicas of some of them, and a wide array of supporting material. At Ladby the ship burial can be seen, displayed behind glass within its burial mound.

The circular camps at Trelleborg and Fyrkat have both been recreated after excavation, and at both there are reconstructions of excavated buildings to be seen. Near to Fyrkat there is also a reconstruction of the farmhouse excavated at Vorbasse.

Jelling is dominated by the complex of monuments that includes the twin mounds, the rune stones and the church; there is an adjacent exhibition outlining the site's history.

At Ravning there is a short reconstructed length of the bridge, and a small exhibition about it. The area around Viborg has the largest concentration of rune stones in Denmark.

Germany

Hedeby (or Haithabu), near modern Schleswig, has notable remains of the semicircular rampart around the Viking Age town, and a good site museum.

At Schloss Gottorp Museum, Schleswig, the pre-Viking Nydam ship is displayed, as are weapons, clothing and other objects recovered from the region's bogs.

Danevirke, the rampart that defined Denmark's southern boundary in the Viking Age, can be visited at several places.

Sweden

The Historiska Museet in Stockholm, and the Museum of Cultural History and the University Museum, both in Lund, have major collections.

A ferry cruise from Stockholm will take you (in summer) to the site of the Viking Age town of Birka. Parts of its enclosing rampart can be seen, and extensive grave fields can be traced. There is an explanatory display.

Sigtuna's museum contains important artifacts from the excavations in the town, including the iconic elk antler carved warrior's head shown on page 68; there are also many rune stones within the historic town. At Old (Gamla) Uppsala the impressive mounds can be visited. Throughout the Uppland area in particular many rune stones remain in their original positions.

The Göteborg (Gothenborg) Museum contains the remains of the Äskekärr ship. The Museum in Visby, on Gotland, has a remarkable collection of silver hoards, and also the definitive collection of picture stones.

On Öland the excavated multi-period fort of Eketorp has been reconstructed.

Norway

The National Museum in Oslo and the principal regional museums, in Stavanger, Bergen, Trondheim and Tromsö, have the main archaeological collections.

The Viking Ship Hall, at Bygdøy, Oslo, displays the Tune, Gokstad and Oseberg ships and the objects found in them. The mound cemetery at Borre, and the reconstituted individual grave mounds at Oseberg and Gokstad, are also visitable.

The site of the trading/manufacturing centre at Kaupang reveals nothing of Viking Age life, but the sites of various cemeteries can be found.

At Borg in Lofoten the remarkable hall has been reconstructed, and there is a display of excavated material.

The remains of the deserted Viking Age settlement at Ytre Moa, Øvre Årdal, Sognefjord, stand on a small terrace high above the valley floor.

France

The Museum of Antiquities in Rouen has a small number of Viking artifacts. The earthworks of the Camp de Péran are impressive, and there is an interpretation board.

The Bayeux Tapestry in Bayeux, Normandy, is a remarkable pictorial guide that includes some elements of life-style that were common to Late Viking Age Scandinavians, Anglo-Saxons and Normans.

Holland

The silver hoards from Vieringen are displayed at the museum in Leiden. The Centraal Museum in Utrecht contains some Viking weaponry and objects excavated in Dorestad, the Rhenish trading centre attacked often by Vikings.

At Burgh, and at Oost-Souburg, Flushing, the fortifications built in the Viking Age can still be seen, the latter completely restored with a defensive wall.

Finland

The National Museum of Finland in Helsinki contains the most significant collection of Viking Age objects.

Russia

In Novgorod it is sometimes possible to see material from the Gorodisce site; see also the Staraja Ladoga Museum and The Hermitage Museum in St Petersburg.

Faeroe Islands

The National Museum in the outskirts of Torshavn houses the only collection of Viking Age archaeological material; the excavated remains of two Viking Age buildings can be visited at Kvívík.

Iceland

The National Museum in Reykjavik has the most important archaeological collections; the Árnastofnun Manuscript Institute displays medieval manuscripts.

The exposed and landscaped remains of the site of Herjólfsdalur on the Westmann Islands can be seen, as can other excavated sites such as that at Stöng; a reconstruction based on this building can be seen at Thjórsárdalur.

There is a reconstruction of Eirik the Red's farm at Eiríksstaðir in Haukadalur. Sites associated with events recounted in sagas can be visited, as can Thingvellir, where the Althing met; the site of Snorre Sturluson's home at Reykholt is also open.

Greenland

The National Museum in Nuuk is currently a disappointment as far as its Viking display is concerned.

Better, if possible, to visit the key sites, of which Brattahlid and Gardar are most often on the itineraries of cruise ships; Hvalsey and Herjolfsnes are also extremely evocative.

Canada

At L'Anse aux Meadows, Newfoundland, the excavated remains of Viking Age settlement have been landscaped and displayed, with an adjacent simulation of one of the halls and its outbuildings. There is also an associated interpretation centre.

About 2 km away is Norstead, a re-enactors' village better for the full-scale replica of the Skuldelev deep-sea trading vessel than for the buildings.

England

Principal artifact collections and displays are in The British Museum, the Museum of London, and The Yorkshire Museum in York. The Castle Museum, Norwich and the Tullie House Museum, Carlisle, also display some material, as do, in limited quantities, other museums in the former Danelaw area.

Derby Museum and Art Gallery houses the material from the Repton Viking camp and cemetery, and The Collection at Danes Terrace, Lincoln, includes Viking Age objects from the city and county of Lincoln.

In York, the Jorvik Viking Centre in Coppergate Walk displays the remains of Viking Age houses excavated on this site by York Archaeological Trust, together with a simulation of the Viking Age streetscape and a selection of objects found there. There are also periodic special exhibitions. A flavour of the archaeological processes of discovery and investigation can be got at DIG, in St Saviourgate. York Minster's Undercroft exhibits a series of decorated stone grave markers found there.

North Yorkshire and Cumbria have the strongest representations of Viking Age sculpture in England, with particularly notable collections at Middleton, Brompton and Lythe in Yorkshire, and at Penrith, Lowther and Gosforth in Cumbria. Many other churches also have significant collections; at Kirkdale in North Yorkshire there is also a dedication inscription from just before the Norman conquest.

The 1066 battle sites at both Fulford and Stamford Bridge require imagination to be exercised, as does the site by the River Ouse at Riccall, North Yorkshire, where the Norwegian invaders moored their ships.

An instructive example of how the landscape can change is provided by the site of the deserted medieval village at Wharram Percy, East Riding of Yorkshire; the earthwork humps and bumps are (mostly) of later medieval origin, but the village and its ruined church flourished in the Viking Age.

Scotland

Major museum collections are in the National Museum of Scotland in Edinburgh, in the Tankerness House Museum in Kirkwall, Mainland, Orkney, in the Shetland Museum in Lerwick, Mainland, Shetland, and in Museum nan Eilean in Stornoway, Lewis, Outer Hebrides. In the Northern Isles there are sites to be seen at Jarlshof, on the south tip of Mainland, Shetland, a multi-period excavation with the outlines of longhouses, and at Catpund Quarry, Cunningsburgh, Mainland, Shetland, where there are remains of soapstone quarrying.

On Mainland, Orkney, the prehistoric tomb called Maeshowe can be visited to see the runic inscriptions, and the locations of other excavated sites are also accessible. St Magnus Cathedral in Kirkwall is replete with Viking associations; the box which contains the relics of St Magnus are displayed in the adjacent museum (which also houses a large amount of Viking material including objects from the Scar burial), and the site of his death on Egilsay is also accessible.

In the Western Isles the sites of previous excavations can be visited, although there is little obvious from the Viking Age to see. The museum at the Iona medieval monastery site contains a decorated rune stone.

Wales

The National Museum in Cardiff has the only notable collection.

Ireland

The National Museum in Dublin has the outstanding collection; there is also a worthwhile display in Waterford Museums, and lesser amounts in Limerick and Cork. Limerick Castle displays traces of late Viking Age buildings discovered on the site. The Ulster Museum, Belfast, also has a small collection.

The Dublinia exhibition opposite Christ Church Cathedral, Dublin, presents the history of Dublin, concentrating on the medieval era but touching on the Viking Age origins. A solitary example of a hogback tombstone is to be found at Castledermot, County Kildare.

Isle of Man

The Manx Museum in Douglas, and the House of Manannan near Peel Castle, are the two critical exhibitions.

The Tynwald parliament (Thing) site is always open to visit, and examples of the characteristic slate sculpture are on display in the churches where they were found.

Grave mounds at Balladoole and Knock-y-Doonee, and the occupation site at the Braaid, are also accessible.

Turkey

The well-known runic inscription is carved into a gallery within Agia Sophia, Istanbul, Justinian's sixth-century church that later became a mosque and is now the St Sophia Museum.

FURTHER READING

This selection focuses on books in English. New archaeological reports are listed in the British and Irish Archaeological Bibliography, accessible via the Council for British Archaeology's website (www.britarch.ac.uk); new discoveries in Britain and Ireland are reported in the Society for Medieval Archaeology's annual journal *Medieval Archaeology*. Another journal, *Nordic Archaeological Abstracts* covers 1976–1998 only.

Each of the chapters' bibliographies (in which book titles are usually self-explanatory) should be supplemented by reference to the following general introductory surveys that cover a broad spectrum of Viking topics:

Roesdahl, E. and D.M. Wilson (eds.), *From Viking to Crusader. The Scandinavians and Europe 800–1200* (New York, 1992); Graham-Campbell, J., *The Viking World* (London, 2001); Graham-Campbell, J. (ed.), *Cultural Atlas of the Viking World* (Oxford, 1994); Graham-Campbell, J., *Viking Artefacts* (London, 1980); Sawyer, P. (ed.), *The Oxford Illustrated History of the Vikings* (Oxford, 1997); Haywood, J., *The Penguin Historical Atlas of the Vikings* (London, 1995); Roesdahl, E., *The Vikings* (London, 1991); Fitzhugh, W.W. and E.I. Ward, *Vikings: The North Atlantic Saga* (Washington, 2000); Haywood, J., *Encyclopaedia of the Viking Age* (London and New York, 2000).

Books and articles are mentioned at the first chapter to which they are relevant; but many relate equally to other chapters.

I · Who Were the Vikings?

Pre-Viking archaeology within Denmark is treated in Hvass, S. and B. Storgaard, *Digging into the Past. 25 Years of Archaeology in Denmark* (Århus, 1993); Hedeager, L., *Iron Age Societies: From Tribe to State in Northern Europe, 500 BC to AD 700* (Oxford, 1992) surveys the Iron Age Viking societies of Scandinavia. Hines, J., K.H. Nielsen, and F. Siegmund (eds.), *The Pace of Change. Studies in Early-Medieval Chronology* (Oxford, 1999) has a section devoted to Scandinavia. Jesch, J. (ed.), *The Scandinavians From the Vendel Period to the Tenth Century: An Ethnographic Perspective* (Woodbridge, 2002) is an eclectic series of essays.

Runes are introduced briefly in Page, R.I., *Runes* (London, 1987); Jansen, S.B.F., *Runes in Sweden* (Möklinta, 1987) and Moltke, E., *Runes and Their Origins: Denmark and Elsewhere* (Copenhagen, 1985) survey within modern geographic boundaries.

Techniques of archaeological dating (and much else) are explained in Renfrew, C. and P. Bahn, *Archaeology: Theories, Methods and Practice* (4th edition, London and New York, 2004).

The early town of Ribe is described in Feveile, C., 'Ribe on the north side of the river, 8th–12th centuries' in Feveile, C. (ed.), *Det ældste Ribe* (Århus, 2006, pp. 65–91).

II · Viking Life and Culture

Sawyer, P. and B. Sawyer, *Medieval Scandinavia. From Conversion to Reformation* (Minnesota, 1993) is useful for Viking history, geography, society, etc; other general works on Viking life and culture include Foote, P.G. and D.M. Wilson, *The Viking Achievement* (London, 1970) and Roesdahl, E., *Viking Age Denmark* (London, 1982).

Viking women are given due attention in Jesch, J., *Women in the Viking Age* (Woodbridge, 1991) and in Jochens, J., *Women in Old Norse Society* (Cornell, 1995).

Sawyer, B., *The Viking-Age Rune-Stones* (Oxford, 2000) discusses the evolving social and political scene in their light. Graham-Campbell, J., *Viking Artefacts* (London, 1980) contains a wide selection of objects, including jewelry and clothing.

Munch, G.S., O.S. Johansen and E. Roesdahl, (eds.), *Borg in Lofoten. A Chieftain's Farm in North Norway* (Trondheim, 2003) covers the site in depth.

Jesch, J., *Ships and Men in the Late Viking Age. The Vocabulary of Runic Inscriptions and Skaldic Verses* (Woodbridge, 2001) ranges widely over the topic. A report of 1882, recently reprinted, is Nicolaysen, N., *The Viking Ship Discovered at Gokstad in Norway* (Sandefjord, 2003); Brøgger, A.W. and H. Shetelig, *The Viking Ships* (London, 1971); Crumlin-Pedersen, O., *Viking Age Ships and Shipbuilding in Hedeby/Haithabu and Schleswig* (Schleswig/Roskilde 1997); and Sørensen, A.C., *Ladby. A Danish Ship-Grave from the Viking Age* (Roskilde 2001) are all useful volumes on the subject of ships. Sailing routes are mentioned in Lund, N. (ed.) *Ohtere and Wulfstan. Two Voyagers at the Court of King Alfred* (York, 1984).

Hårdh, B., *Silver in the Viking Age* (Stockholm, 1996) covers Scandinavia and the Baltic. Arwidsson, G. and G. Berg, *The Mästermyr Find: A Viking Age Tool Chest from Gotland* (Stockholm, 1983) reports an important collection of blacksmiths' and carpenters' tools.

Crafts and technology are discussed in various volumes of *The Archaeology of York* series, including Rogers, P.W., *Textile Production at 16–22 Coppergate* (1997); Ottaway, P., *Anglo-Scandinavian Ironwork from Coppergate* (1992); Bayley, J., *Non-Ferrous Metalworking at Coppergate*; Morris, C., *Wood and Woodworking in Anglo-Scandinavian and Medieval York*; McGregor, A., *Bone and Antler from Anglo-Scandinavian and Medieval York*; Mould, Q., I. Carlisle, and E. Cameron, *Leather and Leatherworking in Anglo-Scandinavian and Medieval York*; and Mainman, A.J. and N.S.H. Rogers, *Finds from Anglo-Scandinavian York* (2000).

Kaupang is investigated in Skre, D. and F.-A. Stylegar, *Kaupang. The Viking Town* (Oslo, 2004) and Skre, D. (ed.), *Kaupang Studies* (Århus, forthcoming). Results of the excavations at Birka from 1990–95 are being published in the series Ambrosiani, B. (ed.), *Birka Studies* (Stockholm).

III · Raiders and Invaders

Stenton, F. M., *Anglo-Saxon England* (3rd edition, Oxford, 1971) remains the standard historical introduction; Smyth, A.P., *Scandinavian Kings in the British Isles 850–880* (Oxford, 1977) is also a historical study.

Graham-Campbell, J., R.A. Hall, J. Jesch, and D.N. Parsons (eds.), *Vikings and the Danelaw* (Oxford, 2001) contains, among other things, key papers on the Vikings' 'great heathen army'.

Ó Corráin, D., *Ireland Before the Normans* (Dublin, 1972) and Ó Cróinín, D., *Early Medieval Ireland 400–1200* (Harlow, 1995) are two historical introductions; Clarke, H.B., M. Ní Mhaonaigh and R. Ó Floinn (eds.), *Ireland and Scandinavia in the Early Viking Age* (Dublin, 1998) also contains papers on Scotland. Etchingham, C., *Viking Raids on Irish Church Settlements in the Ninth Century* (Maynooth, 1996) and O'Brien, R., P. Quinney and I. Russell, 'Preliminary Report on the Archaeological Excavation... of the Hiberno-Scandinavian Site of Woodstown 6, County Waterford' in *Decies. Journal of the Waterford Archaeological and Historical Society* 61, (2005, 13-122) are also useful sources.

Ritchie, A., *Viking Scotland* (London, 1993); Graham-Campbell, J. and C.E. Batey, *Vikings in Scotland* (Edinburgh, 1998); and Redknap, M. *Vikings in Wales* (Cardiff, 2000) cover those countries in depth. Price, N. S., *The Vikings in Brittany* (Viking Society for Northern Research, London, 1989); Willemsen, A., *Vikings! Raids in the Rhine/Meuse region 800–1000* (Utrecht, 2004); and Simek, R. and U. Engel (eds.), *Vikings on the Rhine* (Vienna, 2004) are worth a look for those areas.

Contemporary records of Viking raids in England are contained in *The Anglo-Saxon Chronicle*, which is available in a variety of translations, including those by Whitelock, D., (London, 1961/1965) and by Swanton, M., (London,

1996). Nelson, J.L., *The Annals of St-Bertin* (Manchester, 1991) makes available a major Carolingian source; Mac Airt, S. and G. Mac Niocaill (eds.), *The Annals of Ulster* (Dublin, 1983) provides the major Irish source.

Harrison, M. and G. Embleton, *Viking Hersir 793–1066* (London, 1993) provides a brief introduction to weaponry; Pierce, I., *Swords of the Viking Age* (Woodbridge, 2002) is a select illustrated catalogue. Other sources on weaponry include Hawkes, S.C. (ed.), *Weapons and Warfare in Anglo-Saxon England* (Oxford, 1989) and Davidson, H.R.E., *The Sword in Anglo-Saxon England* (Oxford, 1962). Depictions of warriors on English sculpture are presented in Bailey, R.N., *Viking Age Sculpture in Northern England* (London, 1980); in Collingwood, W.G., *Northumbrian Crosses of the Pre-Norman Age* (London, 1927); and in the volumes of (ed. Cramp, R.) *The British Academy Corpus of Anglo-Saxon Sculpture* (Oxford, continuing).

IV · Invaders and Settlers

Hines, J., A. Lane and M. Redknap (eds.), *Land, Sea and Home* (Leeds, 2004) embraces most of the Viking world; Davies, W. (ed.), *From the Vikings to the Normans* (Oxford, 2003) discusses Britain and Ireland. Mortensen, A. and S.V. Arge, *Viking and Norse in the North Atlantic* (Torshavn, 2005) and Lewis-Simpson, S. (ed.), *Vinland Revisited. The Norse World at the Turn of the First Millennium* (St Johns, 2003) include essays on England, Ireland and Scotland.

The many useful volumes on the Vikings in England include Roesdahl, E. et al. (eds.), *The Vikings in England* (London, 1981); Richards, J.D. *Viking Age England* (2nd edition, Stroud, 2000); Hadley, D.M. and J.D. Richards (eds.), *Cultures in Contact. Scandinavian Settlement in England in the Ninth Century* (Turnhout, 2000); Hadley, D.M., *The Northern Danelaw. Its Social Structure c. 800–1100* (London, 2000); Townend, M., *Language and History in Viking Age England* (Turnhout, 2002); Edwards, B.J.N., *Vikings in North-West England* (Lancaster, 1998); Margeson, S., *The Vikings in Norfolk* (Norwich, 1997); and Cavill, P., S.E. Harding and J. Jesch, *Wirral and Its Viking Heritage* (Nottingham, 2000).

Hall, R.A., *Viking Age York* (London, 1996) and Hall, R.A. (ed.), *Aspects of Anglo-Scandinavian York* (York, 2004) cover that important Viking settlement, the latter being one of many reports in *The Archaeology of York* series that presents relevant material. Crawford, B.E (ed.), *Scandinavian Settlement in Northern Britain* (London, 1995) focuses on place-name evidence in Scotland and Northern England.

Crawford, B.E., *Scandinavian Scotland* (Leicester, 1987) and Owen, O., *The Sea Road. A Viking Voyage Through Scotland* (Edinburgh, 1999) introduce this subject. Batey, C.E., J. Jesch and C.D. Morris (eds.), *The Viking Age in Caithness, Orkney and the North Atlantic* (Edinburgh, 1993); Graham-Campbell, J., *The Viking-Age Gold and Silver of Scotland* (Edinburgh, 1995); and Owen, O. and M. Dalland, *Scar. A Viking Boat Burial on Sanday, Orkney* (East Linton, 1999) are also useful.

Larsen, A-C (ed.), *The Vikings in Ireland* (Roskilde, 2001) is a wide ranging series of introductory essays; Johnson, R., *Viking Age Dublin* (Dublin, 2004) concentrates on the latest archaeological discoveries. The National Museum of Ireland's excavations in Dublin are reported in the Royal Irish Academy's series *Medieval Dublin Excavations* (continuing). Connolly, M. and F. Coyne, *Underworld. Death and Burial in Cloghermore Cave, Co. Kerry* (Bray, 2005).

For the Isle of Man read C. Fell et al. (eds.), *The Viking Age in the Isle of Man* (London, 1983) and Kermode, P.M.C., *Manx Crosses* (1907/1994). The 'pagan lady' and other Viking Age burials are reported in Freke, D., *Excavations On St Patrick's Isle, Peel, Isle of Man 1982–88* (Liverpool, 2002).

Bates, D., *Normandy Before 1066* (London, 1982) covers that area. Davidson, H.R.E., *The Viking Road to Byzantium* (London, 1976) is a general introduction to Viking activity eastwards; Franklin, S. and J. Shepard, *The Emergence of Rus 750–1200* (London, 1996) also focuses on the documentary evidence. Brisbane, M.E. (ed.), *The Archaeology of Novgorod, Russia* (Lincoln, 1992), and Brisbane, M. and D. Gaimster, *Novgorod: the Archaeology of a Russian Medieval City and its Hinterland* (London, 2001) each contain an article by E. Nosov on Gorodisce.

V · New Found Lands

Jones, G., *The Norse Atlantic Saga* (2nd edition, Oxford, 1986) provides a historical framework. Bigelow, G.F (ed.), *The Norse of the North Atlantic* (Acta Archaeologica 61, 1990); Hansen, S.S. and K. Randsborg (eds.), *Vikings in the West* (Acta Archaeologica 71, 2000); and Barrett, J.H. (ed.), *Contact, Continuity and Collapse. The Norse Colonization of the North Atlantic* (Turnhout, 2003) are all useful. Lewis-Simpson, S. (ed.), *Vinland Revisited. The Norse World at the Turn of the First Millennium* (St Johns, 2003), and Mortensen, A. and S.V. Arge, *Viking and Norse in the North Atlantic* (Torshavn, 2005) are collections including relevant essays.

Byock, J., *Viking Age Iceland* (London, 2001) is a good source; Einarsson, B.F., *The Settlement of Iceland; A Critical Approach* (Reykjavik, 1995) focuses on ecological approaches; Friðriksson, A., *Sagas and Popular Antiquarianism in Icelandic Archaeology* (Aldershot, 1994) is a critical review of interpretation in Icelandic archaeology. Pálsson, H. and P. Edwards, *The Book of Settlements Landnámabók* (Manitoba, 1972) provides a translation of this text.

Arneborg, J. and Gulløv, H.C. (eds.), *Man, Culture and Environment in Ancient Greenland* (Copenhagen, 1998) includes interim reports on the GUS site; Lynnerup, N., *The Greenland Norse: A biological-anthropological study* (Copenhagen, 1998) is also worth a look.

General works on the Vikings in America include Ingstad, A.S., *The Norse Discovery of America* (Oslo, 1985); Wahlgren, E., *The Vikings and America* (London and New York, 1986); and Fitzhugh, W.W. and E.I. Ward, *Vikings: The North Atlantic Saga* (Washington, 2000). Magnusson, M. and H. Pálsson, *The Vinland Sagas. The Norse Discovery of America* (London, 1965) introduce and translate two key sagas.

VI · Expressions of Identity: Religion and Art

Among many books on the art of the Vikings are Wilson, D.M. and O. Klindt-Jensen, *Viking Art* (London, 1966); Fuglesang, S.H., *Some Aspects of the Ringerike Style* (Odense, 1980); Hedeager, L., 'Beyond Mortality: Scandinavian Animal Styles AD 400–1200' in Downes, J. and A. Ritchie, (eds.), *Sea Change. Orkney and Northern Europe in the Later Iron Age AD 300–800* (Balgavies, 2003); and Nylen, E. and J.P. Lamm, *Stones, Ships and Symbols* (Stockholm, 1988).

Norse mythology is covered in Page, R.I., *Norse Myths* (London 1990); Orchard, A., *Dictionary of Norse Myth and Legend* (London, 1997); Davidson, H.R.E., *Gods and Myths of Northern Europe* (London, 1964); and Price, N., *The Viking Way* (Uppsala, 2002).

VII · The Later Viking Age

Useful sources include Rumble, A. (ed.), *The Reign of Cnut* (London, 1994); Lawson, M.K., *Cnut. The Danes in England in the Eleventh Century* (London, 1993); Cooper, J. (ed.), *The Battle of Maldon, Fiction and Fact* (London, 1993); and Scragg, D. (ed.), *The Battle of Maldon AD 991* (Oxford 1991). Magnusson, M. and H. Pálsson, *King Harald's Saga* (London, 1966) translate the saga.

Carver, M., (ed.), *The Cross Goes North AD 300–1300* (Woodbridge, 2003); Clarke, H. and B. Ambrosiani, *Towns in the Viking Age* (Leicester, 1991); Hurley, M.F., O.M.B. Scully and S.W.J. McCutcheon, *Late Viking Age and Medieval Waterford. Excavations 1986–1992* (Waterford, 1997); and Iversen, M., D.E. Robinson, J. Hjermind and C. Christensen, *Viborg Søndersø 1018–1030* (Moesgård, 2005) are also relevant to this chapter.

VIII · The End and After

McDonald, R.A., *The Kingdom of the Isles. Scotland's Western Seaboard c. 1100–c. 1336* (Phantassie, 1997) and Hudson, B., *Viking Pirates and Christian Princes. Dynasty, Religion and Empire in the North Atlantic* (Oxford, 2005) both provide a document-based background. Pearson, M.P., N. Sharples and J. Symonds, *South Uist. Archaeology and History of A Hebridean Island* (Stroud, 2004) puts the Viking and Norse periods into a wider chronological context.

Stratford, N., *The Lewis Chessmen* (London, 1997); Crawford, B.E (ed.), *St Magnus Cathedral and Orkney's 12th Century Renaissance* (Aberdeen, 1988); and Barnes, M.P., *The Runic Inscriptions of Maes Howe* (Uppsala, 1994) are the best sources on these important finds and sites. Pálsson, H. and P. Edwards, *Orkneyinga Saga* (London, 1978) translates the history of the Earls of Orkney.

Duffy, S. (ed.) *Medieval Dublin* (Dublin, continuing) annually presents useful articles. Byock, J.L., *Medieval Iceland* (Berkeley, 1988) is also useful. For the Herjolfsnes garments, turn to Østergård, E., *Woven into the Earth. Textiles from Norse Greenland* (Århus, 2004).

IX · Nationalists, Romantics, Madmen and Scholars
The best sources are Klindt-Jensen, O., *History of Scandinavian Archaeology* (London, 1975); Wawn, A., *The Vikings and the Victorians* (Cambridge, 2000); Björnsson, Á., *Wagner and the Volsungs* (London, 2003); Wahlgren, E., *The Vikings and America* (London, 1996); Seaver, K., *Maps, Myths and Men. The Story of the Vinland Map* (Stanford, 2004); and Barnes, G., *Viking America. The First Millennium* (Cambridge, 2001).

ILLUSTRATION CREDITS

a = above, b = below, l = left, r = right, c = centre

1 Werner Forman Archive/Statens Historiska Museum, Stockholm; 2 © Ted Spiegel/Corbis; 4–5 Statens Historiska Museum, Stockholm; 6 Museum of Cultural History – University of Oslo, Norway; 8 Werner Forman Archive/Viking Ship Museum, Denmark; 9c Lesley Collett © Thames & Hudson Ltd; 9b E. Malkie; 10 British Museum, London; 11 Landsbókasafn Íslands; 12 NASA; 13 Arne Knudsen; 14a Moesgard Museum, Photo Lars Foged Thomsen; 14b National Museum of Denmark, Copenhagen; 15c National Museum of Denmark, Copenhagen; 15b Lesley Collett © Thames & Hudson Ltd; 16 Riksantivvarieämbetet, Stockholm; 17a Statens Historiska Museum, Stockholm; 17bl Historiska Museet, Lund University, Photo Bengt Almgren; 17br National Museum of Denmark, Copenhagen; 18 Museum of Cultural History – University of Oslo, Norway; 20 Werner Forman Archive/Statens Historiska Museum, Stockholm; 21 Ragnar L. Børsheim/Arkikon; 22c Statens Historiska Museum, Stockholm; 22b Bjorn Ambrosiani; 23a Wikinger Museum, Haithabu; 23b Den Antikvariske Samling I Ribe; 24 Viking Ship Museum Denmark, Photo Werner Karrasch; 25 © Museum of Cultural History – University of Oslo, Norway; 28–29 ML Design © Thames & Hudson Ltd; 30 Moesgard Museum, Photo Lars Foged Thomsen; 32 ML Design © Thames & Hudson Ltd; 33 Courtesy Else Roesdahl; 34a © Charles & Josette Lenars/Corbis; 34b Museum of Cultural History – University of Oslo, Norway; 35l Statens Historiska Museum, Stockholm; 35r Ragnar L. Børsheim/Arkikon; 36al National Museum of Denmark, Copenhagen; 36ar © Mytte Fertz; 36b Werner Forman Archive/Statens Historiska Museum, Stockholm; 37 Wikinger Museum, Haithabu; 38a York Archaeological Trust; 38b © Martin Biddle and Birthe Kjolbye-Biddle, all rights reserved; 39 Museum of Cultural History – University of Oslo, Norway; 40 Drazen Tomic © Thames & Hudson Ltd; 41 Ragnar L. Børsheim/Arkikon; 42 Werner Forman Archive; 43a Courtesy Else Roesdahl; 43b Lesley Collett © Thames & Hudson Ltd; 44a Peter Harholdt, National Museum of Natural History, Smithsonian Institution, Washington, D.C.; 44b Statens Historiska Museum, Stockholm; 45 Museum of Cultural History – University of Oslo, Norway; 46a Historic Scotland; 46b York Archaeological Trust; 47 Museum of Cultural History – University of Oslo, Norway; 48a Collections Picture Library, Photo © Dick Clark; 48b Statens Historiska Museum, Stockholm; 49a National Museums of Scotland, Edinburgh; 49bl Statens Historiska Museum, Stockholm; 49br York Archaeological Trust; 50a Statens Historiska Museum, Stockholm; 50b National Museum of Denmark, Copenhagen; 51 Museum of Cultural History – University of Oslo, Norway; 52 Viking Ship Museum Denmark, Photo Werner Karrasch; 53 Viking Ship Museum Denmark, Photo Werner Karrasch; 54a Viking Ship Museum Denmark; 54c Wikinger Museum, Haithabu; 54b National Museum of Denmark, Copenhagen; 55 Viking Ship Museum Denmark; 56 © Karl Haar; 57 County Museum of Gotland, Sweden; 58 Richard A. Hall; 59 Ragnar L. Børsheim/Arkikon; 60 Museum of Cultural History – University of Oslo, Norway; 61 Wikinger Museum, Haithabu; 62 Wikinger Museum, Haithabu; 63 Wikinger Museum, Haithabu; 64 Bjorn Ambrosiani; 65al Statens Historiska Museum, Stockholm; 65ar © Carl O. Löfman; 66cl Richard A. Hall; 66cr © Carl O. Löfman; 66 Bibliothèque Nationale de France, Paris; 68 Statens Historiska Museum, Stockholm; 69 Richard A. Hall; 70 British Museum, London; 71a Giant Screen Films; 71b Anders Lorange (1889); 72 ML Design © Thames & Hudson Ltd; 73a Airfotos Ltd; 73b English Heritage Photo Library; 74 National Library, Stockholm; 75 National Trust for Scotland; 76a ML Design © Thames & Hudson Ltd; 76b Rijksmuseum van Oudheden, Leiden; 77 Rijksmuseum van Oudheden, Leiden; 78 Michael Groothelde; 79 National Museum of Denmark, Copenhagen; 80bl Photo RMN; 80br Richard A. Hall; 81 Jean-Louis Paute; 82 Pierpont Morgan Library, New York; 83a © Martin Biddle and Birthe Kjolbye-Biddle, all rights reserved; 83b Richard A. Hall; 84b © Martin Biddle and Birthe Kjolbye-Biddle, all rights reserved; 85 © Martin Biddle and Birthe Kjolbye-Biddle, all rights reserved; 86 Richard A. Hall; 87 Margaret Gowan; 88 Margaret Gowan; 89 Glasgow Art Gallery and Museum; 90 National Museum of Denmark, Copenhagen; 91 National Museums of Scotland, Edinburgh; 92 National Museums & Galleries of Wales; 93a Léon Cathedral Treasury; 93b ML Design © Thames & Hudson Ltd; 94 Michael Jenner; 96 ML Design © Thames & Hudson Ltd; 97a State Hermitage Museum, Saint Petersburg; 97b Neil Price; 98a Werner Forman Archive/Biblioteca Nacional Madrid; 98bl Neil Price; 98br State Hermitage Museum, Saint Petersburg; 99 Academy of Sciences, Saint Petersburg; 100 © Ted Spiegel/Corbis; 101 K.Hamann, ZIAGA; 102 York Archaeological Trust; 103 York Archaeological Trust; 104a English Heritage Photo Library; 104b National Monuments Record, Swindon; 105 ML Design © Thames & Hudson Ltd; 106a York Archaeological Trust; 106b Richard A. Hall; 107ar John Byford; 107c&b Norwich Castle Museum; 108 British Museum, London; 109l&c British Museum, London; 109ar York Archaeological Trust; 110 Richard Bailey; 111 Oxford Archaeology; 112 British Museum, London; 113 Werner Forman Archive; 114–117 York Archaeological Trust; 118 National Museums & Galleries of Wales, Cardiff; 119 National Museums & Galleries of Wales, Cardiff; 120 Michael Connolly; 121 National Museum of Ireland, Dublin; 122 ML Design © Thames & Hudson Ltd; 123a Margaret Gowan; 123b National Museum of Ireland, Dublin; 124 Drazen Tomic © Thames & Hudson Ltd; 125 National Museum of Ireland, Dublin; 126a Richard A. Hall; 126b British Museum, London; 127l Mick Sharp; 127r National Museums of Scotland, Edinburgh; 128 National Museums of Scotland, Edinburgh; 129 RCAHMS, Edinburgh; 130 National Museums of Scotland, Edinburgh; 131 National Museums of Scotland, Edinburgh; 132 Historic Scotland, Edinburgh; 133 National Museums of Scotland, Edinburgh; 134a National Museums of Scotland, Edinburgh; 134b Mick Sharp; 135 National Museums of Scotland, Edinburgh; 136 Mick Sharp; 137 RCAHMS, Edinburgh; 138–142 Manx National Heritage, Douglas, IOM; 143 Musée Departmental des Antiquités, Rouen; 144 National Museum, Oslo; 146a ML Design © Thames & Hudson Ltd; 146b S.V. Arge, Føroya Fornminnissavn; 147a S.V. Arge, Føroya Fornminnissavn; 147b Jesar

Hansen; **148** D.L. Mahler, Føroya Fornminnissavn; **149a** S.V. Arge; **149b** S.S. Hansen, Føroya Fornminnissavn; **150a** ML Design © Thames & Hudson Ltd; **150b** Dr Margaret Hermannsdottir; **151a** © Mats Lund; **151b** Richard A. Hall; **152** © Mats Lund; **153a** British Museum, London; **153b** © Mats Lund; **154** © Mats Lund; **155** Arnamagnaeanske Samling, Copenhagen; **156** ML Design © Thames & Hudson Ltd; **157** Richard A. Hall; **158** Lesley Collett © Thames & Hudson Ltd; **159** Jette Arneborg; **160** Richard A. Hall; **161** Parks Canada; **162a** Courtesy Maine State Museum, Augusta, Maine; **162b** Parks Canada; **163a** Parks Canada; **163b** Richard A. Hall; **164** Werner Forman Archive/Statens Historiska Museum, Stockholm; **166** Arnamagnaeanske Samling, Copenhagen; **167a** Richard A. Hall; **167b** Werner Forman Archive; **168** Statens Historiska Museum, Stockholm; **169** Werner Forman Archive/Statens Historiska Museum, Stockholm; **170** National Museum of Denmark, Copenhagen; **171a** Richard A. Hall; **171b** Lesley Collett © Thames & Hudson Ltd; **172** Courtesy Else Roesdahl; **173** © Ted Spiegel/Corbis; **174** Statens Historiska Museum, Stockholm; **175a** Museum of Cultural History – University of Oslo, Norway; **175c&b** Statens Historiska Museum, Stockholm; **176** Statens Historiska Museum, Stockholm; **177l** National Museum of Denmark, Copenhagen; **177r** Museum of Cultural History – University of Oslo, Norway; **178** National Museum of Denmark, Copenhagen; **179a** Museum of Cultural History – University of Oslo, Norway; **179cr** National Museum of Iceland, Reykjavik; **180** © Carmen Redondo/Corbis; **182** Werner Forman Archive; **183** National Museum of Denmark, Copenhagen; **184** Scanpix; **185** Werner Forman Archive; **186** Morten Kustchera; **187a** Lesley Collett © Thames & Hudson Ltd; **187b** Statens Historiska Museum, Stockholm; **188a** National Museum of Denmark, Copenhagen; **188b** ML Design © Thames & Hudson Ltd; **189** Private Collection/Bridgeman Art Library; **190** Mick Sharp; **191a** British Museum, London; **191b** Museum of London; **192a** British Museum, London; **192bl** ML Design © Thames & Hudson Ltd; **192br** © Martin Biddle and Birthe Kjolbye-Biddle, all rights reserved; **193a** Statens Historiska Museum, London; **193b** Museum of London; **194** British Library; **195** Trondheim Cathedral; **196** Sigtuna Museum; **197** Arhus Museum; **198** Manchester Art Gallery/Bridgeman Art Library; **200** York Archaeological Trust; **201** Musée de la Tapisserie, Bayeux; **202bl** Manx National Heritage, Douglas, IOM; **202br** Museum of Cultural History – University of Oslo, Norway; **203** British Museum, London; **204** Mick Sharp; **205** RCAHMS, Edinburgh; **206a** Mick Sharp; **206b** Orkney Library; **207** RCAHMS, Edinburgh; **208** Historic Scotland, Edinburgh; **209a** Michael Jenner; **209b** Mick Sharp; **210a** National Museum of Ireland, Dublin; **210b** National Museums & Galleries of Wales, Cardiff; **211l** Arnamagnaeanske Samling, Copenhagen; **211r** Stofnun Árna Magnússonar, Reykjavik; **212–213** National Museum of Denmark, Copenhagen; **214** © Wolfgang Kaehler; **215** National Museum of Denmark, Copenhagen; **216** © Kieran Doherty/Reuters/Corbis; **218** Decca; **219a** © Catherine Karnow/Corbis; **219c** Statens Historiska Museum, Stockholm; **220** © Reuters/Corbis; **221al** Richard A. Hall; **221ar** Roskilde Museum Archive; **221cr** Richard A. Hall; **222–223** National Museum of Denmark, Copenhagen; **224a** Arnamagnaeanske Samling, Copenhagen; **224b** Statens Historiska Museum, Stockholm; **225** Museum of Cultural History – University of Oslo, Norway; **226** © Rose Hartman/Corbis; **227** Beinicke Library, Yale University, New Haven, Connecticut; **228a** Minnesota Historical Society; **228b** Richard A. Hall; **229l** Nordiska Museum Archives, Stockholm; **229r** John Norris.

The extract from *Heimskringla* (edited by S. Laing, revised by J. Simpson) on page 202 is used with the permission of J.M. Dent and Sons, a division of The Orion Publishing Group.

ACKNOWLEDGMENTS

Anyone compiling a book on the Vikings relies on the expertise and insights of present and former scholars, in many disciplines, and in many places across the Viking world, who have contributed to our ever-expanding understanding of this period.

I am particularly grateful to everyone with whom, over the years, I have discussed aspects of the Vikings and their contemporaries, and for the insights they have given me. I alone am responsible for any errors, mis-representations of fact or mis-interpretations in this book.

In gathering information and illustrations for this book I have received generous help from many people including Mark Ainsley, Jette Arneborg, Margrét Hermanns Auðardóttir, Bjorn Ambrosiani, Brian Ayers, Richard Bailey, Geoffrey Banbrook, Michiel Bartels, Martin Biddle and Birthe Kjølbye-Biddle, Jan Bill, John Byford, Lesley Collett, Mytte Fentz, Claus Feveile, Allison Fox, Maurice Gautier, Christopher Godfrey, Michel Groothedde, Jesper Hjermind, Birgitta Hårdh, Ruth Johnson, Christine Kyriacou, Alan Lupton, Rachel Newman, Guðmundur Olafsson, Jakob Kieffer-Olsen, Lars Pilø, Mark Redknap, Niall Sharples, Linzi Simpson, Dagfinn Skre, Tinna Damgård-Sørensen, Jan Stobbe, Sten Tesch, Patrick Wallace and, in particular, Else Roesdahl.

I must thank Colin Ridler at Thames & Hudson both for commissioning the book and for his exemplary patience over its long gestation; in the production stages it has been a pleasure to have Ben Plumridge co-ordinating and prompting progress with calm efficiency. I am also grateful to two anonymous readers for their comments and suggestions; and to Sally Nicholls for practical assistance in obtaining illustrations.

INDEX

Page numbers in *italic* refer to illustrations.